ISBN 978-0-243-10332-4
PIBN 10761954

1 MONTH OF
FREE
READING

at
www.ForgottenBooks.com

By purchasing this book you are
eligible for one month membership to
ForgottenBooks.com, giving you
unlimited access to our entire
collection of over 1,000,000 titles via
our web site and mobile apps.

To claim your free month visit:
www.forgottenbooks.com/free761954

English
Français
Deutsche
Italiano
Español
Português

www.forgottenbooks.com

Mythology Photography **Fiction**
Fishing Christianity **Art** Cooking
Essays Buddhism Freemasonry
Medicine **Biology** Music **Ancient**
Egypt Evolution Carpentry Physics
Dance Geology **Mathematics** Fitness
Shakespeare **Folklore** Yoga Marketing
Confidence Immortality Biographies
Poetry **Psychology** Witchcraft
Electronics Chemistry History **Law**
Accounting **Philosophy** Anthropology
Alchemy Drama Quantum Mechanics
Atheism Sexual Health **Ancient History**
Entrepreneurship Languages Sport
Paleontology Needlework Islam
Metaphysics Investment Archaeology
Parenting Statistics Criminology
Motivational

REPORT

OF

THE DIRECTORS .

TO

THE TWENTY-FOURTH GENERAL MEETING

OF

𝕮𝖍𝖊 𝕸𝖎𝖘𝖘𝖎𝖔𝖓𝖆𝖗𝖞 𝕾𝖔𝖈𝖎𝖊𝖙𝖞,

USUALLY CALLED THE

LONDON MISSIONARY SOCIETY,

On Thursday, May 14, 1818.

68 lxxiv

PRINTED BY ORDER OF THE GENERAL MEETING.

LONDON:

SOLD BY WILLIAMS AND CO. STATIONERS' COURT, LUDGATE STREET;
J. NISBET, CASTLE STREET, OXFORD STREET;
A. BROWNE AND T. D. CLARKE, BRISTOL; M. RICHARDSON, MANCHESTER;
OLIPHANT, WAUGH, AND INNES, HUNTER SQUARE, EDINBURGH;
AND LA GRANGE, NASSAU STREET, DUBLIN.

1818.

J. Dennett, Printer, Leather Lane,
Holborn, London.

Contents.

LIST OF DIRECTORS.

ANNUAL REPORT of the Proceedings of the Directors for the preceding Year.

MISSIONS.

CONTENTS.

𝔐𝔦𝔰𝔰𝔦𝔬𝔫𝔞𝔯𝔶 𝔖𝔬𝔠𝔦𝔢𝔱𝔶,

ESTABLISHED IN 1795.

—=◦●●◦|◆|◦●●◦=—

PLAN.

I. *THE NAME.**—THE MISSIONARY SOCIETY.

II. *THE OBJECT.*—The sole object is to spread the knowledge of Christ among heathen and other unenlightened nations.

III. *THE MEMBERS.*—Persons subscribing one guinea, or more, annually—every benefactor making a donation of ten pounds—one of the executors, on the payment of a legacy amounting to fifty pounds, or upwards; and Ministers, or other representatives of congregations in the country, which subscribe or collect for the use of the Society five pounds annually.

IV. *GENERAL MEETINGS.*—To be held annually in London on the second Wednesday of May, and oftener if necessary, to chuse a Treasurer, Directors, Secretary, and Collectors, and to receive reports, audit accounts, and deliberate on what farther steps may best promote the object of the Society. At every such meeting, one sermon, or more, shall be preached by one or more of the associated Ministers, and notice given, as usual on such occasions. The President for the day shall open and conclude the meeting with prayer, and sign the minutes of the proceedings. All matters proposed, shall be determined by the majority of the members present.

V. *THE DIRECTION.*—To consist of as many Directors, annually chosen out of its members, as circumstances may require. At the first meeting twenty-five shall be elected, with power to associate with themselves such an additional number as may be judged by them expedient, when the extent of the Society is ascertained. Three-fifths, and no more, of these Directors shall reside in or near London; where all monthly meetings shall be held for transacting the business of the Society. Not less than seven shall constitute a board. For greater facility and expedition, they may subdivide into committees, for managing the funds, conducting the correspondence, making reports, examining Missionaries, directing the missions, &c. but no act of these committees shall be valid till ratified at a monthly meeting. No expenditure exceeding £100 shall be made without consulting all the Directors, or £500 without calling a general meeting of the subscribers. Annual subscribers of £10 or upwards, and bene-

---

* 14th May, 1818. Resolved, That the title of this Society be in future, " THE MISSIONARY SOCIETY, USUALLY CALLED, THE LONDON MISSIONARY SOCIETY."—(Vide close of the Report.)

* A

factors of £100 or more, may attend, if they please, with the Directors, at any of the monthly meetings. On any emergency the Directors shall call a general meeting of the Society, to whom their arrangements shall be submitted: nor shall they enter upon a new mission till they obtain the general concurrence.

VI. THE FUNDS.—Arising from donations, legacies, subscriptions, collections, &c. shall be lodged, as soon as collected, in the hands of the Treasurer. The Directors shall place in the public funds all monies so paid, whenever they exceed £300, until they are required for the use of the mission; excepting it appears to them prejudicial to the interests of the Society.

VII. SALARIES.—The Secretary shall receive such a salary as the Directors may appoint; but the Directors themselves shall transact the business of the Society without any emolument.

At the annual meeting, held the 12th of May, 1814,
Resolved, That a copy of the Fundamental Principle, adopted at the first annual meeting in May, 1796, be printed at the end of the Plan.

FUNDAMENTAL PRINCIPLE.

As the union of God's people of various denominations, in carrying on this great work, is a most desirable object; so to prevent, if possible, any cause of future dissension, it is declared to be a *fundamental principle* of the Missionary Society, that our design is not to send Presbyterianism, Independency, Episcopacy, or any other form of Church order and government (about which there may be difference of opinions among serious persons), but the glorious Gospel of the blessed God, to the Heathen; and that it shall be left (as it ought to be left) to the minds of the persons whom God may call into the fellowship of his Son from among them, to assume for themselves such form of Church government as to them shall appear most agreeable to the Word of God.

At the annual meeting, held the 14th of May, 1812,

Resolved, That those Ministers in the country who are annual subscribers, or whose congregations send an annual collection to the Society; and all presidents, or principal officers, of country auxiliary Societies, who may be in London occasionally, shall be Directors *pro tempore*, and be entitled to meet and vote with the Directors.

LIST OF DIRECTORS,

1818.

————✦•◦◦◦•❘⟨❈⟩❘◦•◦◦•————

LONDON.

Rev. J. Bodington
R. Bowden
J. Brooksbank
George Burder
William Chapman
Thomas Cloutt
George Collison
E. A. Dunn
George Greig
Samuel Hackett
John Hawksley
Thomas Harper
Rowland Hill, A. M.
John Hyatt
Thomas Jackson
John Innes
John Leifchild
W. Manuel D.D.
W. F. Platt
Benjamin Rayson
J. P. Smith, D.D.
William Smith
William Strutt
John Townsend
S. W. Tracy
Alexander Waugh, D.D.
Robert Winter, D.D.
Matthew Wilks

Rev. John Yockney
Mr. John Ballance
William Bateman
Alexander Birnie
John Fenn
George Gaviller
Thomas Gillespie
George Hammond
W. Alers Hankey
Joseph Hardcastle
Alfred Hardcastle
Thomas Hayter
John Honyman
Samuel Houston
T. P. Oldfield
Thomas Pellatt
William Reid
Joseph Reyner
Alexander Riddell
Samuel Robinson
William Shrubsole
J. G. Simpson
Robert Steven
Joseph Tarn
Thomas Walker
Thomas Wilson
Thomas Wontner

COUNTRY.

Rev. Richard ....Alliot, Nottingham
    D. W..............Aston, Buckingham
    James ....Bennett, Rotherham
    James ....Boden, Sheffield
    David ....Bogue, D. D. Gosport
    Samuel..........Bottomley, Scarborough
    Samuel..........Bruce, Wakefield
    John ....Bruce, Newport, Isle of Wight
    W. T...........Bull, Newport Pagnell
    John ....Burder, A. M. Stroud
    William ....Carver, Melbourn
    Michael ....Castleden, Wooburn, Bed s.
    P. S. ....Charrier, Liverpool
    Thomas ....Cope, Launceston
    J. H. ....Cox, Hadleigh
    Thomas ....Craig, Bocking
    John ....Day, A.M. Bristol
    Charles.........Dewhirst, Bury St. Edmund's
    Archibald ......Douglas, Reading
    John ....Durant, Poole.
    Joseph ....France, Lancaster
    James ....Gawthorn, Derby
    George ....Gill, Harborough
    George ....Gladstone, Lincoln
    Thomas ....Golding, Poundsford Park
    Samuel ....Greatheed, Bishopshull, near Taunton
    John ....Griffin, Portsea
    Thomas ....Haweis, L.L.B. M.D. Bath
    Samuel.........Hillyard, Bedford
    J. T. ....Holloway, D.D. Whitby
    John ....Hudson, West Bromwich
    Robert ....Jack, D. D. Manchester
    J. A. ....James, Birmingham
    Joseph ....Julian, A. B. Trimley, near Ipswich
    William ....Jay, Bath
    James ....Knight, Kingston, Surrey
    Edward ....Lake, Worcester
    Charles.........Maslen, Hertford
    Thomas ....Mason, Sunderland

DIRECTORS.

Rev. Alexander ⁓Stewart, Dingwall
       Ralph ⁓Wardlaw, Glasgow
       John ⁓Willison, A.M. Forgandenny
       George ⁓Wright, Markinch
Mr. James ⁓Carlile, Paisley
       John ⁓Laird, Greenock
       David ⁓Morrison, Perth
       Alexander ⁓Murray, Ayton

IRELAND.

Rev. John ⁓Burnett, Cork
       James ⁓Carlile, Dublin
Mr. —— ⁓Dill, Newton Limavady
Rev. Samuel ⁓Hanna, Belfast
       John ⁓Johnston, Elmfield, near Armagh
       Thomas ⁓Loader, Dublin
       Thomas ⁓Miller, Cookstown
       B. W. ⁓Mathias, A.B. Dublin
       John ⁓Pelherick, Limerick
       David ⁓Stewart, Dublin
       William ⁓Urwick, Sligo
       William ⁓Woolseley, Saintfield
Mr. William ⁓Seymour, Dublin
       Robert ⁓White, Ditto
       James ⁓Ferrier, Ditto
       W. C. ⁓Hogan, Ditto

FOREIGN DIRECTORS.

Europe.

The President of the Religious Society at Basle.
The President of the Missionary Society at Rotterdam.
Mr. Bernardus Ledeboer, Rotterdam.
The President of the Society for promoting the Gospel in Denmark.
Rev. John Jœnicke, Berlin.
Mr Gilbert Vander Smissen, Altona.
Dr. Cleardo Naudi, Malta.
Rev. Francis Perrot, Jersey.
Rev. Clement Perrot, Guernsey.

DIRECTORS.

America.

The President of the Missionary Society in Connecticut.
The President of the Missionary Society in New York.
Rev. Dr. Mason, New York.
Rev. Dr. Romeyn, New York.
Mr. Divie Bethune, New York.
The President of the Board of Foreign Missions in
    Massachusetts.
Mr. Robert Ralston, Philadelphia.

South Africa.

Mr. Richard Beck, Cape Town.
Mr. Kuyper, Stellenbosch.
Mr. De Lange, Roodesand.

New South Wales.

Rev. Samuel Marsden, M.A.

TREASURER.

Mr. William Alers Hankey, Fenchurch Street.

SECRETARY.

Rev. George Burder.

ASSISTANT SECRETARY.

Mr. George Hodson.

ASSISTANT SECRETARY AND ACCOMPTANT.

Mr. David Langton.

COLLECTOR.

Mr. Thomas Adams.

---

*It is requested that all Letters on the Business of the Society, be sent to
the Missionary Rooms, No. 8, Old Jewry, London.*

REPORT OF THE DIRECTORS

TO THE

Twenty-fourth General Meeting

OF

The Missionary Society.

MAY 14, 1818.

Beloved Brethren,

THE Divine Redeemer, whose we are, and whom, in this Institution, we are associated to serve, permits us once more to enjoy the privilege of assembling together, to promote the single object of our union—the glory of Christ in the salvation of the heathen. May He, whose interests we espouse, and in whose name we meet, be in the midst of us, while we rehearse what God hath wrought by our Missionaries, and how he hath opened the door of faith unto the Gentiles.

The Directors will now proceed to give a concise account of the labours of our brethren, and the various degrees of success with which it hath pleased God to follow them.

SOUTH SEA ISLANDS.

AT the last Annual Meeting of this Society, the Directors had the pleasure of communicating the interesting intelligence they had received from respectable individuals in New South Wales, concerning the state of the South Sea Mission; they have now the satisfaction of reporting, that the whole of that information has been abundantly confirmed by an official letter from the Society of Missionaries, dated at Eimeo, August the 13th, 1816, and received in January last.

B

It will be recollected, that when Pomare, the King of Otaheite, returned to that island from Eimeo, to resume his government, and to reinstate his friends in the possessions which they had been obliged by a rebellious party to abandon, he was assailed on the beach by a number of the insurgents, but who appeared for a season to be pacified by his conciliatory behaviour. In a short time afterwards, however, they renewed their hostility, and made a desperate assault on the king and his people, while they were assembled for worship on the morning of the Lord's day; but the assailing party, soon losing their chief, were thrown into confusion, and completely routed. Contrary, however, to the usual practice in their wars, the king issued strict orders that the fugitives should not be pursued; that the women should not be injured; and that the slain should be decently interred. This humane conduct, which he had learned from the Gospel, produced the most salutary effect on the people. They were won by his kindness; and many of them united in the public thanksgivings offered to Jehovah on the evening of that Sabbath, declaring that their idols had deceived them, and that they would trust them no longer.

Pomare was now, by universal consent, restored to the government of Otaheite and its dependencies. In his progress through the several districts, to replace his friends in their estates, he constituted, as chiefs, many of those who had long attended the ministry of the Missionaries, and who had made a public profession of their faith. The people at large, assisted and encouraged by their chiefs, demolished the Morais, overthrew the altars, and burned their gods in the fire. Idolatry was at once completely abolished, and the worship of Jehovah substituted in its place. Numerous buildings for that purpose were immediately erected, in every district,* and meetings for prayer held in them thrice on the Lord's-day, (which is strictly and universally observed) and once on the Wednesday.

* A private letter says there are about fifty places of worship in Otaheite alone; and that family worship is general among the inhabitants.

The king, after having destroyed the public idols, sent those which had long been held sacred in his family to the Missionaries, leaving it to their option, either to burn them or send them to this Society, "that the people in England might see what foolish gods," as he calls them, "they had formerly worshipped." The latter measure was determined upon by our brethren; who were aware what a high degree of satisfaction (may we not say of pious exultation) the public exposure of them would produce.

As soon as circumstances would admit, some of the Missionaries from Eimeo visited Otaheite, at the request of the people, and preached in every district to large and attentive congregations, who readily assembled wherever they went, and whose decorous behaviour was highly encouraging.

The school at Eimeo, notwithstanding former discouragements, now prospers greatly; and many hundreds of those who had received instruction in it, being by various circumstances dispersed, have become the teachers of others; and thus the knowledge of reading and writing has been spread far and wide.

When the Missionaries wrote, (which is now twenty-one months since) it was calculated that *three thousand persons* were in possession of books, and able to make use of them; many hundreds could read well. They are also in possession of about 400 copies of the Old Testament History, and 400 of the New, which is an abridgment of the four Evangelists, and part of the Acts. Many chapters also of St. Luke's gospel, in manuscript, are in circulation, together with about 1000 copies of the Catechism, composed and printed for their use, and which several hundreds of the people can perfectly repeat. The call for more spelling-books was urgent, and we hope has long since been answered by a new edition printed at Port Jackson. But their own press will now supply their wants, so that Otaheite, and several other islands, will soon be furnished with parts of the Holy Scriptures, and with elementary books, in their own language.

But the blessings of this spiritual revolution are by no

means confined to the two islands of Otaheite and Eimeo, they appear to be rapidly extending to several islands adjacent. The small islands of *Tapua-manu* and *Tetaroa* are, in profession, "*Christian islands;*" and there also the Morais are destroyed, human sacrifices and infant murder abolished,* while the natives are urgent to obtain the instruction of the Missionaries.

In the islands which they call "the Leeward Islands," the same hopeful symptoms appear. TAPA, the principal chief, has openly renounced idolatry, and embraced Christianity; and his example has been followed by most of the other chiefs, and by a large majority of the people in the four "Society Isles," *Huaheine, Taha, Borabora,* and *Raiatea.* One of the Missionaries, in a letter to a friend, says, that in *Huaheine, Raiatea,* and *Barabora,* there are nearly 4000 who embrace the Gospel.

Mr. Hayward, in a letter to a friend, says, "In every district round the island (Otaheite) we found a house erected, where the natives on the Sabbath assemble three times, and on every Wednesday evening, for prayer; and here they met with us to hear the word of the true God. Our congregation often exceeded 400, and were never less than 100, all, in general, attentive hearers. We commenced our mission at Oparre, and closed it at Matavai, our old residence. We had not been long in this district before our old neighbours came, and requested Brother Nott to preach to them; they likewise informed us, that the ground where our houses and gardens formerly stood, and the whole of the district from *Taraa* to *Tapahi,* the boundaries of the district, should be ours, if we would return to reside among them again. This happened on the 6th of March, the same day, 19 years, since the first Missionaries landed on Taheite from the ship Duff. Some of the chiefs of these islands have sent repeated messages, requesting the brethren to come and teach them; and one of them re-

* The abominable Society, called AREOI, is said to be suppressed. This society was composed of a privileged order, who indulged in extreme lewdness, and uniformly murdered the fruits of their licentious intercourse.

minded the Missionaries that " Jesus Christ and his apostles did not confine their instructions to one place or country." Such an intimation from a heathen chief (if such he may now be called) carries with it prodigious force.

The Directors are happy in reflecting upon the measures they have adopted, in sending out ten more Missionaries, (including Mr. Crook from Port Jackson, and Mr. Gyles) to assist in this great, and, they trust, growing work; they have reason to believe that they all are now at their post, diligently engaged in acquiring that language, in which it will be their privilege to publish, to attentive thousands, the glad tidings of salvation by Jesus Christ—in preaching to a people who appear to be " prepared for the Lord."

The Directors cannot pass on to another branch of their Report without making a pause, and presenting a few reflections on these great and glorious events. They cannot but consider the work of God among these distant islanders as forming not only a remarkable era in the history of this Society, but as furnishing a memorable event in the general history of the Christian church. The event appears to them to be almost, if not altogether, without a parallel in ecclesiastical history. These islands, it is true, are not very populous, but they are numerous; and it may be expected that, when the intelligence spreads, as it will from island to island, and numbers of the converts are dispersed among the inhabitants, general enquiry will be excited, and the knowledge of Christ be widely diffused. Together with the blessings of the Gospel, the useful arts of civilization will doubtless be communicated; idolatry, cruelty, and war will be suppressed, and the multitudes of isles become obedient unto the faith.

May we not also indulge the expectation that future Missionaries, in various parts of the world, will, from the example of our brethren in Otaheite, learn patiently to persevere in well-doing, and not abandon their stations because they do not immediately perceive the fruit of their labours. It will not soon be forgotten that the Missionaries in these islands laboured for seventeen or eighteen years, amidst all kinds of discouragement, yet, after all, were crowned with a success which far exceeded all their expectations."

In fine, the Society cannot but feel itself called upon to unite this day in offering up the most ardent praises and thanksgivings to the God of all grace, who, in answer to prayer, has poured down his Holy Spirit in such a copious measure, and has turned the barren desert into a fruitful field: to Him be the glory wholly ascribed, while with grateful hearts we renew the dedication of ourselves to him, encouraged by his goodness to continue and redouble our efforts to spread abroad throughout the whole habitable earth the sweet savour of the knowledge of Christ.*

CHINA.

OUR Missionary, Dr. Morrison,† perseveres in the laborious and important task of translating the sacred volume into the language of China. In addition to the whole of the New Testament, which has been for several years in circulation, he has finished the books of Exodus, Ruth, and the Psalms, and has entered upon the prophecy of Isaiah. His labours suffered a suspension of a few months by his journey to Pekin, as one of the interpreters who accompanied his Excellency Lord Amherst, the British Ambassador to the Emperor of China. This interruption will, however, we trust, be compensated by the additional

. * The state of the few inhabitants of Pitcairn's Island, the descendants of the mutineers on board the Bounty, as reported by some of our countrymen who touched there in Sept. 1814, could not but engage the attention of the Directors, who therefore gladly embraced an opportunity of sending, by a vessel bound to the South Seas, a present of Bibles, prayer-books, spelling-books, &c. with a letter to John Adams, expressing the good-will of the Society towards them, and their hope that they shall be enabled to send them a Missionary to instruct them in the knowledge of the gospel.

† The title of Doctor in Divinity was unanimously and gratuitously granted by the *Senatus Academicus* of the University of Glasgow, as a reward of his philological labours.

knowledge which his journey through several provinces, and his intercourse with the natives of all ranks, enabled him to acquire of the language, customs, and especially of the religious views, of the vast population of that extensive empire.

Dr. Morrison and Mr. Milne having finished the translation of several books of the Old Testament, have made such arrangements with regard to the rest, that they hope, if it please God to give them health, to complete the whole in the course of the present year.

We regret exceedingly that the opposition of the Chinese Government to the labours of Dr. Morrison still continues, and that his progress in printing has thereby been impeded; it is, however, pleasing to learn that the work is going forward to Malacca, Dr. Morrison having committed to the care of Mr. Milne, the superintendence of a large edition of the New Testament, consisting of *eight thousand* copies in duodecimo, and *fifteen hundred* in octavo.*

MALACCA.

We are sorry to state that Mr. Milne has suffered much by severe illness. Fears were entertained lest his valuable services should be speedily terminated. But we indulge a hope that his voyage to China will be beneficial. Mrs. Milne, who had been very dangerously ill, had previously taken a voyage to that country.

Mr. Milne had paid a visit to Penang (or Prince of Wales's Island), where he was most kindly received by Governor Petrie and many other gentlemen,† was favoured

* See Appendix, No. II.

† While Mr. Milne was at Penang, he met with Sabat, a man of talent, who some years renounced the religion of Mahomet, and professed to embrace that of the gospel. The religious public formed sanguine expectations of his extensive usefulness. But he became an apostate, and wrote against Christianity. He professed, however, to repent, and again to receive the gospel. He wrote an affectionate letter to Mr. Milne on the subject. In consequence of his espousing the cause of an usurper, he was taken prisoner, and it is said, by order of the King of Achcen, drowned in the sea. See Appendix, No. III.

.with many excellent opportunities of sending copies of the
Chinese new Testament, catechisms, and tracts to Siam,
where it is said 20,000 Chinese reside, to Rhio, Cochin-
China, and various other places where the Chinese are
found in great numbers, as well as of conversing on religious subjects with the sailors belonging to the vessels by
which they were conveyed. In Penang only, there are
said to be 8,000 Chinese inhabitants, among whom Mr.
Milne went from house to house, distributing the scriptures
and tracts. Mr. M. calculates, that in China and Malacca
together, there have been printed and circulated not less
than 36,000 Chinese pamphlets and tracts, exclusive of the
Holy Scriptures. May we not hope that some of the good
seed so liberally disseminated will spring up, and produce
much fruit to the glory of God and the salvation of souls.
Towards the great expense of printing Chinese tracts, the
Religious Tract Society in London have liberally contributed the sum of £500.

Mr. Milne's labours appears to have been abundant. He
has translated the books of Genesis and Deuteronomy,
and part of Joshua, into the Chinese language ; he has also
paid considerable attention to the Malay, in which he can
read with tolerable facility. He has now two Chinese
schools, into which he has introduced the Lancastrian
plan, as far as it was practicable. The children learn Dr.
Morrison's Chinese Catechism.

Mr. Thomsen, we trust, has returned to Malacca, and
is proceeding with the Malay mission. He has translated
the Ten Commandments, and Dr. Watts's First Catechism.
Mr. Milne wrote an introduction to the Ten Commandments, explaining their design ; judging that the holy law
of God, as expressed in the Decalogue, is peculiarly calculated to strike at the root of their false principles, base
practices, and abominable idolatries.

The arrival of Mr. Medhurst at Malacca, in July last,
afforded great satisfaction to Mr. Milne, as he appears to
be well qualified to superintend the press, having been
brought up to the business of a printer, and having made

some proficiency in the learned languages.* This settlement has now the advantage of possessing two presses, with suitable workmen, and an able superintendant. Mr. Thomsen, who obtained in England a knowledge of letter-founding, will materially assist in this department. The buildings necessary for the several purposes of the mission have lately been much extended; but the expenditure, though considerable, will, we trust, be richly compensated by the utility of this very important institution, from which, throughout the numerous and populous regions of India beyond the Ganges, we trust the waters of the sanctuary will issue to fertilize the vast and dreary waste.

The Directors, urged by the solicitation of Dr. Morrison and Mr. Milne, have lately sent out four additional labourers, Messrs. Milton, Fleming, Beighton, and Ince,† the first of whom is designated to the Chinese mission, the other three to such stations in the East as may be deemed the most necessitous and the most promising.

AMBOYNA.

Accounts received from Mr. Kam, at Amboyna, are very encouraging. His stated ministry in the Dutch church appears to have been greatly blessed, as well as his preaching to the heathen, in the Malay tongue. In the year 1816, he baptized nearly 200 adults, who had relinquished the religion of Mahomet, and professed to embrace the gospel of Christ. The number of heathens and Mahometans, who have made a profession of Chris-

---

* Mr. Medhurst, while at Madras, was appointed agent of the British and Foreign Bible Society at Malacca and Penang, and was furnished with a quantity of Dutch, Portugueze, and Arabic Bibles for distribution.

† These Missionaries, with the wives of Mr. B. and Mr. J. were exposed for several weeks to severe storms, and particularly to that which happened on the 4th of March. Their apparent danger was extremely great, and their preservation demands the thanksgivings of the Society to their great Preserver. They embarked at Gravesend, Feb. 18, but were driven about by stormy wind until the 24th of March, when they left Spithead, with a fair wind.

tianity through his instrumentality, since his arrival in,
Amboyna, exceeds 1200. Mr. Kam has commenced the
building of a place of worship for the use of the heathen
slaves, but the work has been impeded in consequence of
the distressing events which have taken place in the island,
which have also occasioned some interruption of his own
labours. The unhappy commotions in Amboyna have occasioned much bloodshed. The insurgents endeavoured to
compel the Christian inhabitants to join them, many of
whom, on their refusal, were cruelly murdered. Mr. Kam
appears to have been in some personal danger, so that he
says, in a letter to the Directors, " O my God, my soul
is cast down within me; all thy waves and thy billows are
gone over me; yet neither my body nor my soul has been
hurt. I have escaped many dangers by land and by sea;
and, out of the darkness which now surrounds me, I have
confidence that light will arise, probably greater than before.
Surely the mercy of the Lord has accompanied my poor
labours from the time of my arrival in Asia! Surely the
time of salvation is at hand, in favour of the numerous
heathen of this colony." In another paper, he says,
" Whenever I am in great distress, then I say in my heart,
and sometimes with a loud voice, Lord be mindful of thy
praying people in England and every where else in Europe,
on our behalf."

Mr. Kam's zealous labours have not been confined to
the island of Amboyna. In the months of September and
October, 1816, he visited several of the Molucca islands,
where his ministry was most joyfully received; and in the
negerys (or villages) of *Aboro, Hulaliuw,* and *Kariou,* the
inhabitants, who had been long devoted to the service of
dumb idols, arose, and with holy indignation destroyed their
false gods. Mr. Kam speaks of this triumph of Christianity
over heathenism with pious exultation; and says, in his
address to British Christians, " Many of you will not see
much of this glorious conquest, but in heaven you will see
thousands of these poor black people, who have been saved
through the Gospel by our precious Saviour, who bled and
died for our sins. There I shall see you again, my dear

brethren, and there you will find that your faithful labours of love for the name and cause of Christ have not been in vain."

The Directors have acceded to the earnest request of Mr. Kam, and have sent out a printing-press, which he much needed, for the purpose of supplying the people with religious tracts, which were before transcribed with great labour; they have also sent out a large number of .tracts in the Malay language, printed in London, for dispersion in Amboyna. We trust that the inhabitants will soon be favoured with a large supply of the Malay Bible, now print‑ing by the British and Foreign Bible Society, of which they are in earnest expectation, and which they will gladly purchase at any price.*

On account of the dangerous state of affairs in Amboyna, the Directors have deferred sending out additional Missionaries to that station; they are also in expectation that the Netherland Society will, ere long, send more labourers into that extensive and promising field.†

JAVA.

It is with the deepest regret we have to record the death of Mr. Supper, at Batavia. His labours in that populous city were useful. He possessed great advantages, which he employed to good purpose. He had been a principal instrument of establishing Auxiliary Societies in behalf of Missions, of Bibles and Tracts, and had the prospect of much usefulness both among the Portugueze and Malay Christians. The loss of so zealous and active a labourer, in the prime of life, is deeply to be lamented; but we bow to the Sovereign Ruler of the world, and say, " Thy will be done." The Society has at present no Missionary in that interesting station; but we trust it will be kept in view by the Directors.

* Mr. Kam says, that he needs at least 20,000 copies of the Bible for the supply of the people in Amboyna and neighbourhing islands. A single copy of the Bible was lately sold by auction for *eight pounds.*

† See Appendix, No. IV.

CEYLON.

Our information from Ceylon during the past year is very scanty. Mr. Palm continues to preach in the Dutch church at Columbo. Mr. Ehrhardt, who was for several years our Missionary at Matura, and afterwards at Cultura, where he preached alternately in Dutch and Cingalese, and superintended schools, has lately been appointed by the Madras Government (on the recommendation of Sir R. Brownrigg) Missionary to the Dutch inhabitants of Cochin. Mr. Reade continues to superintend a school.

INDIA.

In this vast and populous region of the globe our Society has now seven stations, occupied by about eighteen Missionaries, who, as far as their health will admit, are diligently employed in preaching the gospel, translating and circulating the Scriptures, and in supporting schools for the native heathen.

CHINSURAH.

We begin with the most northerly station, which is Chinsurah. Here Mr. May has long laboured in the ministry of the word, and is now assisted in his work by Mr. Pearson, who was sent out last year, and by Mr. Harle, an European, who has resided some years in India.

The providence of God has favoured Mr. May with extensive opportunities of being useful in that line of service to which he was always partial, and for which he had peculiar talents. The native schools in the neighbourhood of Calcutta, under his superintendence, were, according to the last accounts, 30 in number, including, on the books, 2663 children, of whom about 1775 were in actual attendance.* The schools, he judged, were likely to be increased, as the

---

* By letters since arrived, it appears, that there are now 36 schools, and that the number of children is nearly 3000.

attention of the public to them had been much excited. About 100 schools, he observes, have been established by different Societies in the last three years; and a Society has been recently formed at Calcutta (to which the Directors have liberally subscribed) for the purpose of furnishing the schools with elementary books—a measure of a very necessary and laudable nature, and which promises to be highly conducive to their prosperity. It is pleasing to observe, that in many villages the Brahmins, as well as, the inferior inhabitants, express great joy on the introduction of a school, as the education which the boys receive, qualifies them for situations in which they may obtain employment and support.

CALCUTTA.

The Directors have much reason to be satisfied with the appointment of Mr. Townley and Mr. Keith to their very important station at Calcutta, the metropolis of British India. Ever since their arrival, in September 1816, they have been labouring diligently to acquire the language; and have already begun to preach, in Bengallee, the glorious gospel of God our Saviour.

It has pleased God to give them favour among our countrymen in Calcutta, to many of whom they preach with much acceptance, and, we trust, usefulness. Their first house for worship, the Freemasons' Hall, being insufficient for the congregation, Dr. Bryce, the minister of the Scot's congregation, with the approbation of the Kirk Session, kindly offered the use of the temporary place he now occupies while the Presbyterian church is building, at any time when not engaged by himself; for which accommodation the Directors feel themselves greatly indebted. Mr. Townley and Mr. Keith have also opened a place for preaching at Hourah, on the other side the river Hoogley, where the attendance is good. Thousands of the natives are employed in the dock-yard, and access may be found to a number of populous villages in the neighbourhood.

Our brethren, agreeably to their instructions, are active in the establishment of schools, as calculated gradually to

undermine that system of error and superstition by which
the millions of Hindoostan are so miserably enslaved.   Mr.
Townley has built a school-room in Calcutta, which will
accommodate about 100 children, and Mr. Keith has engaged a poojah-house (a place for pagan worship) for
another.   A Sunday school is also commenced, in which
the children learn the Catechism; and some of their parents
also attend.   Missionary prayer-meetings are held alternately in the different places of worship ; and our Missionaries cordially unite with their Baptist brethren on these
occasions.

GANJAM,

(369 *miles south of Calcutta.*)

The malignant fever which long raged at Ganjam, has
put a stop, for the present, to the missionary efforts of
Mr. Lee, who had laboured there with acceptance, and for
whom a church had been built, and schools established;
but both his congregation and the scholars have been dispersed.   His own constitution has suffered so severe a
shock, that he has been under the necessity of retiring
from all labour for a time.   Indeed it was providential that
he was obliged by his illness to withdraw from Ganjam;
for had he resided there at the time it was invaded by the
Pindarees, it is probable, that he and all his family would
have been murdered.   Two thousand of that party visited
Ganjam on the 24th of Dec. 1816, and his house, in which
he had left most of his effects, was plundered.   Mr. Lee,
after having taken a voyage to Vizagapatam and Madras,
not finding his health restored, was strongly advised, by
medical and other friends, to remove with his family to the
Cape of Good Hope, where they have arrived, and are
gone to reside for a time at Stellenbosch ; where we pray
and hope that his health may be recovered, and that he
may yet be spared as a useful Missionary, either in Africa
or in India.

VIZAGAPATAM,

(*About 557 miles south of Calcutta.*)

Three brethren, Messrs. Gordon, Pritchett, and Dawson, occupy this station, which was commenced in the year 1805, by those truly valuable Missionaries, Messrs. Cran and Desgranges, long since deceased. Mr. Gordon's health, which had been so extremely reduced that it was expected he must have declined the Mission and returned to Europe, has been completely restored, so that he now is enabled to exert himself in the missionary work with renewed vigour. Mr. Pritchett also labours incessantly in teaching, translating, and superintending schools. They are now assisted by Mr. Dawson, who, we are sorry to hear, has been much indisposed, but we hope is recovered.

The brethren are in the habit of associating and conversing with the natives, who are more and more inquisitive about the truth, and with whom very interesting conversations frequently take place.

The influence of the Gospel appears to be gradually diffused in the country; so that the attachment of many to their superstitions is evidently diminished, and their attention to the Gospel increased. Having heard that at *Chicacole*, a town about 60 miles north of Vizagapatam, some persons had been induced to forsake the pagoda, and throw away a favourite ensign of their idolatry, which they used to wear on their persons, one of the brethren paid them a visit; and upon ascertaining the fact, enquired into the cause, when he found, that by reading the true VEDAS, (or the New Testament, which they had sent them) and by conversation with *Anundaraya*, the Brahmin, who had formerly visited them from Vizagapatam, they had made this promising advance towards the religion of Christ. The brethren are very desirous that a Missionary may be sent to this place.

The brethren have made considerable progress in the translation of the Scriptures into the Telinga (or *Telugo*) language; and they hoped to complete the whole of the New Testament by the close of the last year. The first

edition of the Gospels which they had printed, was wholly
disposed of, and the call for more copies was very urgent,
especially to the southward of their station, and at Madras.

The native schools at this place continue to be well attended, and promise to be very useful ; many of the children
make a surprising proficiency, and acquire much knowledge
of divine things. The principal school, which is now kept
in the heart of the town, and is open to all passengers,
excites much attention. The novelty of catechising the
children publicly, and the promptitude of their answers,
never fail to bring many adult persons to hear them, and
thus affords many topics for enquiry and conversation.
Adults and children are thus instructed at the same time.
The Missionaries here are of opinion, that it is practicable,
though difficult at first, to introduce Christian books and
Christian principles into the seminaries, and thereby lay a
solid foundation for much future benefit.

MADRAS.

At this Presidency, and in a city said to contain, with its
vicinity, nearly half a million of souls, Mr. Knill, who went
out in 1816, now labours together with Mr. Loveless, who
has been many years at this station. A considerable revival seems to have taken place, to which the presence and
assistance of several Missionaries who were waiting for
opportunities to repair to their appointed stations, happily
contributed ; and our brethren, uniting harmoniously with
Missionaries from other Societies, were at the very time of
our last Anniversary in London, joyfully engaged in similar
services at Madras. Probably so pleasing a scene was
never before witnessed in India. This Meeting appears
to have been delightful and beneficial in no small degree.
An Auxiliary Missionary Society has been formed, and
about £200 transmitted to the Parent Society. " No
congregation in Britain (says Mr. K.) of equal size can
boast of such a sum." More labourers are needed. Mr.
K. says, " The Missionaries here are but as a drop to the
ocean." In another letter, the brethren say, " Our calls
for labour continue and abound. There is an amazing

field at Madras. Great concern is excited by the preaching of the Gospel; and we hope that our labours are not in vain in the Lord."

The word of God is statedly preached at the chapel (erected in 1810 by Mr. Loveless) in the Black Town, and elsewhere occasionally, especially at the Fort and at the Mount, in English, at which latter place a few individuals raised 50 pagodas for fitting up a chapel. Mr. Loveless's school-room at *Vepery* is well attended on Lord's-day evenings. Among the natives there appears to be a desire to hear the Gospel. Mr. Gordon freely conversed with them in the streets, and at the pagodas, on religious subjects; to which they paid much attention.

The Missionary Prayer-meeting on the first Monday of the month is statedly observed and well attended. There are also circulating prayer-meetings held in private houses, to which the neighbours are invited, and where the Scriptures are expounded.

Much attention is paid to the schools.* There are 147 names on the books of the free-school for boys; a free-school for girls has been recently commenced, in which there are about 40. The school-rooms are erected in the chapel garden.† The schools for natives contain about 400 children; and the New Testament is introduced, and some parts of it are learned and repeated.

Mr. Knill is studying the Tamul language, which begins to be familiar to him; and he hopes soon to be able to preach in it. He is of opinion, that immense congregations of the heathen may be collected to hear the Gospel, when preached in their own tongue. The people receive books and tracts gladly, and the Missionaries are earnestly desirous of gratifying them; " the distribution of them (say

* " The number of our schools might be greatly augmented, were it not for the expence attached to them. We might have thousands of children; but teachers, rooms, &c. are very dear."

† Mrs. Loveless and Mrs. Mead, who were the principal superintendants of the female school, give a pleasing report of its state. Several gentlemen and ladies at Madras contribute liberally to its support.

they) is recreation to our bodies, relaxation to our spirits, and joy to our souls."

On the whole, we have much cause to be thankful for the present state of the mission at Madras, and for the pleasing prospect of future and extensive usefulness. The Directors will probably think it expedient to increase the number of their Missionaries at this very interesting station, the second, perhaps, in importance in India.

BELLARY,
(About 500 miles N. West of Madras.)

The progress of the Gospel at this station, by the blessing of God on the indefatigable labours of Mr. Hands, our first Missionary there, and of Mr. Taylor and Mr. Reeve, who now assist him, affords us great satisfaction. The ministry of the brethren among the British soldiers of the 84th regiment has been remarkably useful, 27 of that corps having lately been added to their society. " Among the heathen in India," says Mr. Hands, " our prospects are gradually brightening, and we hope you will, ere long, hear that the Lord is doing a great work. O send us more labourers, and let your intercessions on behalf of the poor Hindoos be fervent and incessant !"

Mr. Hands, during the last year, paid a visit to Madras, and took with him the gospels of Matthew and Mark, which he had translated into the Canada language, ready for the press, and was in expectation of getting them printed by the Calcutta Auxiliary Bible Society, which is connected with, and assisted by, the British and Foreign Bible Society in England. The Gospels of Luke and John, the Epistle to the Ephesians, and extracts from other parts of the scriptures are also translated, and it is hoped that in the course of a year or two more, the translation of the whole Bible will be accomplished. Our brethren have not yet obtained a press at Bellary, nor is it certain whether that privilege will be granted, although the public authorities of India have every reason to be assured that it would not be abused.

Mr. Taylor is studying the *Canada* and *Tamul* languages,

and has translated a part of the New Testament from the Tamul into the Canada, and several tracts. These, with Dr. Watts's Catechism, our Lord's Sermon on the Mount, and other tracts which have been distributed among the people, have produced a considerable sensation. Old and young apply for books, which they receive with great thankfulness, and many are beginning to express doubts about the verity of their own religion.

Mr. Reeve makes good progress in learning the language, and bids fair to be a useful Missionary. His labours in English have been greatly blessed. Mrs. R. is also a valuable acquisition to the Missionary family, among the whole of which the utmost harmony prevails.

The schools are carried on with spirit; there are at least seven of these seminaries in the town and neighbourhood, containing about 400 children.* It affords us great satisfaction to learn, that the Scriptures are read in all the schools, and the catechism taught. Prejudices against this measure prevailed at first, but soon subsided; and there is great reason to believe that the instruction afforded has been blessed to many of the children. The brethren feel much interest in this department of their work, and indulge the hope of seeing much good fruit of their labour.

The distribution of tracts and portions of the sacred

---

* The schools at Bellary are as follow :—

1. The Boarding School in Mr. Hands' house, 24 children, some of whom appear to be seriously inclined.

2. The Bellary Charity School in the fort, 34 children; five of whom are boarded, &c. This seminary, in which 200 children have been educated, has been a blessing to many.

3. A Native School in the Mission Garden ; 50 children instructed in the Scriptures and Catechism.

4. An English School for Natives in the Mission Garden, in which 26 are learning the English language.

5. A Native School in the Coul Bazaar, about a mile from the Mission House, in which 55 children are instructed in their own language, and in the principles of Christianity.

There are also Native Schools at Ruggool, Assoondy, Hurriall, and Paltoon, neighbouring villages, in which about 150 children are instructed.

Scriptures has been extensive. Thousands have been dispersed in town and country, and scarcely a day passes without applications for them : this affords a good opportunity of conversing with the natives on their contents. The brethren are also informed that their Catechism is introduced and taught in many schools in the country beside their own.

An Auxiliary Missionary Society, and a Tract Society, are established, together with a Reading Society, composed of about forty members, in which many good books have been read, and more are wanted.

Mr. Hands, in his journey from Bellary to Madras, visited many schools, and distributed a number of Telinga tracts, but was not furnished with a sufficient quantity to gratify all the applicants; but he was delighted to observe the attention with which they were read. Mr. Hands, on his way home, distributed many Canada tracts, and preached frequently in the Ghauts, wherever he halted: great numbers listened attentively to him, while he taught them in their streets; and many followed him to his lodgings, desiring him to explain more fully what he had delivered, and to prolong his stay among them. Surely these are fields already white to the harvest; and who does not wish that many more such labourers may be employed?

TRAVANCORE,

(About 450 miles south of Madras.)

We are happy to inform the Society, that the very important missionary station in this country, which had been relinquished by Mr. Ringeltaube, and which was vacant for some time, is (or, we trust, soon will be) again occupied by Mr. Mead, who, with Mrs. M. and their infant, proceeded thither in September last, from Madras, where he had resided for about a year after his arrival in India.* He was kindly recommended by the Rev. Mr. Thompson,

* We are extremely concerned to hear of the death of Mrs. Mead. See Appendix

of Madras to that distinguished friend of missions, Colonel Monro, the British Resident at Travancore. We trust he will gather together again the scattered sheep, and bring many others into the fold of Christ; but it is necessary he should be joined by another Missionary as soon as pos·sible.*

SURAT,

(A great city on the west coast of India, about 180 *miles north of Bombay.)*

We now cross the great peninsula of India to the populous city of Surat, on the north of the western shore. The brethren Skinner and Fyvie have devoted themselves to the study of the Guzerattee language, in which we believe they have made considerable progress, and in which they hope ere long to be able to publish the gospel of peace: they also intend to compile a Grammar and Dictionary, but not to attempt a publication of them until they are greater proficients in the language. They are, however, preparing for the press a small Catechism, and a few short Scripture Extracts, which they intend to print at Bombay, the American Missionaries having a press, with Guzerattee and Mahratta types. Those valuable men, who are now able to preach to the natives in their own tongue, have begun to print a correct edition of the Scriptures in Mahratta. Our brethren are in expectation of having a printing press at Surat, which they greatly need. They have public worship in their own house, in English, on Sundays, and on Wednesday evenings, when some of the natives occasionally attend, and enquire into the meaning of their service: the Missionaries gladly embrace this opportunity of explaining to them the great things of God.

It is their intention to establish schools as numerously as they can with propriety and prudence, as they have many prejudices to combat. In their English school there are about 50 boys, and about half that number in the native school. We are glad to find, that in Bombay, and we

* Mr. Smith, another Missionary, is appointed to this station.

hope in Surat also, no objection is made to the use of the Scriptures as a school-book.

Mr. Donaldson, who was sent out to aid this mission, informs us, in a letter dated Sept. 19, 1817, that he had arrived safely at Bombay, after a passage of eighteen weeks, and was graciously received by his Excellency Governor Nepean, who promised him a letter of introduction to the principal officers at Surat. Mr. D. was extremely affected with a view of the wretched superstitions of the heathen, of which he observes, that those who are not actual spectators can form no adequate idea, and longed to proceed to his ultimate destination, where he might acquire their language, and be able to preach to them Christ crucified.*

MAURITIUS, or ISLE OF FRANCE.

Mr. Le Brun, who has occupied this station about three years, persists in his labours, but amidst considerable opposition, arising chiefly from the dreadful state of morals in the island. He has, however, the satisfaction of perceiving a great change wrought in some, by the instrumentality of the word. Twenty-five persons are united in a Christian society, and meet for social worship and conference. Mr. Le Brun was also employed by his Excellency Governor Farquhar, in giving religious instruction to the two brothers of a principal chief of Madagascar, and who made considerable progress in a short time. They have since returned to that island, and we hope will be friendly to the Missionaries when they arrive at their station.

MADAGASCAR.

To this very important station the Directors have long turned their attention, and are now happy to state that two young men, Mr. Bevan and Mr. Jones, who received the rudiments of their education under the Rev. Mr. Phillips, of Neuaddlwyd, in Wales, and who have since attended to

* Mr. Donaldson has since joined the Missionaries at Surat.

missionáry studies at Gosport, sailed for the Mauritius in March last, intending to proceed from thence to Madagascar, where we hope a wide and effectual door will be opened to them, for the promulgation of the everlasting Gospel. The principal chief, who sent his brothers to the Mauritius for instruction, and who is said to be anxious for improvement in the arts of civilization, will, we trust, patronise the efforts of our brethren, who will endeavour to impart to him, and to his people, the most important and useful kind of knowledge—that of the Saviour of the world.*

SOUTH AFRICA.

THE Directors will next present to the Society a compendious view of the different missions which have been established in South Africa, among a race of people more generally despised than any other on the face of the globe, but among whom the sovereign Lord of all nations has been pleased to gather into his fold a goodly number of his sheep; and to manifest the riches and power of his grace, in raising more than a few from the lowest state of civil and moral degradation, to the dignity and privileges of the children of God.

CAPE TOWN.

Mr. Thom, who resides in the metropolis of the colony, perseveres in his various labours in the cause of religion,

* This island is said to contain *four millions* of inhabitants, and is in a partial state of civilization. Governor Farquhar, of the Mauritius, has taken much laudable pains in preparing a Vocabulary, Grammar, and Dictionary of the language, collected by a French gentleman, by many years' labour. Three places, Fort Bourbon, St. Luce, and Tamataff, have been occupied by the English; and from these places the Mauritius and Bourbon receive supplies of cattle, &c. The island produces food in abundance: the lower lands near the coast are said to be unhealthy, but not the interior.

both among the colonists and the slaves, of the latter of whom there are multitudes disposed to hear the gospel. Mr. Thom takes a lively interest in the African missions at large, and is enabled, by his residence at the seat of government, to render important services to the cause. But his labours are not restricted to the town; he has again made a tour of about 1800 miles, in which he visited the stations of Mr. Seidenfaden and Mr. Pacalt, and had an opportunity of preaching in Dutch to thousands of colonists, hottentots, and slaves. We doubt not that his labours have been blessed to the conversion and edification of many.

Mr Thom has lately made an application to the Governor for permission to build a chapel in Cape Town, for the instruction of slaves. Mr. Thom's letter was referred by his Excellency to the consistory of the Reformed Church at the Cape, who met to consider it, but broke up without coming to any determination.

He has since hired a dwelling-house, and intends to preach four times every week, in Dutch, and to hold three English Prayer-meetings. His own English congregation has considerably increased lately.

STELLENBOSCH,

(26 miles north-east of Cape Town.)

Mr. Bakker who has faithfully laboured at this station many years, continues to be useful in the town; but, on account of his infirmities, is not able to extend his labours, as he wishes, into the surrounding country.

Mr. Bakker labours under considerable restraint, not being allowed to baptize the converts, or admit them to the Lord's table. This he feelingly laments, and longs to have these unreasonable restrictions removed. He thus expresses his pious sentiments, " I am happy that to me, the least of all saints, is given grace to preach the unsearchable riches of Christ to perishing Heathens; and although I have reason to be thankful, that now and then a blessing is given to my labours, still I wish it were more abundant and I cannot but think, that the use of the sacraments might lead to that end, for although God certainly does not attach salvation to the use of them, yet he can never approve the neglect of commands so especially given. I, therefore, request my honoured brethren to do every thing in their power to settle this point."

The Directors hope, that if a deputation be sent to visit our Missionary stations in Africa, a measure which they have long had in view, and have anxiously endeavoured to accomplish, this impediment may be removed.

The friends of the Missionary cause in this place lament, that, in consequence of the state of the times, they were not enabled to renew the anxiliary donation of the preceding year.

BOSJESVELD,

(In the Drosdy of Tulbagh.)

We have received no information from Mr. Kramer for a long time; in his last letter he tells us, that he was employed in preaching to the slaves, hottentots, and colonists, the latter of whom, being far from any church, greatly needed his assistance, and that, though he expects to derive his support from the people among whom he labours, he still wishes to be considered in connection with this Society.

CALEDON,

(120 miles East of Cape Town.)

This station, which has been occupied by Mr. Seidenfaden about six years, appears to be nearly in the same state as reported last year; the number of baptized adults being about 60, and the children who attend the school, about 50. Considerable improvements have been made by large inclosures for cultivation, especially for kitchengardens, and by making better roads and fences.* The

* Mr. S. says he has planted a *quince-hedge* in the valley, 1800 feet in length, which answers the double purpose of defending the kitchen-gardens, and in two or three years will yield a quantity

E

people belonging to the settlement are about 400. In the long evenings of the winter months, Mr. S. catechised the people every other evening, and was much encouraged by the progress that many of them made in the knowledge of the truth.

HIGH KRAAL,

(Near George Town, 300 miles East of Cape Town.)

Mr. Pacalt's station, which is well situated in the midst of a large plain, about two miles from the sea, and three from George Town, is reported to be in a flourishing state. Much good has been done here in a few years. A place of worship, and two small but good houses have been erected, beside the cottages of the Hottentots, which are placed in regular rows. Mr. Pacalt has two large and fruitful gardens, with good pasture and corn land; the people also have gardens attached to their houses, which they are taught both by precept and example diligently to cultivate. Mr. P. is a laborious Missionary, having a school to attend, as well as to minister the word to the people.

Mr. Evan Evans, who, with other brethren on their way to Bethelsdorp, rested at this place, speaks with delight of the affectionate regard which the people paid to Mr. Pacalt, on his return from a journey; and of their strong expressions of gratitude to this Society for sending them Missionaries; with their astonishment that any could be induced to leave their parents and brothers and sisters in England, to come and live among poor wretched Hottentots. He speaks highly, as many others have done, of the engaging melody of their voices in singing the praises of God.

Mention also is made of the holy triumphs of a Hottentot converted to God at the age of 90, and who, in the

---

of fruit for the use of the poor people. This was planted chiefly by the baptized females, the men being employed in working for the inhabitants in ploughing, &c. and in cultivating their own grounds.

expectation and hope of death, rejoiced with joy unspeakable and full of glory.

BETHELSDORP,

(About 600 miles east of Cape Town.)

The official account of the state of Bethelsdorp for the year 1816, did not reach us in time for insertion in our last Report. From that account we learned, that though the settlement had laboured under some severe discouragements, especially from the sterility of the soil, scanty supply of water, and a bad season for corn ; yet many pleasing instances had occurred of the power of divine grace in the conversion of the Heathen. In the course of that year, the Missionaries had baptized 143 adults, of whose conversion they had no doubt. Surely this ought to be considered as no inconsiderable success, but as an occasion both to them and to us of abundant thanksgiving to God. They had also baptized 100 children. The brethren inform us, that civilization is also progressive among the people, though not in the degree which they earnestly desire.* The knitting-school, under the care of Mrs. Messer, flourishes. Many stockings have been made and sold, and a quantity was ready for sale. Mr. Hooper, who has the care of the school, containing, we believe, more than 300 children, reports favourably of their progress.

The Report of Bethelsdorp for the past year is just come to hand. This station has been strengthened by the accession of Mr. Hooper and Mr. Evan Evans, who are now able to preach in Dutch, and the latter will be eminently serviceable to the cause, by his acquaintance with the art of printing. The Report contains a striking specimen of the talents of one of the native preachers. A new church

* Mr. Messer, in a letter to Mr. Campbell, says, "If you were *now* to visit our kloof, you would see most excellent gardens, of which one belongs to me, where there are many vines, which at this time (January, 1817) are full of grapes nearly ripe. There are also many peach-trees laden with fruit. Last week I gathered a quantity of figs. Between our houses and the mill are excellent gardens, planted with fruit trees, and fenced with high walls.

is now building. The brethren preach occasionally to the military at Algoa Bay. During the last year 15 adults have been baptized, and 34 children; 43 have been born, and 16 have died; 24 couples were married. The settlement includes 45 well cultivated gardens. We hope that this station, the external appearance of which has excited so much censure, is now in an improving state. The spot, indeed was ill chosen, and labours under great disadvantages; but the spiritual benefits received by many persons have far exceeded in real importance, all its external defects.

THEOPOLIS,

(About 60 miles N. E. of Bethelsdorp.)

By letters from our brethren, Ullbricht and Barker, we find, that both have been much indisposed, and the latter almost wholly incapacitated for labour. Mr. Ullbricht expresses much thankfulness to God for his goodness ever since this settlement was formed, as a branch from Bethels-dorp, in the year 1814. The situation, being but two miles from the sea, and near rivers and a wood, is very advantageous, and affords many facilities for a comfortable subsistence. The external circumstances of this station are generally encouraging; much land is cultivated, and but for frequent droughts the produce would be abundant. Their cattle is much increased, and they hope soon to improve their houses; there are now upwards of 80 gardens, each containing about an acre of ground, and additional ones are forming.*

* "In 1814," says Mr. Ullbricht, "we sowed 20 bushels of corn, and gathered but little, on account of the drought. In 1815 we sowed 60 bushels—gathered 608 (of 8 bushels I gathered 224.) In 1816 we sowed 212 bushels, and for my own use 20, but did not gather so much as the last year from the 8. This year (1817) we sowed 252 bushels." It is pleasing to observe the increase of cultivation, and it is a proof that the Missionaries have not been idle or inattentive, as the opposers of the African Missions say, to civilization.

" As to our privileges," says Mr. Ullbricht, " the greatest of all is, that our labour has not been in vain ; many souls have been brought to the knowledge of the Lord: this lightens all our burdens. Our church consists of 87 members (39 men and 48 women)." They have been occasionally plundered by the neighbouring Caffres, whose incursions occasion some degree of apprehension ; but they repose confidence in the Divine Saviour.

Mr. Barker proceeds with the school, though much hindered by extreme illness ; some of the children have begun to write on paper.

An Auxiliary Missionary Society has been formed, which last year produced about £15. besides eight rix dollars contributed by the children of the school.

We entertain much hope that this Settlement will prove a great blessing to the country.

STATIONS BEYOND THE COLONY.

CAFFRARIA,

(Kat River, about 200 miles N. E. of Bethelsdorp.)

To this new, distant, and arduous station, Mr. Williams, with no other assistant than Jan Tsatzoe, a converted native, repaired in July, 1816, where he built a house for himself and family, formed a garden, inclosed ground for corn, and prepared for conducting water to it from a distance. His labour has been very considerable. About 100 Caffres attend his ministry on the Lord's day, and about 70 on other days. He has commenced a school for the native children, about 150 of whom have learned the alphabet ; some could spell, and most of them have committed to memory an excellent hymn. The attention of the people while he preaches is remarkably great; not a word is heard, nor a smile perceived. Mr. Williams entertained some hope of a few persons being under concern for their souls: many continue steadily to attend the word, and unite in prayer; and though their knowledge is yet but small, he had reason to believe that his labour was not wholly in vain.

Mr. Williams greatly needs further assistance; and we hope that Mr. Brownlee, a Missionary originally intended for Lattakoo, and who was inclined to join him, has obtained permission from the Government at the Cape to proceed to Kat River for that purpose.

HEPHZIBAH,

(In Namaqualand, about five days' journey North of Graaf Reynett.)

Mr. Corner and J. Goeyman occupied this station for a short time after Mr. Smit, but were ordered to leave it, and have retired for the present to Bethelsdorp. But we are glad to hear that his Excellency the Governor has permitted Mr. Moffat and Mr. Kitchingman to proceed to this spot, where the people are earnestly desirous of hearing the word.*

GRIQUA TOWN,

(North of the Great, or Orange River.)

We are happy to state, that the mission at Griqua Town appears to be in more favourable circumstances than during the two preceding years. Some persons, who had behaved ill and left the settlement, and whose conduct threatened much mischief, have repented and returned to the settlement, after which the work prospered; and Mr. Anderson, in a letter dated Griqua Town, 15th Jan. 1817, says, " Scarcely a Sabbath passes but we receive one or more by baptism." The revival is chiefly among the females, who have now a social meeting among themselves, in which Mrs. Anderson and Mrs. Helm preside. Mr. Anderson

---

* Mr. Kitchingman is gone to Bethany; he had proceeded on the 3d of December last as far as Byzondermeid, with Mr. Moffat, who who was going to Peace Mountain to join Mr. Ebner.

had baptized 50 adults, chiefly young persons, whose hearts the Lord had powerfully impressed, even at the time in which the enemy of souls was permitted so to rage, as threatened to destroy the whole settlement; but by the preaching of the word, several of the most violent opposers had returned, asking forgiveness,· and promising to do every thing in their power for the good of the station.

A great quantity of corn was sown the last year, and much new land cultivated. All things considered, we have great cause for thankfulness.

BETHESDA,

(On the Great River, between Griqua Town and Pella.)

Mr. Sass relates, in his Journal, many pleasing instances of the power of divine grace in the hearts of the poor *Corannas*, many of whom appear to be truly pious. About 20 adults were baptized in the course of the year, besides children.

The converted people of this settlement, in their intercourse with kraals of Bushmen and others, frequently take occasion affectionately to speak of Christ and salvation to them, and sometimes apparently with much effect. In one place they found a large kraal of Bushmen, and were surprised to hear their Chief speaking to them of the things of God, which he had occasionally heard at Bethesda, and conducting divine service in an orderly manner.

They frequently suffer by the incursions of the wild Bushmen, who steal their cattle. In one instance they apprehended several men, who some months before had robbed them; but instead of punishing them, as was expected, they treated them with kindness, and made them a present of several sheep and goats. They were astonished and ashamed; and one of them, trembling, said to some others, " I shall not believe they will spare my life, until I get home in safety; for though they deal thus kindly with us at present, they will certainly kill us as we return." They found, however, that the benign principles of the Gospel prevailed; and thus the Christians " overcame evil with good." Who can tell what a happy effect such an instance of love may produce; how powerfully it may prevent future assaults, and prepare the hearts of the people to receive the lovely religion of Christ!

Mr. Sass concludes his journal by saying, " Much reason have we to praise and glorify the Lord, our most beloved Saviour, for what he has done among a people so uncivilized. Brethren and fathers, let us have a part in your sincere payers."

LATTAKOO,

(About 800 miles North of the Cape..)

After two unsuccessful attempts to commence a mission in this city, the Missionaries, on their third visit, succeeded. When they arrived there, on the 28th of December, 1816, they found the King sitting in the midst of his Chiefs, and upon informing him that they were come in consequence of the permission he had given to Mr. Campbell, and his promise that he would be a father to them, he began to repeat the objections formerly stated; but having pleaded the King's promise, and that the good people over the great waters had sent them on purpose to do them good, the King gave them leave to unyoke their oxen under the great tree, which amounted to a permission for them to remain. On the very next day one of the brethren who understood the Bootsuanna language commenced preaching to the people.

Not long after the arrival of the Missionaries, the King, with about a thousand of his people, armed, set out on a predatory expedition against a northern tribe, contrary to the earnest solicitations of the brethren, to whose care, however, he committed his queen and family during his absence. When the conflict took place, his forces were immediately routed, about 200 were killed, and himself hurt in his feet in the retreat. He returned with difficulty to Lattakoo, heartily repenting of the ill-judged and unfortunate expedition.

The Missionaries having now obtained his favour and friendship, he requested their continuance with him; though this measure was not agreeable to some of his principal people. And judging that the present scite of the town, which had long been found inconvenient, would become more so by the accession of the Missionaries and those who accompanied them, he determined to remove to a more eligible spot, situated on the banks of the Krooman river, about three days journey nearer to Griqua Town. On the 4th of June, the Missionaries removed to the Krooman, and commenced their preparations for the settlement. Mr. Hamilton's mechanical operations in the structure, of a water-mill filled them with astonishment.*

In a letter, dated May 23, 1817, it is stated, that some of the king's family were very attentive to religious instruction; and that one of them, on hearing a person complain that he could not understand the word, advised him to retire, and say, " Lord Jesus, open my heart to understand and love thy word," assuring him that he would hear his prayer.

The printing-press for Lattakoo is arrived at Griqua Town; and the Missionaries have begun to compile a dictionary and catechism in the Bootsuanna language. We hope ere long to hear that reading, writing, and printing have been commenced at Lattakoo.†

* When they saw Mr. H. make a hole through the millstone, they were astonished, that they thought he must be more than a man. The iron chain of the waggon also filled them with surprise, they could not conceive how the links were put together ; and one of the chiefs seeing a Missionary form a steel, and strike fire with it, insisted he must be a god. Some of the people from the neighbourhood of Lattakoo, observing the superior knowledge of the Missionaries, said to the inhabitants, that they were highly favoured, for God had come to visit them.

This is mentioned only to shew that the avowed superiority of the Missionaries in the knowledge of the useful arts, may prepare the minds of the people for listening to their spiritual instruction.

† Mr. John Evans, who was intended to settle at Lattakoo, has relinquished his work as a Missionary, and is settled as a Dutch minister at Cradock.

The Directors think it is equitable, that he should repay to the Missionary Society their expences on his behalf.

F

MAKOON'S KRAAL, &c.

Mr. Campbell having given the people of Malapeetzee and Makoon's Kraal reason to expect that Missionaries would be sent to them, one of the brethren determined, as soon as possible after arriving at Lattakoo, to pay them a visit. It appeared, that the Corannas had left *Malapeetzee,* and removed to the *Matslakoo River.* The Missionary was received with open arms, and the people immediately flocked to hear the word. They declared that they had waited impatiently for the fulfilment of the promise made them four years ago ; that they had tried to live without the word of God, but found it impossible, and insisted upon the Missionary continuing with them ; they had heard, they said, that the word was going to every nation, and they were afraid of being too late. The Missionary could not possibly stay with them, but promised to send a preacher very shortly.

Makoon also was most earnestly desirous that the Missionary who visited them from Lattakoo should abide with them ; which being impracticable, they were rejoiced when *Cupido* agreed to stay with them. One of the chiefs appears to be a man of prayer, and worships God devoutly with his family ; and such was his attachment to the word, that he had resolved to accompany the Missionary to Lattakoo, but he was providentially hindered. Cupido was, by solemn prayer, separated to the work at this station ; and it is hoped he will become the instrument of much good. Thus far the Society has endeavoured to fulfil the promise made to these poor heathen, that Missionaries should be sent to preach to them the word of life.

BETHANY,

(In Namaqua Land, about two days' journey north of the Great River.)

By a letter from Mr. Schmelen, dated 10th March, 1817, we are informed, that on his return from the Cape, whither he had been on business, he learned on the road, that he should not be able immediately to proceed to his distant station, in consequence of the want of water for his oxen, which were wearied out; he therefore wrote to his people at Bethany, to send more oxen, to help him onward. In the mean time, he proceeded to Pella, to settle the affairs of the Mission there.

At the place from which he writes, formerly called *Byzondermeid*, but now *Steinkopff*, he informs us, that there is among the people a general desire to hear the word, and that a praying spirit prevails among them; a place of worship is built, and service regularly performed, morning and evening. But of the state of the Mission at Bethany, we have not received any particulars.*

JERUSALEM,

(Formerly called Peace Mountain, and Africaner's Kraal.)

Mr. Ebner, who resides at this station, informs us, that about 400 people attend the place of worship, which is now too small for the accommodation of all who wish to hear. " Since I came," says Mr. Ebner, " to Africaner's kraal, which I have named Jerusalem, I have baptized 40 persons, converts, and their children, and married about 40 couple. I have received 100 Bibles and 100 Testaments from the British and Foreign Bible Society, for the use of those who can read the Dutch language. He reports several instances of the converting grace of God, and says, that the converts continue to be much attached to the Gospel, and to himself as their teacher; and that they maintain among themselves social meetings for prayer and conference, in which they express their religious views and feelings with remarkable animation.

* On his journey Mr. Schmelen met a Namaqua chief, who was going to the Cape, there, if possible, to procure a Missionary for his people, when Mr. Shaw, of the Wesleyan connexion, who had resided some time at Cape Town, and was travelling with Mr. Schmelen, agreed to accompany that chief to the place of his residence (Camies Mountain,) and abide with the people, which he accordingly did; and we gladly learn that his prospects are very pleasing.

Civilization, which always accompanies the introduction of the Gospel, is also making progress. Mr. Ebner has introduced potatoes, and other useful vegetables, which prosper beyond his expectation ; he speaks also favourably of the crops of corn, and rejoices, in hope, that the natives will soon reap abundant advantage from the increase of the comforts of life among them, as well as from the superior blessings of the Gospel of grace : and thus is presented to the world another proof of the truth of what one of the Missionaries before asserted, that in Africa "the Bible and the plough go together."

On a review of the state of our Missions in Africa, we find occasion to sing both " of mercy and of judgment." With grief we have heard of the lamentable fall of one of our Missionaries into immorality, and to learn, at the same time, of a few instances of less flagrant misconduct in others ; but the feelings excited by this afflictive intelligence have since been alleviated by intimations of repentance on the part of the offenders, which it is hoped will be followed by satisfactory evidence of its reality. It has, consequently, been the painful duty of the Directors to mark their detestation of the faults committed, in such a way, as will, it is hoped, maintain the honour of the cause, and prove an admonition to others. They also trust, that some irregularities in the management of our affairs in that part of the world, will be fully remedied by the wisdom and prudence of the Deputation, which they hope soon to send to Africa.

When we consider the numerous perils and strong temptations to which our Missionary brethren in Africa are exposed, we cannot but recommend them to the constant and fervent prayers of all the members of the Society. Let them not be forgotten in your daily supplications. They greatly need them ; they earnestly entreat them. O! pray that God may keep them, by his mighty power, through faith, unto salvation!

MALTA.

Mr. LOWNDES, who arrived in Malta in November 1816, has continued there, as at first proposed, for the purpose of acquiring the Italian and modern Greek languages. While thus employed, he has embraced every opportunity of preaching the Gospel, and, we have reason to think, not in vain. Several persons appear to have derived solid advantage from his ministry; and he is very desirous that, when he leaves Malta for the Greek Islands, another minister from England may fill his place. It is probable, that he will soon be enabled to proceed to Corfu or Zante, to pursue the original object of his mission—the revival of pure religion in Greece and in the Greek Islands. The Directors intend soon to send another Missionary to Malta.

WEST INDIES.

DEMERARY.

THE accounts received from Mr. Davies, Mr. Elliot, and Mr. Smith, who labour in different parts of this extensive and populous colony, are peculiarly gratifying. Several thousands of the negro slaves, as permitted, in rotation, by their masters, attend on Mr. Davies, at George Town, on Mr. Elliot, on the West Coast, and on Mr. Smith, at Le Resouvenir. These people gladly hear the word, and in many cases, it is believed, with the best effect. We are grieved to find, that the opposers of missions have defamed our brethren in the public newspapers; on which account they have judged it necessary, in vindication of their character, to appeal to the justice of their country. We are persuaded, however, that their blameless conduct, and the good effects of their instruction on the slaves, will finally prevail against the unhappy prejudices entertained by some of their owners, whose interest, we are confident, would be best promoted by the universal instruction of the negroes.

The congregation at Le Resouvenir, formerly under the care of Mr. Wray, has been much revived and increased. The chapel built by Mr. Post, is now insufficient for those who desire to attend, and a larger, in a more eligible situation, is about to be built; the negroes have offered all the assistance in their power towards its erection. Great attention is paid to catechetical instruction; and the negroes are very diligent in learning the catechism. It is peculiarly pleasing, that those who learn of the Missionaries, take pains to teach others who cannot personally attend; so that the knowledge of divine truth is rapidly and widely extend. ing. Mr. Smith has baptized 70 or more negroes, after due examination, and upon receiving a recommendation from their respective masters, who readily acknowledge the good effect of religious instruction, apparent in their diligence and the improvement of their morals.*

The success of our brethren in this colony, and the earnest desire generally expressed by the negroes to be instructed, have induced the Directors to determine on sending two more labourers into this promising part of the vineyard, one of whom is to be stationed at *Mahaica*, where the people have long enjoyed occasional instruction. Mr. Smith says, " the poor slaves bless and pray for the Directors and friends of the Missionary cause."

---

* While some of the masters are apprehensive that the religious instruction of the slaves will prove injurious to their interests, and therefore forbid their attendance, others are fully satisfied that religion will make their slaves more docile and useful. A pleasing instance of this kind is related by Mr. Smith : " There is a slave, of the name of *Gingo*, whose master gives him, as he does many others, *task work*. When this is appointed, he says, ' Now, Gingo, when you have done this, you may go and pray.' Gingo replied, " Me glad massa know now dat pray do every ting." The death of this valuable slave, who used to lead the singing in the chapel, is much lamented by his sable brethren.

A planter, who complained that one of his slaves was too religious, admitted, however, that " in every other respect he was a good servant, and that he would not sell him for 6,000 guilders," above £400; a sufficient proof that religion had not spoiled him,

BERBICE.

The laborious efforts of Mr. Wray in behalf of tho
slaves of this colony promised much usefulness. Many of
the slaves on the crown estates, on which he resided for
some time, had been taught to read; and not a few of them
appeared to have received the truth in the love of it. Many
of them had been baptised, and admitted into the visible
church of Christ. These estates, however, having been
restored about two years ago, by a special convention to
the Dutch Company, to whom they had formerly belonged,
Mr. Wray was soon wholly excluded from them by the new
managers; and the poor slaves were not only deprived of
the benefit of his personal instructions, but the Bibles,
hymn books, and other good books he had given them,
were forcibly taken away, and all communication with him
prohibited.

Since this painful occurrence, Mr. Wray has been engaged in the instruction of a large body of slaves, about
300 in number, who belong to the British government, and
reside in the town of New Amsterdam, where they are
employed chiefly as mechanics. In the pursuit of this
object, he has hitherto enjoyed the countenance and aid of
the British Government; and the Directors are led to hope
that these will be continued to him. Some very embar-
rassing and perplexing difficulties, however, have been
thrown in his way, by persons on the spot; and, with a
view to their removal, he has been induced to visit England.
He will shortly return to Berbice, and resume his labours,
where Mrs. Wray, during his necessary absence, has continued to instruct, with great assiduity, the young and
female part of his congregation. The situation in which
Providence has placed him is highly important; for besides
the Crown slaves already mentioned, among whom he
labours with the direct sanction and encouragement of the
British Government, his preaching is attended on Sundays
by a number of other slaves, by many free people of colour,
and even by some whites. Divine service has hitherto been
performed by Mr. Wray in a large room; but it is intended

that a chapel shall be built for the accommodation of the congregation.

TRINIDAD.

Mr. Adam continues in this island, and statedly preaches in the town of Port of Spain, where there are some who attend very seriously; and among whom, during the past year, he has seen some pleasing instances of conversion. The unfounded apprehension of danger from the meetings of negro slaves, which prevails in the West Indies, has induced his Excellency the Governor to impose peculiar restrictions upon the labours of the Missionaries in Trinidad, to which Mr. Adam thought it his duty respectfully to object; but the result we have not yet heard.

Mr. Adam meets with more encouragement at a place on the coast, which he frequently visits, where the word appears to make very powerful impressions, and where the planters have proposed to support a preacher. The Directors have therefore acceded to the earnest and repeated request of Mr. Adam, and in February last sent out Mr. Mercer, who was for a time under the instruction of the Rev. Mr. Newton, at Witham.

A few months ago, Mr. Adam, in an excursion into the interior of the island, had an opportunity of paying a visit to a new settlement, consisting of upwards of 600 negroes, who were formerly slaves in North America; but having been taken prisoners in the late war, by the British, were brought to Trinidad, where they were made free, and had land assigned them, which they cultivate for their support, assistance being afforded them until that could be accomplished. These people, some of whom had acquired the knowledge of the Gospel in America, now occupy ten or twelve villages, where they maintain, as well as they are able, the worship of God. They are well reported of as quiet, sober, and industrious people. Mr. Adam was greatly delighted with their appearance; and they were highly gratified by his friendly visit, and his preaching among them. He is desirous of establishing schools, and procuring a minister for them.

BRITISH NORTH AMERICA.

From the brethren who went to various places in British North America, very little has been heard during the past year. Mr. Spratt remains, we believe, at Quebec.

Mr. Smart informs us that he is about to build a chapel in Brockville, and intends to come to England for the purpose of soliciting subscriptions towards the expence of its erection.

Mr. Pigeon, who has resided for some years in Prince Edward Island has accepted the charge of St. Peter's parish, which is extensive and populous. He expresses his hope that the expence of the Society, in sending him out to that part of the world, and his own labours and hardships, will now be amply rewarded.

Mr. Sabine, who succeeded Mr. Hyde, at St. John's, Newfoundland, is under the necessity of removing to the United States, on account of the inability of the congregation to support his large family, in consequence of those dreadful conflagrations which took place in that town in the commencement of last winter. The Directors, taking into consideration the importance of continuing the ministry of the gospel at St. John's, and the liberal contribution which the congregation afforded some years ago to this Institution, have voted £100. towards the support of another minister.

IRKOUTSK, IN SIBERIA;

(About 4000 miles east of St. Petersburgh.)

At our last Annual Meeting, Mr. Stallybrass, a Missionary intended for this distant and important station, had an opportunity of taking leave of the Society, and requesting their prayers for his success. Soon after that day he embarked, with Mrs. S. for St. Petersburgh, where they safely arrived; and Mr. S. applied himself with ardour to

G

the acquirement of the Russian language, as well as to the preaching of the word among the English residents, to many of whom, we trust, his ministry was not less useful than acceptable. Many persons being desirous of hearing the gospel, Dr. Paterson has been induced to preach to them; and another minister, (Mr. Swan) who may also promote the Missionary cause, in connection with the Missionaries already sent to Irkoutsk, will soon depart from hence, and reside, at least for a time, at St. Petersburg.

While the Directors were anxiously enquiring for a second Missionary to unite with Mr. Stallybrass in his great undertaking, they were highly gratified by the generous offer of a pious and well-established clergyman, the Rev. Cornelius Rahmn, of Gottenburg, who, on the representation of this interesting subject to him by our valuable friend Dr. Paterson, on his return from England to St. Petersburg, and on our earnest invitation, readily relinquished all his respectable connections and pleasing prospects, to devote himself to the service of Christ among the Heathen. These brethren, having received all possible encouragement and assistance from Dr. Paterson and other friends, and aided by the officers of government at St. Petersburg, left that city on the 3d of January last, and arrived at Moscow on the 15th. His Imperial Majesty, having expressed a wish to see them, they had the honour of an interview with the Emperor, who received them most graciously, and conversed with them freely on the object of their journey, which he warmly approved. His Majesty assured them, that every possible facility should be afforded them on their journey, and that his prayers should ascend to God on their behalf. After taking leave of his Excellency Prince Gallitzin, who had promoted their interest with the most friendly and pious ardour, and of his Excellency M. Papoff, who had also been their zealous friend, they proceeded on their journey towards Irkoutsk, on the 19th. By a letter, which has been received, dated 27th Feb. we have had the satisfaction to learn, that Mr. Stallybrass and his companions had, on the preceding day, reached the city of Tobolsk in Siberia.* They had accomplished rather more than half their long and arduous journey, and, through the preserving care and goodness of their Divine Protector, with much less fatigue and inconvenience than, considering the season of the year in which they travelled, could have been expected. Every thing that human care and kindness could effect, had been done for them by order of the most excellent Emperor of Russia and his Government, and they were received and treated with the utmost respect and attention by persons in authority throughout their whole route. They were looking forward earnestly to the intended place of their labours, at which, we trust, they have, ere this, arrived.†

CALMUCKS.

The Directors have lately granted one hundred pounds, in addition to three hundred formerly given, in aid of the Moravian Mission to the Calmucks, of the Torgutsk tribe, where the brethren *Schill* and *Huebner*, having now acquired their language, are beginning to preach the Gospel; and from whom very agreeable communications, holding out pleasing prospects, have been received.

SEMINARY.

It is with a high degree of satisfaction, that the Directors are enabled, by the report of their deputation, who lately visited Gosport,‡ to state, that the Seminary under the

* From St. Petersburg to Moscow is 530 English miles.

Moscow to Perm	979
Perm to Tobolsk	607
Tobolsk to Tomsk	777
Tomsk to Irkoutsk	1047
Total	3940

From Irkoutsk to Pekin, in China, about 1,500 miles.

† They arrived at Irkoutsk, March 30th, 1818, in good and improved health.

‡ The Deputation consisted of the Rev. Dr. Winter, the Rev. John Humphrys, and the Rev. George Collison.

direction of our venerable brother Dr. Bogue, now assisted
by his son Mr. David Bogue, is in a very prosperous state.
We transcribe a part of the Report. " Your deputation
has great pleasure in reporting the encouraging state of
the Missionary Seminary at Gosport. Of the assiduous
attention of the respected theological tutor to the formation
and improvement of the minds of his pupils, they cannot
speak too highly. His mode of lecturing on theological
subjects, appears to them peculiarly adapted to impart information, to meet and vanquish objections, to excite talent,
and to direct every accession of knowledge to the great
purpose of preparing the young men for the arduous employment before them." They speak also in terms of com-
mendation of Mr. David Bogue, of his qualifications for
the classical branch of education, and of his useful method
of teaching; and they observe, that the superior attention
now paid to the languages, promises to be of great advantage to those students who may be required to translate the
Holy Scriptures into the language of the heathen.

The Deputation, together with the Tutor, report very
favourably also of the students ;—as to their acquisition of
knowledge, the correctness of their doctrinal views, and
of their decided piety and devotedness to the work of God.

There are now nineteen students in the seminary, several
of whom will probably soon depart to their various scenes
of labour.

It should here be noticed, and with great thankfulness,
that some of the students now at the seminary, as well as
some who have lately finished their studies there, had received the benefit of classical instruction at other academies,
before their admission at Gosport; and the Society has
lately enjoyed the services of some others, who have already
completed their education. They receive it with gratitude,
as " a token for good," that the Lord has inclined the hearts
of pious young men, whose talents have already been tried
and approved, to devote themselves to Missionary labours,
and to consecrate to Christ their literary attainments, in
order to promote his kingdom among the heathen. And
they indulge the hope, that many more, in the various col-

leges and seminaries of England, Wales, Scotland, and Ireland, will be actuated by the same noble and disinterested motives.

During the past year, the Directors have sent forth into the field of labour ten Missionaries:—Mr. Stallybrass and Mr. Rahmn, to Irkoutsk; Mr. Mercer to Trinidad; Messrs. Milton, Fleming, Beighton, and Ince, to Malacca; and Messrs. Bevan and Jones to Madagascar; and Mr. Gyles, as a cultivator, to Otaheite. Eight of these brethren went out married.

FUNDS.

The Funds of the Missionary Society form a subject which its Directors must ever regard with peculiar earnestness; and its intelligent friends will fully share in their feelings.

In reference to this important topic, the Directors are sensible that they have reason, and they are conscious that they have the best inclination, to express their obligations to the friends of the Society throughout the kingdom, for the liberality which they have always manifested towards it. The propriety of their making this acknowledgment will not be considered, however, as lessening the expediency of their offering some observations on the present state of their Funds, and on the relative proportion which they bear to the present and future operations of the Society. The importance of such considerations will indeed be obvious after the Directors have stated, that there is a diminution in the Income of the Society, so far as it arises from Annual Subscriptions and other Voluntary Contributions for the year just expired, when compared with that of the preceding year; and a still greater defalcation in the same source of supply, when compared with the proceeds of the year, ending April 1, 1816. That such would be one of the results of the serious distresses which have prevailed during the last two years, through the country at large, it was natural to expect; and it leads the Directors as confidently to look for the return of former abounding liberality, in proportion as the pressure which has restrained it is removed; and that the realization of this hope is not of less moment to the progress of the Society's operations, than it is desirable to the feelings of its friends, the following observations will, it is presumed, sufficiently evince.

It was an expectation formed by the founders of the Society, and long cherished by its Directors, and also one which appeared so reasonable, that nothing but contradictory experience could have weakened it,—that the expences of our Missionary settlements, and especially of those formed in countries where a considerable population is found, would be merely temporary; and that a few years would, at least, render the several stations self-supported, if not contributory to the expences of spreading the Gospel embraced by themselves, among their kindred heathen. Thus, it was presumed, that the Funds, disengaged from the earlier stations, would be applicable to the formation of new ones; and an unlimited progress in the Society's operations be provided for, without any considerable progressive augmentation of income. But this hope has not been realized in the case of any mission yet undertaken by the Society. On the contrary it is found, not only that the Missionaries derive little or no support from the places in which they reside, but that their claims on the Society augment in proportion as their families enlarge. It may also be observed (as it stands in near relation to the subject) that the families of the Missionaries are occasioning further and very serious demands on the Funds of the Society, which are urged upon the Directors with considerable importunity, not merely by various Missionaries abroad, but by their friends at home; and which, if met, even to a limited extent, will, from the large and increasing number of those to whom they refer, become a heavy and growing charge upon them. These circumstances afford weighty points of consideration to the members of the Society at large; and they impose upon the Directors the necessity of distinguishing, in their estimates of the expences and income of the Institution, between those charges which, arising from the missions already established, must be considered as *permanent,* and those which, depending on the undertaking of new missions, may be regarded as *conditional* or *contingent.* The charges of the first class, while they are peremptory, as having the force of positive engagements, to which all the resources of the Society are pledged, are already of a very great amount; and they will be augmented every year by each new mission, in which expences of the latter class are incurred. Indeed, it may be stated, as a point not to be viewed with indifference, that, added to the cost of the education of the Students already engaged, and the charges of management (which must also be considered of the same class) the actual amount of this division in the expenditure of the Society, during the last year, amounts to three-fourths of its revenues from ordinary sources It follows, therefore, that limitations are approaching, and that not slowly, to the extension of the Society's operations, which will ill comport with the enlarged and benevolent hopes and expectations of its members; or that the re-served Funds, which afford solidity to the system, must be progressively absorbed, unless the growing dispropor-tion be checked by a decrease in the expenditure of the existing missions, or by a renewed and progressive advance in the income of the Society. It will be the duty of the Directors to do every thing in their power consistently to economize, as well as enlarge the Funds; but in the latter of these labours, especially, they must chiefly rely, in due dependence on Divine Providence, on the zeal and energy of their Christian brethren through the United Kingdom, by whom the Institution has been founded, and is sup-ported. And it is in order to shew to their constituents in every part of the country, more clearly than they would most probably otherwise apprehend it, the need which really exists, not merely for the continuance, but the augmen-tation of liberality, that this view of the financial prospects of the Society has been given by the Directors; judging that, as their close inspection of its affairs causes them to foresee the advancing evil, it is their duty to give timely notice of it to the members at large, in order that, by their zealous efforts in supporting the Funds, they may coun-teract its silent though certain operation.

It is besides proper, on the part of the Directors, not longer to defer placing before the Society at large, a view of its financial prospects, inasmuch as mistaken opinions of an existing superfluity have been formed, and objections founded on them have been avowedly urged for the purpose of restricting the liberality of the religious public.

As to the means of effecting the desired end, the Directors cannot but look with earnestness to the increase of Voluntary Associations throughout the country. Experience has proved such Associations to be among the most effective means of replenishing the funds of all institutions of magnitude which have been called into action. Nor is the value of the principle on which they are founded to be estimated by its influence in merely a pecuniary respect, important as that is; it is of still higher utility, as a source of those feelings of interest in the *object* itself, which are best maintained by a visible relation to the instruments and measures by which that object is promoted. It enlarges the sphere of the privileges of the great Christian community; it makes a personal co-operation in the measures by which the Gospel of Jesus Christ is to be promoted, the happiness and the honour of the many, which, till of late years, were regarded as the exclusive property of the few; and as it precludes no rank, so it debars no age from that distinction. There is also another ground on which a zealous activity in the formation of Auxiliary Institutions may be pressed on the friends of the Missionary Society;—that it is necessary, in order to preserve the just proportion between the progress of our Society and that of others following in the same career of Christian philanthropy, whose energy and activity in applying the principle to their respective Institutions, ought not only to be admired, but also imitated.

Leaving with their zealous friends these observations, the Directors beg to assure them, that no inference resulting from them shall induce them to relax in their best endeavours to fulfil, to their greatest extent, the hopes and expectations of the Society, in carrying into effect the plans already formed for new and interesting missions, and in embracing those farther opportunities which the Great

Head of the Church may open to them, relying on his continued favour, and the affectionate support of British
Christians.

Having recited the proceedings of this Society in the
great work of evangelizing the heathen, we cannot refrain
from expressing our unfeigned pleasure in witnessing the
progress and success of other Societies in our own country,
and abroad; we perceive with delight the zeal with which
they are animated, the liberality with which they are sup-
ported, and the blessed effects which have already attended
their labours. The great object which for many ages and
generations seemed to be unnoticed, or was thought unat-
tainable, has now taken full possession of the minds of our
fellow Christians, of almost all denominations, and we hope
will become a kind of national—of universal concern. We
cannot, therefore, but indulge the hope, that the glorious
season, long predicted, is at hand, when the name of Jesus
shall be exalted in every land and by every tongue.

Whilst the Directors reflect with pleasure on the extent
to which the efforts of the Society have been carried, and
on the continuance of that efficient support which has been
derived from the annual subscribers, from numerous congregations, and the auxiliary societies in town and country,
to whom we most thankfully make our acknowledgments,
we beg leave to remind our friends, that what has already
been achieved bears no proportion, or at most a very small
proportion, to the crying necessities of a perishing world,
" lying in wickedness."

The countries in which our Missionaries are now placed,
require many additional labourers. India Proper, and
India beyond the Ganges, as well as Africa and the West
Indies, demand many, many more Missionaries, there being
almost every where a disposition to hear the Gospel; while
islands and countries yet unattempted by us, Sumatra,
Borneo, and Penang; Persia, Tartary, Abyssinia, Egypt,
Greece, South America—regions containing hundreds of
millions of souls, excite the commisseration and claim the

H

help of British Christians. Let us therefore, beloved brethren, steadily persist in the course we have commenced; and instead of relaxing our efforts, let us redouble our zeal; let us abound yet more and more in the work of the Lord, for as our labour has not been, so are we confident it will not be, in vain in the Lord.

TITLE OF THE SOCIETY.

At the last General Meeting of the Society, held at Spa Fields Chapel, on Thursday the 14th of May, 1818, it was unanimously

' *Resolved,*

'That the Title of this Society be in future " THE MISSIONARY SOCIETY, USUALLY CALLED THE LONDON MISSIONARY SOCIETY." '

APPENDIX.

No. I.

SOUTH SEA ISLANDS.

Letter from the Missionaries at Eimeo to the Directors.

Honoured Fathers and Brethren,   *Eimeo, Aug.* 13, 1816.

THE last letter we received from you was dated July 23, 1814, and reached us in May 1815, as we have mentioned before. And our last to you was dated Sept. 5, 1815, a duplicate of which, as usual, accompanies this. We gladly embrace the present opportunity of giving you a further account of the state of the Islands and of the Mission. At the time the above-mentioned letter was written, the state of affairs in these Islands was full of confusion and uncertainty; the balance, as far as we could perceive, was nearly equipoised; it appeared very doubtful whether the heathen party, who had taken up arms to avenge the cause of their gods, and the ancient customs of their forefathers, might not prevail, and occasion either the extermination or banishment of all who had embraced Christianity, together with ourselves, at least from these Islands of Tahiti and Eimeo. The months of July and August, previous to the date of our letter, had been with us and our poor people a time of trouble and great anxiety. The 14th of July we had set apart as a day of humiliation, fasting, and prayer, and were joined by several hundreds of our people, in seeking mercy and protection from Him who has the hearts of all men in his hand, and to whose control all actions and events are subject. It was ' a day of trouble ' with us; and we and our persecuted people called upon Jehovah : and we think there is no presumption in saying our supplications were regarded, our prayers were answered; for, according to his promise, He sent us ' deliverance,' though not in the way which we anticipated or expected.

The people at Tahiti, who had embraced Christianity, having providentially made their escape, and joined us at Eimeo, their enemies, as we mentioned before, quarrelled among themselves. The Atahura party having fought with and vanquished the Porionu, Teharoa, &c. they and the Taiarabu party, who had assisted them, quarrelled again among themselves, and fought; when the Taiarabuans were conquered, and driven to the mountains. After this there was a prospect of peace being established; and the people who, on account of religion, had fled to Eimeo to save their lives, were invited to return to Tahiti, and take re-

H 2

possession of their respective lands. This made it necessary for the king and his people, and most of those about us, to go over to Tahiti, in company with the different parties of refugees, and, according to an ancient custom of the country, to reinstate them in a formal manner in their old possessions.

On the arrival of the king, and those who followed him, at Tahiti, the idolatrous party appeared on the beach in a hostile manner; seemed determined to oppose the king's landing, and soon fired on his party; but ,by the king's strict orders, the fire was not returned, but a message of peace sent to them, which was productive of the exchange of several messages, and at last apparently issued in peace and reconciliation.

In consequence of this, several of the people returned peaceably to their different lands; but still fears and jealousies existed on both sides. This state of things continued till Sabbath-day, November 12th, 1815, when the heathen party, taking advantage of the day, and of the time when the king and all the people were assembled for worship, made a furious, sudden, and unexpected assault, thinking they could at such a time easily throw the whole into confusion. They approached with confidence, their Prophet having assured them of an easy victory. In this, however, they were mistaken. It happened that we had warned our people, before they went to Tahiti, of the probability of such a stratagem being practised, should a war take place; in consequence of which they attended worship under arms; and though at first they were thrown into some confusion, they soon formed for repelling the assailants: the engagement became warm and furious, and several fell on both sides.

In the king's party there were many of the refugees from the several parties who had not yet embraced Christianity; but our people, not depending upon them, took the lead in facing the enemy, and as they were not all engaged at once, being among bushes and trees, those who had a few minutes of respite fell on their knees, crying to Jehovah for mercy and protection, and that he would be pleased to support His cause against the idolatry of the heathen. Soon after the commencement of the engagement *Upufara*, the Chief of Papara, (the principal man on the side of the idolaters,) was killed; this, when known, threw the whole of his party into confusion, and Pomare's party quickly gained a complete victory. However, the vanquished were treated with great lenity and moderation; and Pomare gave strict orders that they should not be pursued, and that the women and children should be well treated. This was complied with; not a woman or child was hurt; nor was the property of the vanquished plundered. The bodies also of those who fell in the engagement, contrary to the former barbarous practice, were decently buried; and the body of the Chief of Papara was taken in a respectful manner to his own land, to be buried there.

These things had a happy effect upon the minds of the idolaters. They unanimously declared that they would trust their gods no longer; that they had deceived them, and sought their ruin; that henceforward they would cast them away entirely, and embrace the new religion, which is so distinguished by its mildness, goodness, and forbearance.

In the evening after the battle the professors of Christianity assembled together, to worship and praise Jehovah for the happy turn which their affairs had taken. In this they were joined by many who had, till then, been the zealous worshippers of the idols. After this Pomare was, by universal consent, restored to his former government of Tahiti and its dependencies; since which he has constituted chiefs in the several districts, some of whom had for a long time made a public profession of Christianity, and had for many months attended the means of instruction with us at Eimeo.

In consequence of these events idolatry was entirely abolished, both at Tahiti and Eimeo; and we had the great, but formerly unexpected, satisfaction of being able to say, that Tahiti and Eimeo, together with the small islands of Tapua-manu and Te-taroa, are now altogether in profession *Christian Islands*. The gods are destroyed, the morais demolished, human sacrifices and infant murder, we hope, for ever abolished; and the people every where calling upon us to come and teach them.

The Sabbath-day is also every where strictly observed, and places for the worship of the true God have been erected, and are now erecting, in every district; and where there is no preaching, the people have prayer-meetings every Sabbath, and every Wednesday evening, all round Tahiti and Eimeo.

But this is not all; we have also good news to communicate as to the Leeward Islands. *Tamotoa*, or, as he is now called, *Tapa*, the principal chief, has likewise publicly renounced idolatry, and embraced Christianity. His example has been followed by most of the other chiefs, and a large majority of the people throughout the four Society Islands; viz. Huaheine, Raiatea (or Reiadea), Tahaa (or Otaha), and Borabora (or Bolabola). Two chiefs of Borabora, named *Tefaaora* and *Mai*, have distinguished themselves by their zeal in destroying the gods, and erecting a house for the worship of the true God. The chiefs of these islands have sent letters and repeated messages to us, earnestly entreating us to send some of our number to them to teach them also; and *Mai*, a chief of Borabora, sent us a letter to remind us, that Jesus Christ and his apostles did not confine their instructions to one place or country.

A war broke out lately at Raiatea also, one principal cause of which was, that *Tapa* and others had cast away and destroyed the gods. The idolaters were resolved to revenge this, and in consequence attacked *Tapa* and his friends, but were themselves, as at Tahiti, entirely defeated, and afterwards treated with much more lenity than they deserved; but though they were then subdued, yet there is still a party at Raiatea talking of war, and the restoration of the gods; but it seems probable that they will not be able to effect any thing of importance, as the great majority of the people appear decidedly in favour of Christianity.

Since the above happy change of affairs at Tahiti, Brother Nott, at the request of the brethren, went over on a visit to Tahiti, accompanied by Brother Hayward. He preached to the people in every district all around the islands. Large congregations readily assembled everywhere, and their attention and behaviour was very encouraging.—At the present time Brother Bicknell is there, partly for the purpose of preaching to the people in the different districts, judging also that the voyage and journey may be conducive to the restoration of his health, which is much impaired, and has been in a very precarious state for many months past.

The school, notwithstanding former discouragements, has prospered exceedingly, and continues to prosper; though, at present, many hundreds of the scholars are scattered through the neighbouring islands, some of whom are teaching others in the different islands and districts where they reside; and thus, through their means, some knowledge of reading and writing has spread far and wide. There are at least 3000 people who have some books, and can make use of them. Many hundreds can read well; and there are among them about 400 copies of the Old Testament History, and 400 of the New, which is an abridgement of the four Evangelists, and part of the Acts of the Apostles.—Many chapters of Luke's gospel, in manuscript, are also in circulation; and 1000 copies of our Taheitean catechism, which several hundreds have learnt, and can perfectly repeat. The spelling-books, which were printed in London, of which we received, we suppose, about 700, having been expended long ago, we had lately 2000 copies of a lesser spelling-book printed in the colony. These we have received and distributed; and there is an earnest call from all the islands for more books, the desire to learn to read and write being universal. We want a new edition of the abovementioned books, and are now preparing the gospel of Luke for the press. We intended to send the catechism and small spelling-book to the colony by this conveyance, and get 2 or 3000 printed; but having heard that a printing-press is sent out for us, we thought it best to wait awhile, notwithstanding the urgent call of the natives, as we wish to prevent expense as much as possible.

From a view of our present circumstances, our deficiencies, and the state of the mission, we rejoiced to learn that the Directors thought proper to accede to our request, and to add to our number; and that among those that are intended for these islands there is a person that understands printing; we hope the others also are such as the present state of the mission particularly requires, and such as we have pointed out in our former letters; viz. 'such as possess a true missionary spirit, suitable abilities to acquire the language, and to engage in the immediate work of the mission, particularly to assist in the translation of the Scriptures.' If this should be the case, and our hope be realized, we, as well as our people, shall have cause to rejoice for such a timely supply—on the other hand, should the case be reversed, our disappointment and regret will be proportionably great.

In our last we mentioned Brother Crook's intention of coming to our assistance, and we suppose that what he wrote himself on the subject has reached you long before this; we are now happy to say that he and his family, after rather a tedious voyage, arrived here in good health on the 8th of May last.

As to ourselves, we are at present, through mercy, upon the whole, in a tolerably good state of health; yet one or another often complains: Brother Bicknell's ill state of health we mentioned before, but we hope his journey to Tahiti will be beneficial to him. We do not think our present situation on this island (Eimeo) so healthy (particularly in the rainy season) as many other places that might be found in the islands; yet circumstances have in a manner confined us to this spot, so that for a long time past we have had no choice.

The little case of medicines and the other articles, mentioned in your letter of July 1814, reached us in the end of December last, and proved a very seasonable supply. We shall quickly want more medicines, as there is often much illness among our people, and they constantly make application to us in their bodily as well as mental distresses. Brother Henry has had an addition to his family, Mrs. Henry being brought to bed of another daughter some months ago. The widow of our late Brother Scott has been lately married to Mr. George Bicknell, nephew of Brother Bicknell.*

Our vessel is still in hand, not finished, partly through want of materials, and partly through illness and want of time to attend to it during many of the past months. Moreover, we have been of late much discouraged as to the prospect of turning it to any good account; for, since we commenced it, things have assumed entirely a different aspect, both as to the mission and the state of mercantile affairs. For now, were we all qualified, and could devote the whole of our time to the immediate work of the mission, there is an urgent call for us all and for many more. On the other hand, during the last three years, the merchants of New South Wales have pursued with eagerness every speculation for profit that they could think of among these islands, so as to bring things apparently to a close, and they know not what further to attempt; in consequence of which some of their vessels are already, and others are likely soon to be without employment, as the voyages will not cover the expenses. Some time ago the pearl-fishery and pearl-shells promised much advantage; but that trade (which we had partly in view when we began the vessel), was soon brought to a close, and now the sandal-wood business is also nearly terminated; but were it otherwise, we

* Since the above was written, Brother Bicknell has returned from Tahiti much improved in his health.

could not in conscience allow our vessel to be any way concerned in it, as we apprehend most, if not all, the sandal wood is used in China or India for idolatrous purposes. The pork-trade likewise is at an end for the present, as most of the hogs have been destroyed in the late wars, and the remainder, that were at all fit for salting, have been purchased by the late vessels that have touched here.

The Active, a vessel belonging to Rev. Mr. Marsden,* and in which Brother Crook and family came hither, is now among the islands in these seas seeking for pork, but we are apprehensive she will not be able to procure much of a cargo. In this state of things we really should not know what to do with our vessel if she were fit for sea. Our motives in attempting to build it were good, whatever may be the result; we had no other view than to serve the purposes of the mission, and lessen the expenses of the Missionary Society, in respect of our support here. If it fail of answering those ends we cannot help it; we have made the attempt in the midst of many difficulties, afflictions, and ill health: but what grieves and perplexes us most at the present time is, that the vessel in a manner prevents our removing from our present residence, while there is such a loud call from all quarters for us to come and teach the poor islanders, who are now truly desirous of instruction.

The present state of the islands makes us decidedly of opinion that there should be at least two Missionary establishments, one for Tahiti and this island, and one for the Leeward Islands; but we are anxiously looking for the arrival of those brethren who are said to be coming to us, and for further information and directions from you, so that we may know better how to act.†

We enclose another friendly letter of his Excellency Governor Macquarrie; as also a letter from Pomare, concerning his family gods, which have been delivered to us, that we might either destroy them, or, if we think proper, send them to you. We have chosen the latter, and send them by this conveyance nailed up in a case, directed to Mr. Hardcastle. These are the king's family gods, and are a good specimen of the whole. The great national ones, which were of the same kind, only much larger, have been some time ago entirely destroyed.

Expecting that we shall soon have another opportunity of writing more fully of our proceedings and future prospects, we shall now conclude, subscribing ourselves, as before,

Honoured fathers and brethren,

Your brethren, and unworthy fellow-labourers,

BICKNELL, HENRY.	HENRY, WILLIAM.
CROOK, WILLIAM.	NOTT, HENRY.
DAVIES, JOHN.	TESSIER, SAMUEL.
HAYWARD, JAMES.	WILSON, CHARLES.

* Towards the support of which the Missionary Society contributes annually.

† Eight more Missionaries have long since been sent out, and, we have reason to believe, are now at their posts.

Translation of a Letter from Pomare, King of Otaheite, to the Missionaries.

Friends,

May you be saved by Jehovah, and Jesus Christ our Saviour. This is my speech to you my friends. I wish you to send those idols to Britane for the Missionary Society, that they may know the likeness of the gods that Tahiti worshipped. Those were my own idols, belonging to our family from the time of *Taaroamana-hune** even to *Vairaatoa* : † and when he died he left them with me. And now, having been made acquainted with the *true God*, with Jehovah, *He is my God*, and when this body of mine shall be dissolved in death, may the Three-One save me! And this is my shelter, my close hiding-place, even from the anger of Jehovah. When he looks upon me, I will hide me at the feet of Jesus Christ the Saviour, that I may escape. *I feel pleasure and satisfaction in my mind ; I rejoice, I praise Jehovah,* that he hath *made known* his word unto me. I should have gone to destruction if Jehovah had not interposed. Many have died, and are gone to destruction, kings and common people ; they died without knowing any thing of the true God ; and now, when it came to the small remainder of the people, Jehovah hath been pleased to make known his word, and we are made acquainted with his good word, made acquainted with the deception of the false gods, with all that is evil and false. The true God Jehovah, it was he that made us acquainted with these things.— It was you that taught us ; but the words, the knowledge, was from Jehovah. *It is because of this that I rejoice,* and I pray to Jehovah, that he may increase my abhorrence of every evil way. The Three-One, He it is that can make the love of sin to cease ; we cannot effect it ; it is the work of God to cause evil things to be cast off, and the love of them to cease.

I am going a journey around Tahiti, to acquaint the Ratiras with the word of God, and to cause them to be vigilant about good things. The word of God does grow in Tahiti, and the Ratiras are diligent about setting up houses for worship ; they are also diligent in seeking instruction, and now it is well with Tahiti.

That principal idol, that has the red feathers of the Otuu is Temeharo,‡ that is his name, look you, you may know it by the red feathers ; that was Vairaatoa's own god, and those feathers

---

* *Taaroamanahune* lived some ages ago, and was one of the ancestors of Pomare's family.

† *Vairaatoa*, one of the names of old Pomare, the king's father, and though a friend to the Missionaries, yet was he a most zealous advocate for the gods, and the old religion.

‡ *Temeharo* was one of the principal *family* gods of the royal family of Tahiti ; but *Oro* was the principal *national* god, and to him alone human sacrifices were offered, at least in modern times. Temeharo is said to have a brother called *Tia :* these were famous men, deified after their death.

were from the ship of Lieutenant Watts ;* it was Vairaatoa that set them himself about the idol. If you think proper, you may burn them all in the fire ; or, if you like, send them to your country, for the inspection of the people of Europe, that they may satisfy their curiosity, and know Tahiti's foolish gods !

This also is one thing that I want to enquire of you : when I go around Tahiti, it may be that the Ratiras and others will ask me to put down their names ; what shall I do then? Will it be proper for me to write down their names? It is with you—you are our teachers, and you are to direct us. We have had our prayer-meeting the beginning of this month, February ; it was at Homai-au-Vahi ; the Ratiras, and all the people of the district assembled, leaving their houses without people. They said to me, ' Write down our names.' I answered, ' It is agreed.' Those names are in the enclosed. paper, which I have sent for your inspection. Have I done wrong in this? Perhaps I have : let me, my friends, know the whole of your mind in respect of this matter.†

May you, my friends, be saved by Jehovah the true God. I have written to Mahine for a house for the use of the Mission-aries; when they arrive, you will let Mabine know where the house is to be, and he will get the people to remove it there. Let it be at Uaeva, near you.

It is reported here, that there is a ship at Morea, and I was thinking it might be the ship with the Missionaries ; but it may be that it is only an idle report. However, should the Mission-aries arrive at Morea, write to me quickly, that I may know. Let me know also, what news there may be from Europe and from Port Jackson. Perhaps King George may be dead, let me know. I shall not go around Tabiti before the month of March.

May you be saved, my friends, by Jehovah, and Jesus Christ the only Saviour by whom we sinners can be saved.

POMARE, King of Tahiti, &c. &c.

Tahiti Mo Tuta, Feb. 19, 1816.

No. II.

CHINA.

MR. MORRISON'S DICTIONARY.

Now Publishing at Macao, in China,

A Dictionary of the Chinese Language ; to consist of three parts. First, Chinese and English, arranged according to the

---

* Lieutenant Watts visited Tahiti in the Lady Penrhyn, 1788.

† This was in imitation of us ; for during 1814 and 1815, after our Monthly Missionary Prayer-Meetings, we used to take down the names of such as renounced Heathenism and embraced Christianity in a public manner; but since the state of affairs is altered in the islands, and the profession of Christianity is become general, we have thought proper to discontinue the practice, as now not likely to answer the ends intended.

radicals; next English and Chinese; and lastly, Chinese and English, arranged alphabetically.

The first part will contain about twenty numbers, and the other two parts taken together, nearly the same, making about forty numbers in all. These are to be sold at half-a-guinea each number. Two numbers are already published. Several years will be required to complete the remainder.

Subscriptions will be received in *London*, by Black, Parbury, and Allen, Leadenhall-street. *Paris*, by Professor Remusat. *China*, by F. H. Toone, Esq. *Malacca*, by the Rev. William Milne. *Bengal*, by Messrs. Colvins, Bazett, and Co. *Madras*, by Messrs. Arbuthnot, D'Monte, M'Taggart, and Co. *Bombay*, by Messrs. Forbes and Co.

Persons who wish to do so, may subscribe to the first part only; it will be a complete Chinese Dictionary in itself, containing about forty thousand characters. It contains many quotations from the Chinese classics, and other original works, which illustrate the opinions and usages of that people.

The Author of the above work, the Rev. R. Morrison, has directed his attention to the collection of materials for it during the last ten years. The Honourable the East India Company, has generously undertaken the whole expense of printing and paper, for an edition of seven hundred and fifty copies, of which six hundred and fifty copies are given to the Author, to be disposed of, as a remuneration for the very considerable labour which he has bestowed upon it, and which he must continue to bestow, should Divine Providence grant him life and health, till the whole be completed.

From a misunderstanding on the part of Mr. Morrison's friends, in England, they have promised that the whole should not exceed ten guineas. To those who have already subscribed on the faith of this, the promise will be inviolably adhered to. But, at the present price, viz. half-a-guinea a number, which is very moderate for a work that contains so much of the Chinese character; twenty numbers will amount to ten guineas, which is only one half of what the three parts are expected to make; the other half then must be given for nothing, or the author must depart from his original fulness of definition, which would render the work comparatively of little value. He purposes, however, to persevere in the same method which he has hitherto observed, in the hope of facilitating to Englishmen, and to the Western World, the acquisition of the Chinese language: which, whether viewed in itself; its peculiar structure; or with respect to its antiquity; its having been for nearly 4000 years the language of so large a portion of the human species; and its still being the written medium, in private and in public life; in literature, in arts and in government, of the most extensive empire on earth;—viewed in any, or in all of these respects, it seems to deserve the attention of every inquisitive and curious mind.

It is therefore to be understood, that the whole work will be faithfully sent to those who have already subscribed, and for the price stated by Mr. Morrison's friends, viz. ten guineas; but to those who may subscribe after the publication of this notice, the work will be sold at half-a-guinea a number. If the work should exceed forty numbers, no charge will be made for those above that. It shall not cost the subscribers more than twenty guineas.

Canton, China, November, 3, 1817.

There have been published by the same Author,

1. A Grammar of the Chinese Language. Price £1.
2. A Collection of Dialogues and Detached Sentences, in Chinese and English, with a Free and Verbal rendering. Price 10s.
3. A View of China for Philological Purposes, containing a Sketch of Chinese Chronology; Geography; Population; Government; Religion; and Customs; with Remarkable Occurrences. The names of Emperors; Places; Officers of the Government, and so on, are given in the Chinese Character. Price £1. 1s.

These Works have all been printed at the sole expense of the Honourable East India Company.

There is reason to fear that many copies of the Dialogues, were lost on their passage to England. But those who wish to become subscribers for any of these Works, may sign their names at any of the above mentioned places, and the number of copies remaining will be delivered to those whose names are first in order of time,

---

Two letters have lately been received from Dr. Morrison, at Canton. He begins the former, dated Sept. 4, 1817, by saying, ' TEN YEARS, this day, have elapsed since I first landed on these shores. To carry into effect the objects of the Missionary Society (which were at the same time objects dear to my own heart), I left my native land. God has been gracious to us; he has borne with our infirmities; he has granted us in part the wish of our hearts, and blessed be his holy name.'

Mr. Milne has been some months with Dr. Morrison, revising with him the translation of Joshua and Deuteronomy, which, with the book of Psalms, will soon be put to press at Malacca,

Dr. Morrison says, ' I have translated the Morning and Evening Prayers of the Church of England, just as they stand in the Book of Common Prayer, altering only the Prayer for the rulers of the land. These I am printing, together with the Psalter, divided for the thirty days of the month. I intend them as a help to social worship, and as affording excellent and suitable expressions for individual devotion. Mr. Milne wished me to modify them, so as to render them more suitable to our peculiar circumstances, and the state of the heathen; but as they possess here no authority but their own general excellence, and are not binding on the practice or conscience of any, and as they are not exclusive, I judged it better to preserve them as they are : additional helps may be afforded if they should not be fully adequate. The heathen at first require help for social devotion; in this, Mr. Milne and I are of the same opinion, and to me it appeared, that the richness of devotional phraseology, the elevated views of the Deity, and the explicit and full recognition of the work of our Lord Jesus Christ, were so many excellencies, that a version of them into Chinese, (as long as they are not exclusive) was better than for me to re-model them. The Church of Scotland supplied us with a Catechism, the Congregational Churches afforded us a simple form of a Christian Assembly ; and the Church of England has supplied us with a Manual of Devotion, as a help to those who are not sufficiently instructed to conduct social worship without such aid. We are of no party. We recognize but two divisions of our fellow-creatures—those who fear God, and those who do not. Grace be with all that love our Lord Jesus Christ in sincerity ! Amen, and Amen."

In a subsequent letter, dated Canton, Jan 18, 1818, he says, " In a few days, my brother and companion in labour, Mr. Milne, together with his family, and it is hoped, two type-cutters, will leave Macao to return to Malacca, there to prosecute the objects of your association."

(Dr. Morrison then intimates, that the strength of Mr. Milne was exceedingly reduced, and serious apprehensions entertained as to the result of his disorder.)

Dr. Morrison next states, that the American Consul at Canton had made arrangements with Mr. Milne, to place under his care at Malacca, a young gentleman from the United States, to learn the Chinese language. " I recommended," says Dr. Morrison, " the adoption of this measure ; I am persuaded that the more we can bring Christendom and China into contact with each other, the more probable will be the diffusion of Divine Revelation in this part of the world. It is in this view of the case, that I am encouraged to persevere in the very dry and irksome task of composing my Dictionary; and I hope the Society will regard it in a similar point of view."

No. III.

An Account of Sabat.

At Penang, Mr. Milne met with *Sabat*, who, after making a zealous profession of Christianity, had apostatized to Mahomedanism. We shall relate what happened, in Mr. Milne's own words.

" Jan. 26. To-day met with Sabat, the Arabian, formerly a convert to Christianity, under the labours of the (late) Rev.

Henry Martyn, and subsequently employed by the Bible Society in Bengal.

"To me his aspect seemed interesting in the highest degree, and his conversation discovered a very acute intellect. I had before heard of his conversion and labours, but knew nothing of his apostasy till he himself mention d it. The causes which led to this unhallowed step, he endeavoured to explain, but I could not well understand them. The facts of his apostasy, and of his having subsequently written a book professedly in favour of Mahomedanism, are, I suppose, generally known; nor did he himself conceal them. On putting some pointed questions to him, he said, 'I am unhappy! I have a mountain of burning sand on my head! When I go about, I know not what I am doing.'

"He says, 'What I did in renouncing Christianity, and writing my book, (which I call *my evil work*) was done in the heat and fury of passion, which is so natural to an Arab; and my chief wish now is, that God may spare me to refute that book, page by page. I know that it contains all that can be said in favour of Mahomedanism; and should I live to refute it, I shall do a greater service to the Gospel than if it had not been written.'

"He spoke with rapture of the Rev. Mr. Martyn, and of several Missionaries. 'Were every hair on my body,' said he 'a tongue, I could not fully tell that man's worth. I knew, and have been with the Rev. Messrs. Cran and Desgranges at Vizagapatam. O what lovely men! I know the Baptists at Serampore also; they are worthy men; but I cannot receive their doctrine of adult baptism.'

"The case of this poor man much affected me, and Major M'Innes, who was also present. We afterwards visited and conversed with him. Before leaving Penang I wrote a letter to him, (he understands English) exhorting him to speedy repentance and turning to the Lord. He wrote an answer to me, after my return to Malacca, which commences thus:—

"'Sabat, the corrupted, turned, and lost servant of the Lord Jesus Christ, to the man of God, the Rev. W. Milne,' &c. Towards the close, he says; 'Though my body be not with the truth, yet my heart, soul, and understanding, are with it; nor shall they ever be turned away from it, by silver, gold, jewels, or the riches of the world, or any pleasure of science, &c. &c.'

"After a little time, he went over to *Acheen*, with the ex-king; for what purpose I know not. But on his way back to Penang, he unfortunately fell into the hands of the Usurper, who seized all his property, and put him in irons. A few days ago I received a letter from him, from which it appears that he is confined day and night in the gun-room of a piratical brig, belonging to the Usurper. During the night he is always in irons. He says, 'When brought before the Usurper, he examined me, and found no fault. He then asked me, 'What is *thy* religion?

Ans. ' My parents were Mahomedans.'—Ques. ' But what is thy religion.' Ans. ' God knows.' ' Thy parents,' said the Usurper, ' were Mahomedans bu thou a t a *Serance,* (*i. e.* Christian) and must be killed.' Sin e that time he has been confined; nor does it appear that he denied his bei g still a Christian. The letter I instantly despatched o Major M'Innes, entreating him to try to procure Sabat's release. May the Lord grant that in his captivity his backslidings may be healed.

" I have purposely enlarged on the case of poor Sabat, for the information of the religious public, who have not themselves had the opportunity of seeing him, or hearing much of him, since his departure from Calcutta. I there not still reason to hope that God will do him good in his latter end?

" He is a man of great natural powers. The clear and evangelical comments which I heard him make on several passages and doctrine of Scripture, shewed that he had not been an inattentive learner, and reflect the greatest honour on the piety, sentiments, and care, of those worthy men under whose instruction he was placed."

No. IV.

MALACCA.

Mr. George Livett, a gentleman who lately visited Amboyna, has favoured the Directors with his observations on the state of religion there, and the necessity of increasing the number of Missionaries. In Amboyna alone it is supposed that there are 20,000 professing Christians, and about the same number of Mahomedans, beside Chinese, &c. The professing Christians attend public worship with great readiness, and appear to be very desirous of instruction. The arrival of Mr. Kam among them occasioned great joy, and he was immediately placed by Mr. Martin, the British resident, as Calvinistic minister, with a handsome salary. Mr. Carey, a son of Dr. Carey, was also engaged to superintend the schools, which he did with great ability and success. On the 5th of June 1815, a public examination took place before the President, &c. when an address was delivered by Mr. Martin (the president), which did him much honour.

Beside the island of Amboyna, there are many other islands where the people would gladly receive the word, but who, for want of Christian instructors, are relapsing into Mahomedanism or Idolatry. Mr. Livett mentions the islands Celebes, Almeiheira (or Gelolo), Manado, Ternate, Tidore, Mortier, Mackion, Kulla Talliabo, Kulla Mangola, Thulla Bessy, Oby Major, Mysole, the beautiful, fertile, and extensive isle of Buero, Ceram, Goram, &c. &c. In many of these islands the Netherland government would not object to the admission of British Missionaries; and Mr. Livett is of opinion that they would be most joyfully received by the people.

No. V.

TRAVANCORE.

Death of Mrs. Mead.

By letters from Mr. Mead and Mr. Medhurst, the Directors are informed of the death of this excellant woman. Mr. Mead, in a letter dated Malacca, Nov. 11, 1817, thus writes:—" I have to convey to you the sad intelligence that my dearest partner departed this life at Penang, on Sunday, October 26. Her death was occasioned by an abscess on the liver. We were on our way to Quilon, in Travancore. Penang being near Malacca, I took the opportunity of the offer of a free passage, and arrived there November 4. I am indeed much afflicted on the event. I have lost the most affectionate of wives, and the church one of the most devoted of Missionaries. She died triumphing in the Lord."

Mr. Medhurst, in a letter, dated Malacca, December 4, 1817, says:—" Our dear departed sister witnessed a good confession, as may be seen by the account her afflicted husband drew up of her experience towards her latter end. She did not shrink at the approach of death, but was strong in faith, giving glory to God. She hailed with joy the heavenly messenger who came to summon her soul away into the realms of bliss. The people at Penang were astonished ; they had never before seen the power of religion exemplified in so striking a manner ; they knew not how to glory in tribulation, or to account death a gain. I trust that God will fasten a conviction of their personal need of a Saviour on the minds of those who had then an opportunity of witnessing the power of his grace, that they also may die the death of the righteous, and their last end be like hers.

" Both at Penang and Malacca God raised them unexpected friends in the season of sorrow, who, though they could not remove, yet, by their kind offices, assisted in lightening their afflictions. Major M'Innes (the tried friend of our Missionaries), without any previous introduction, sought them out immediately on their arrival in Penang-harbour, and persuaded them to come on shore, and take up their reidence at the house of a person who had volunteered his kind services on the occasion. He continued to visit and assist them during Mrs. Mead's illness, and entreated them to draw on him for every pecuniary aid they would require during their stay in Penang. He afterwards defrayed the expenses of Mrs. M.'s funeral, and begged the acceptance of a present for the little boy. A medical gentleman (Mr. Henderson) attended Mrs. M., gratis, with that assiduity and concern which has left a deep impression on the mind of the afflicted husband.

" On our dear brother's arrival here, about a month ago, his health was considerably impaired, being afflicted with the liver complaint, brought on by constant anxiety, watchfulness, and sorrow. He was obliged to submit to an immediate course of calomel, and has been, through God's blessing, so far restored, as to be able to prosecute his voyage to Bombay. He embarked yesterday on board the Pascoe, Captain Nicholl, with some hopes of being set down on the Malabar coast in their way up, but will proceed to Bombay if that should be impracticable ; he will there meet with Christian friends, and may have an additional opportunity of recruiting both his mental and bodily strength before entering on his solitary mission ;—this he certainly needs. His mind in his present state would sink in solitude ; and his poor body is not yet capable of enduring the hardships of the Juinvelly mission. His only comfort now is the little infant (about ten months old), the fruit of a union now dissolved for ever :— its interesting smiles and playful gambols serve in some measure to soothe the father's heart. He needs, dear Fathers and Brethren, your earnest entreaties at a throne of grace, that, under his domestic afflictions and missionary difficulties, he may be able to bear up without weariness and without fainting. May the almighty Angel of the covenant now go with him in his journeyings, and the Eternal God be his refuge."

No. VI.

BETHELSDORP.

Conversation with a Converted Hottentot, on his former State of Ignorance.

(Extracted from the Journal of Mr. Evan Evans, July 15, 1817.)

July 15.—Experienced much pleasure this morning in conversing with the driver of our waggon, concerning the state of ignorance in which his nation was plunged previously to the time in which Missionaries came among them. He shewed me a small insect, which the farmers call *the Hottentots' God ;* and which, in fact, they used to worship. This man said to me, ' Oh ! Sir, it is impossible for me to say how thankful I am to the good men over the great waters, because they have sent you, his servants, to teach poor Hottentots. But it is God, the Almighty God, who put this in the hearts of the good men in England. He said to them, The poor Hottentots in Africa know nothing of me, the true God ; they worship a poor insect that even they themselves can tread to death with their naked foot. Yes, here he is !—here he is ! This was our god, before God's servants came among us. Yes, the farmers told us before you came, that we were nothing but baboons or monkeys ; and if they saw us listening when they were reading the book, (the Bible) they would immediately cry out, What do you want, you baboons ? begone, you have no business to look in our houses.' *

I asked, Did you ever worship this insect, then ? He answered, ' Oh ! yes, a thousand times ; always before I came to Bethels-

* This, however, is, we trust, not the general character of the Boors, (or African farmers,) many of whom are pious and benevolent, and encourage the instruction of their Hottentot servants.

dorp: whenever I saw this little creature, I would fall down on my knees before him and pray." What did you pray to him for? ' I asked him to give me a good master, and plenty of thick milk and flesh.' Did you pray for nothing else? ' No, Sir, I did not then know that I wanted any thing else.' Did not you know then that you had an immortal soul? ' Oh, no; the farmers used always to say that Hottentots had no souls, and that they were made by the Devil, and not by the God of the Christians. They would never allow us to go to Church; I was never in a church till I came to Bethelsdorp, nor ever heard one word out of the book (the Bible.) Before I came there, I was as ignorant as these oxen, and knew nothing. Whenever I used to see this insect,' holding the creature still in his hand, ' I used sometimes to fall down immediately before it; but if it was in the waggon-road, or in a foot-path, I used to take it up as gently as I could, to place it behind a bush, for fear a waggon, or some men or beasts should tread it to death.' If a Hottentot by some accident killed or injured this creature, he was sure to be unlucky all his lifetime, and could never shoot an elephant or a buffalo afterwards.

It is impossible to describe the thankfulness which this poor man manifested, because the Lord hath remembered his wretched and despised nation, and had sent his servants to teach them the knowledge of the true God, and the way of salvation through Jesus Christ, instead of worshipping this poor creature, which, as he observed, he could squeeze to death between his fingers, and which could not deliver itself out of his hands. How true are the Apostle's words!—' For ye see your calling, brethren, how that not many wise men after the flesh, not many mighty, not many noble, are called: but God hath chosen the foolish things of the world to confound the wise; and God hath chosen the weak things of the world to confound the things which are mighty; and base things of the world, and things which are despised, hath God chosen; yea, and things which are not, to bring to nought things that are: that no flesh should glory in his presence.' Who more foolish, who more weak, who more base, and who more despised than poor Hottentots were? Yet I have no doubt that they would be able to confound many wise philosophers, princes, and warriors, if they were set to converse with them respecting the things of God. Although they are poor, and as ' the offscouring of all things'—yea, though they ' are not,' as it were, yet I doubt not there are hundreds of them rich in grace and faith, heirs of everlasting glory, who shall be for ever rich, even when the riches of this world shall be consumed. I never saw the beauty of this passage so much, as since I came to South Africa.

Missionary Society's Stations & Missionaries.

MAY 1818.

SOUTH SEAS.

OTAHEITE AND EIMEO.—John Davies, William Henry, Samuel Tessier, Henry Nott, James Hayward, Charles Wilson, Henry Bicknell, W. P. Crook.—To assist whom have been sent, William Ellis, Laun. Edw. Threlkeld, J. M. Orsmond, Charles Barff, David Darling, Robert Bourne, George Platt, John Williams, and Mr. John Gyles, sent out as a cultivator.

SOUTH AFRICA.

BETHELSDORP—J. G. Messer, Evan Evans, F. G. Hooper.

GRIQUA TOWN—William Anderson, Henry Helm.—B. Berend, P. David, J. Hendrick, Piet Sabba, *Natives.*

STELLENBOSCH—J. Bakker.

TULBAGH DROSDY—Cornelius Kramer, Ariel Vos, John Taylor, *(pro tempore.)*

BETHESDA—Christopher Sass.

CALEDON—John Seidenfaden.

HOOGE (or High) KRAAL—Charles Pacalt.

THEOPOLIS—J. G. Ullbricht, G. Barker.

GRACE HILL—Erasmus Smit.

BETHANY, *Namaqualand*—H. Schmelen, James Kitchingman, J. Marquard.

PEACE MOUNTAIN, *formerly known by the name of Africaner's Kraal*—E. Ebner, Robert Moffat.

CAFFRARIA—Joseph Williams, Jan Tzatzoo, *a Native.*

HEPHZIBAH—W. F. Corner, J. Goeyman.

LATTAKOO. *Krooman's River*—Robert Hamilton.

CAPE TOWN—George Thom.

MAURITIUS—John Le Brun.

MADAGASCAR—David Jones, Thomas Bevan.

EAST INDIES.

TRAVANCORE—Charles Mead.

VIZAGAPATAM—John Gordon, Edward Pritchett, James Dawson.

MADRAS—W. C. Loveless, Richard Knill.

CEYLON—J. D. Palm, W. Reade.

BELLARY—John Hands, Wm. Reeve, Joseph Taylor.

GANJAM—William Lee, returned to England.

CHINSURAH—Robert May, J. D. Pearson, John Harle.

SURAT—James Skinner, William Fyvie, John Donaldson.

CALCUTTA—Henry Townley, James Keith.—Two Missionaries are on the point of sailing for this station, viz. Messrs. Hampson and Trawin.

EXTRA GANGES.

CHINA.

CANTON—Robert Morrison, D. D.

AMBOYNA—Joseph Kam.

MALACCA—W. Milne, C. H. Thomsen, W. H. Medhurst, John Slater.

RUSSIA.

IRKOUTSK, *in Siberia, about* 4000 *miles east from St. Petersburg.* —Edward Stallybrass and Cornelius Rahmn.

RUSSIAN TARTARY.

J. G. Schill, Christian Huebner.

WEST INDIES.

DEMERARA.

LE RESOUVENIR—John Smith.

GEORGE TOWN—John Davies, Richard Elliot.

BERBICE—John Wray.

TRINIDAD—Thomas Adams, James Mercer.

GREEK ISLANDS.

Isaac Lowndes.

AN ALPHABETICAL ACCOUNT

OF

Subscriptions, Donations, &c.

TO THE

MISSIONARY SOCIETY,

1818.

⟿ₒₒₒₒ⃰|◀❖▶|ₒₒₒₒ⇐

IN LONDON AND ITS VICINITY.

⟿ₒₒₒₒ|◀❖▶|ₒₒₒₒ⇐

	Donations.			Annual Subscriptions.		
	£	s.	d.	£		d.
Abraham, Mr. Great Marlbro'-street ··	–	–	–	1	1	0 L. Day
Adam, Mr. A. Lower Thames-st. 1815	10	10	0	–	–	–
Adams, Mr. T. Kennington..............	–	–	–	1	1	0 Mich
Addison, Mr. Ludgate-street	–	–	–	1	1	0 Xmas
Aitcheson, Mr. Poland-street	–	–	–	1	1	0 L. Day
Aitkens, Mr. Chapel-st. Grosvenor-place	–	–	–	1	1	0 Xmas
Aldersey, Mr. Homerton 1796	10	0	0	–	–	–
Ditto 1800	20	0	0	–	–	–
Allardyce, Mr. Homerton..............	–	–	–	1	1	0 L. Day
Allardyce, Mr. Domingo-st. Old-street	–	–	–	1	1	0 Do
Allen, Mr. St Catherine's	–	–	–	1	1	0 Do
Allen, Mrs Martha, Brick-lane	–	–	–	1	0	0 Do
Allison, Mrs Blackheath	–	–	–	1	1	0 Xmas
Anderson, Mr. R. Clapham-road.........	–	–	–	1	1	0 Do
Anderson, Mrs. Exeter-st. Sloane-st. ...	–	–	–	1	1	0 L. Day
Arding, Mr James, Dorset-street	–	–	–	1	1	0 Do
Arding, Mr. W. Old Boswell-court......	–	–	–	0	10	6 Do
Arnold, Mr Kingsland-road..............	–	–	–	1	1	0 Do
Arrowsmith, Mr. Soho-square	–	–	–	1	1	0 Do
Atley, Rev Mr. Stepney	–	–	–	1	1	0 Xmas
Austin, Mr. Cumberland-st. Curtain-r.	–	–	–	1	1	0 L. Day
Austin, Mr Golden-square	–	–	–	1	1	0 Xmas
Ayscough, Mrs. Holloway	–	–	–	1	1	0 L. Day
Bacchus, Mr. Upper Thames-street ...	–	–	–	1	1	0 Do
Backler, Mr Apothecaries-hall..........	–	–	–	1	1	0 Do
Baddeley, Mr Oxford-street	–	–	–	1	1	Mich
Bagster, Mr. James, per Mr. Mosely...	–	–	–	1	1	0 L. Day
Bailey, Mr. St. Paul's Church-yard, 1796	10	10	0	–	–	–
Bainbridge, Mr. Guildford-street.........	–	–	–	2	2	0 Do
Baker, Miss, Basinghall-street.............	–	–	–	1	1	0 Do
Ballance, Mr. Hackney	–	–	–	2	2	0 Mid
Ballance, Mrs. Ditto	–	–	–	1	1	0 Do
Ballance, Mr. J. Jun. Stewart-st. Spital.	–	–	–	1	1	0 Do
Bampton, Mr. J Brackley-street	–	–	–	1	1	0 L. Day
Banger, Mr. Jos. Hackney	–	–	–	1	1	0 Mich
Banger, Mr. M. Ditto	–	–	–	1	1	0 Do
Baber, Mr. Knightsbridge 1799	10	0	0	–	–	–
Ditto Ditto 1800	20	0	0	–	–	–
Barber, Mr. S. Cheapside	–	–	–	1	1	0 L. Day
Barnard, Mr. W. Walworth..............	–	–	–	1	1	0 Xmas
Barnes, Mr. Copthall-court	–	–	–	1	1	0 L. Day
Barnett, Mr. W. Bridge-st. Westminst.	–	–	–	2	0	0 Do
Barton, Mr. Swallow-street	–	–	–	1	1	0 Do
Bateman, Mr. P. Bunhill-row	–	–	–	1	1	0 Do
Bateman, Mr. W. Ditto	–	–	–	1	1	0 Xmas

B

	Donations.			Annual Subscriptions.		
	£	s.	d.	£	s.	d.
Bates, Mrs. Davies-street, Berkely-sqr.	0	10	0	–	–	–
Bayford, Mr. Knight Ryder-street	–	–	–	1	1	0 Mid
Bayly Mr. Clarence-row, Camberwell...	–	–	–	1	1	0 Mich
Bayley, Mr. R. Queen-square	–	–	–			0 Mid
Bealby, Mr. Drury-lane	–	–	–			0 L. Day
Beams, Mr. Great Carter-lane............	–	–	–			Mid
Beazley, Mr. C. Whitehall	–	–	–			Xmas
Beazleay, Mrs. Surrey-road	–	–	–			L. Day
Beckett, Mr. Barbican	–	–	–			Mid
Belgrave, Mrs. Camden-town......1810	10	0	0			L. Day
Bernard, Mr. Queen-str. Edgware-road	–	–	–			Do
Berridge, Mr. Greenwich..................	–	–	–			L. Day
Bevan, Mr. Walthamstow 1815	21	0	0			Xmas
Bickersteth, Rev. Mr. Salisbury-square	–	–	–			Mid
Bickley, Mrs. Kentish-town...............	–	–	–			Xmas
Binks, Mrs. Bedford-street	–	–	–			L. Day
Bittleston, Mr. Norton-st. Maryl. 1814	10	10	0	–	–	–
Birnie, Mr. Great St. Helens	–	–	–	2	2	0 Mid
Black, Mr. J. York-str. Covent-garden	–	–	–	1	1	0 Xmas
Blades, Mr. Piccadilly	–	–	–	1	1	0 L. Day
Blades, Mrs. Ditto	–	–	–	1	1	0 Do
Blair, Mr. Great Russell-street	–	–	–	1	1	0 Do
Bland, Mr. Newington-causeway........	–	–	–	2	2	0 Do
Bliss, Mr. Barbican	–	–	–	1	1	0 Do
Blunt, Mr. Red Cross-street, Borough	–	–	–	1	1	0 Do
Bly, Mr. Dacre-street, Westminster ...	–	–	–	1	1	0 Do
Bogie, Mr. St. Martin's-lane.............	–	–	–	1	1	0 Do
Bond, Mr. Stoke Newington.............	–	–	–	1	1	0 Mid
Bond, Mr. Hampstead	–	–	–	5	0	0 L. Day
Bound, Mr. Ray-street	–	–	–	1	1	0 Xmas
Bradbee, Mrs. Newgate-street............	–	–	–	1	1	0 L. Day
Brecknell, Mr. Tavistock-square	–	–	–	1	1	0 Do
Brett, Mr. T. Camberwell 1799	10	0	0	–	–	–
Ditto 1800	30	0	0	–	–	–
Ditto 1801	10	0	0	–	–	–
Brewin, Mr. Kent-road....................	–	–	–	1	1	0 Xmas
Britten, Mr. Cateaton-street.............	–	–	–	1	1	0 L. Day
Brocklesby, Mr. Newman-street	–	–	–	2	2	0 Do
Brodie, Mr. Frederick-place	–	–	–	1	1	0 Do
Brogden, Mr. Camden-street, Islington	–	–	–	1	1	0 Xmas
Brooks, Mrs. Camberwell-green	–	–	–	1	1	0 L. Day
Brown, Mr. Stoke Newington ...1796	10	0	0	–	–	–
Brown, Mr. Pudding-lane 1797	10	0	0	–	–	–
Brown, Mr. Drury-lane....................	–	–	–	0	10	6 Do
Brown, Mr. Titchfield-street	–	–	–	1	1	0 Xmas
Brown and Stokes, Misses, Peckham ...	–	–	–	2	2	0 L. Day
Browning, Mrs. Newington-green	–	–	–	1	1	0 Mid
Browning, Mr. Munday-st. Hoxton-sq.	–	–	–	1	1	0 L. Day
Broyden, Mr. Old-street-road	–	–	–	2	2	0 Do
Bruton, Mr. T. Ironmonger-lane.........	–	–	–	1	1	0 Xmas
Budden, Mr. W. Budge-row...............	–	–	–	2	2	0 Do
Budden, Mr. J. per Mr. W. Budden ...	–	–	–	1	1	0 Do
Bunnell, Mr. J. Southampton-row	–	–	–	5	0	0 L. Day
Bunnell, Mr. Z. New-street, Covent-gar.	–	–	–	1	1	0 Mid
Bunyon, Messrs. R. & J. Tower-street	–	–	–	1	1	0 Mich
Burchett, Mr. Paul's-chain	–	–	–	1	1	0 L. Day
Burden, Mr. E. Bedford-st. Covent-gar.	–	–	–	1	1	0 Xmas
Burden, Mr. T. Ditto	–	–	–	1	1	0 Do
Burder, Rev. G. Camberwell-grove, 1796	10	10	0	5	0	0 Do
Burder, Rev. H. F. Hackney	–	–	–	1	1	0 L. Day
Burder, Miss E. Charter-house	–	–	–	1	1	0 Xmas
Burgess, Lieut. Col. Grove-pl. Hackney	–	–	–	1	1	0 L. Day
Burkitt, Mr. J. T. Coleman-street	–	–	–	1	1	0 Do

	Donations.			Annual Subscriptions.		
	£	s.	d.	£	s.	d.
Burkitt, Mr. Poultry 1810	10	0	0	–	–	–
Ditto 1813	10	10	0	–	–	–
Ditto..	–	–	–	1	1	0 Xmas
Burnell, Mr. Whitechapel-road	–	–	–	1	1	0 L. Day
Burrup, Mr. Jun. Clapham-road...	–	–	–	1	1	0 Do
Burt, Mr. J. per Mr. Francis	–	–	–	1	1	0 Do
Burt, Mrs. Howland-street	–	–	–	1	1	0 Do
Burton, Mr. Leadenhall-street.............	–	–	–	1	1	0 Xmas
Burton, Mr. Newington-place	–	–	–	1	1	0 L. Day
Butcher, Mr. Haydon-square	–	–	–	1	1	0 Do
Butterfield, Mr. Strand.....................	–	–	–	1	1	0 Do
Byfield, Mr. Charing-cross	–	–	–	1	1	0 Do.
Byrchmore, Mr. Somer's Town	–	–	–	1	1	0 Do
Campbell, Rev. Mr. Shacklewell.........	–	–	–	1	1	0 Xmas
Capel, Mr. Cornhill 1814	10	10	0	–	–	–
Carlill, Mr. J. Leman-street 1810	10	10	0	–	–	–
Carroll, Mrs. by Mr. D. Langton	–	–	–	5	0	0 Do
Carruthers, Mr. Bucklersbury ...1800	10	10	0	–	–	–
Carter, Mr. W. Peckham	–	–	–	2	2	0 L. Day
Carter, Mr. S. Ditto	–	–	–	2	2	0 Do
Carter, Mr. Royal Exchange	–	–	–	1	1	0 Mich
Carter, Mr. Cold Bath-square	–	–	–	1	1	0 Xmas
Cattley, Mr. Camberwell............1800	50	0	0	–	–	–
Cecil, Mr. Thames-street	–	–	–	1	1	0 Mich
Chandler, Mr. St. Paul's Church-yard...	–	–	–	1	1	0 L. Day
Chatteris, Mr. Lombard-street.............	–	–	–	1	1	0 Mich
Christie, Mr. J. Pallmall	–	–	–	1	1	0 Do
Christie, Mr. W. Wapping........1800	10	0	0	–	–	–
Churchill, Mr. Hatfield-street	–	–	–	1	1	0 L. Day
Churchill, Miss, Ditto	–	–	–	1	1	0 Do
Clack, Rev. Mr.	–	–	–	1	1	0 Xmas
Clark, Mrs. Brick-lane, Spitalfields......	–	–	–	0	10	6 L. Day
Clark, Mrs. Hackney......................	–	–	–	0	10	6 Do
Clark, Mr. J. Strand	–	–	–	1	1	0 Xmas
Clark, Mr. W. Borough 1796	10	10	0	10	10	0 L. Day
Ditto 1800	50	0	0	–	–	–
Ditto 1810	10	0	0	–	–	–
Clayton, Rev. G. Walworth	–	–	–	1	1	0 L. Day
Clayton, Rev. J. Jun. Hackney	–	–	–	1	1	0 Do
Clayton, Mrs. Highbury-place.............	–	–	–	1	1	0 Do
Clunie, Mrs. Castle-street, Oxford-str...	–	–	–	1	1	0 Do
Coade, Mrs. Peckham	–	–	–	2	2	0 Do
Cock, Mr. A. Mile End-road 1796	10	10	0	–	–	–
Coe, Mr. North-street, Tottenham-ct.-r.	–	–	–	0	10	6 Do
Cole, Mr. Prince's-street, Drury-lane...	–	–	–	1	1	0 Do
Collison, Rev. Mr. Hackney.............	–	–	–	1	1	0 Mid
Collier, Mr. Long-lane, Bermondsey ...	–	–	–	1	1	0 Do
Collyer, Rev. Dr. Walworth........1816	10	10	0	–	–	–
Compigne, Mr. Camberwell	–	–	–	1	1	0 L. Day
Comyn, Mr. S. Serjéant's-inn, Fleet-str.	–	–	–	1	1	0 Xmas
Conn, Mr. London-street	–	–	–	1	1	0 L. Day
Cook & Hammond, Messrs. Wood-street	–	–	–	5	5	0 Do
Cook, Mr. H. Walthamstow...............	–	–	–	1	1	0 Do
Cooper, Mr. J. Walworth 1816	10	10	0	–	–	–
Cooper, Mr. Highbury-place 1816	10	0	0	–	–	–
Cope, Mr. Upper Thames-street	–	–	–	1	1	0 Do
Corp, Mr. Tower-street.....................	–	–	–	1	1	0 Mid
Corsbie, Mrs. Artillery-place 1810	10	10	0	–	–	–
Cowie, Mr. R. Surrey-square 1796	50	0	0	–	–	–
Ditto 1797	21	0	0	–	–	–
Ditto 1800	100	0	0	–	–	–
Ditto 1805	10	10	0	–	–	–

	Donations.			Annual Subscriptions.			
	£	s.	d.	£	s.	d.	
Cowie, Mr. G. Great St. Helen's 1797	10	10	0	2	2	0	L. Day
Cowie, Mrs. Falcon-square	–	–	–	1	1	0	Do
Cowell, Mr. Camberwell-green.............	–	–	–	1	1	0	Do
Crawford and Lindsay, Earl of, Richmond 1802	100	0	0	–	–	–	
Creak & Co., Bermondsey 1810	21	0	0	–	–	–	
Creed, Mr. Whitechapel-road	–	–	–	1	1	0	Mich
Cross, Mr. T. Castle-street, Holborn '...	–	–	–	1	1	0	L. Day
Crossley, Mr. Borough......................	–	–	–	1	1	0	Xmas
Curling, Mr. Jesse, Bermondsey...1800	10	10	0	2	2	0	L. Day
Curling, Mr. A. Fish-street-hill	–	–	–	1	1	0	Do
Curling, Mr. W. Ditto	–	–	–	1	1	0	Do
Curling, Mrs. Camberwell-grove...1817	10	10	0	1	1	0	Do
Curling, Mr. D. Cheapside 1818	10	10	0	–	–	–	
Cutbush, Mr. 30, Whitechapel.............	–	–	–	1	1	0	Xmas
Daker, Mr. Whitecross-street	–	–	–	1	1	0	L. Day
Dale, Mrs. Prince's-street, Spitalfields	–	–	–	1	1	0	Xmas
Dalton, Mr. Camberwell-grove.............	–	–	–	2	2	0	Do
Davenport, Mr. E. Lime-street	–	–	–	1	1	0	L. Day
Davenport Mr. S. Ditto.................	–	–	–	1	1	0	Do
Davidson, Mr. Kensing. Gravel-pits 1797	20	0	0	–	–	–	
Davidson, Mr. Fish-street-hill ...1800	10	10	0	–	–	–	
Davidson, Mr. J. Doctors Commons 1808	10	10	0	–	–	–	
Davies, Mr J. Hackney 1814	10	10	0	–	–	–	
Davies, Mr. Islington......................	–	–	–	2	2	0	Xmas
Davies, Mr. Shoreditch	–	–	–	1	1	0	Do
Davis, Mr. Whitechapel	–	–	–	1	1	0	L. Day
Davis, Mr. Houndsditch	–	–	–	1	1	0	Do
Davey, Mr. per Mr. Roberts	–	–	–	1	1	0	Do
Daukes, Mr. Friday-street	–	–	–	1	1	0	Xmas
Dawson, Mr. R. Borough, by Mr. J. Bunnell 1813	10	10	0	–	–	–	
Dawson, Mrs. T. Billiter-square	–	–	–	1	1	0	L. Day
Dawson, Mrs. J. Ditto	–	–	–	1	1	0	Do
Deere, Mr. King's-head-street ...1800	10	0	0	–	–	–	
Dennett, Mr. Leather-lane	–	–	–	1	1	0	Mid
Dent, Mr J. Hackney-grove	–	–	–	2	2	0	
Denyer, Mrs. Dulwich	–	–	–	1	1	0	Do
Desbois & Wheeler, Messrs. Gray's-inn-p.	–	–	–	2	2	0	Do
Devey, Mr. Surrey-square.................	–	–	–	1	1	0	L. Day
Dexter, Mr. Whitechapel.................	–	–	–	1	1	0	Mich
Dickers, Mr. James, Strand	–	–	–	1	1	0	Xmas
Dimock, Mr. J. 160, Holborn	–	–	–	2	2	0	Do
Dixie, Mr. Falcon-square	–	–	–	1	1	0	Do
Dixon, Mr. R. Fenchurch-street	–	–	–	1	1	0	Mich
Dixon, Mr. J. Aldersgate-street	–	–	–	1	1	0	L. Day
Dixson, Mr. Cheapside	–	–	–	1	1	0	Do
Dobson, Mr. per Mr. Thompson	–	–	–	1	1	0	Mich
Dodson, Mrs. Great Coram-street	–	–	–	1	1	0	Mid
Downes, Mr. Limehouse	1	0	0	–	–	–	
Dresser, Mr. Prince's-square.............	–	–	–	1	1	0	Xmas
Drury, Mr. Red-lion-street	–	–	–	1	1	0	L. Day
Dunkin, Miss, West-square	–	–	–	2	2	0	Do
Dunn, Rev. E. A. Pimlico.................	–	–	–	1	1	0	Xmas
Durant, Mr. E. Copthall-court	–	–	–	1	1	0	Mich
Dyson, Mr. G. Hackney............1800	10	10	0	–	–	–	
East, Mr. Budge-row......................	–	–	–	1	1	0	L. Day
East, Mr. New-street, Covent-garden...	–	–	–	1	1	0	Do
Edelman, Mr. Queen-street, Cheapside	–	–	–	1	1	0	Xmas
Eland, Mr. Islington	–	–	–	1	1	0	L. Day
Elliott, Mr. Friday-street	–	–	–	1	1	0	Do

	Donations.			Annual Subscriptions.			
	£	s.	d.	£	s.	d.	
Emerson, Mr. Whitechapel	–	–	–	1	1	0	L. Day
Emerson, Mr. S. S. Ditto	–	–	–	1	1	0	Do
Emslie, Mr. Dalston	–	–	–	1	1	0	Do
Evans, Mr. J. one of Rev. Mr. Newth's Pupils, Bennett-street, Surrey-road	–	–	–	1	1	0	Do
Everard, Mr. Whitechapel road	–	–	–	1	1	0	Mich
Eyre, Mrs. Hackney	–	–	–	2	2	0	L. Day
E. C. per Mr. Davies, Shoreditch.........	–	–	–	1	1	0	Xmas
E. D. Walworth, Produce of a Missionary Box...................................	1	1	0	–	–	–	
Faden, Mr. Charing-cross	–	–	–	1	1	0	L. Day
Falconer, Mr. Craig's-court	–	–	–	1	1	0	Xmas
Fallowfield, Mr. Scotland-yard...........	–	–	–	1	1	0	L. Day
Farmer, Mr. R. Kennington 1799	10	10	0	–	–	–	
Favell, Bousfield, and Co. Messrs. St. Mary-axe 1799	10	0	0	–	–	–	
Favell, Mr. St. Mary-axe	–	–	–	1	1	0	Mich
Fearn, Mrs. Spital-square	–	–	–	1	1	0	Do
Fenn, Mr. J. Peckham...............1796	10	0	0	–	–	–	
Ditto 1797	25	0	0	–	–	–	
Fenn, Mr. Botolph-lane 1800	50	0	0	–	–	–	
Fenton, Mr. per Mr. D. Cook	–	–	–	1	1	0	L. Day
Ferris, Mr. J. Petticoat-lane	–	–	–	1	11	6	Do
Ferris, Mr. Charles, Ditto	–	–	–	1	11	6	Do
Field, Mr. Frith-street	–	–	–	1	1	0	Do
Filby, Mr. Pilgrim-street	–	–	–	1	1	0	Do
Filling, Mr. Sun Tavern-fields ...1800	10	0	0	1	1	0	Do
Flanders, Mrs. Colebrook-row, Islington	–	–	–	1	1	0	Mich
Forbes, Mr. Camberwell	–	–	–	1	1	0	L. Day
Ford, Rev. Mr. Stepney	–	–	–	1	1	0	Xmas
Fowler, Mrs. Walworth......................	–	–	–	1	1	0	L. Day
Fox, Mr. T. Lewisham 1800	20	0	0	–	–	–	
Fox, Mr. Islington............................	–	–	–	1	1	0	Do
Foyster, Mrs. Charlotte-st. Tot. Ct. rd.	–	–	–	2	2	0	Do
France, Mr. J. Bank	–	–	–				D
Francis, Mr. Wellclose-square	–	–	–				D
Freeman, Mr. Suffolk-street...............	–	–	–				D
Freeman, Mr. London-Wall 1801	20	0	0				D
Freshfield, Mr. New Bank-buildings ...	–	–	–				Xmas
Friend, by Mr. Bland	–	–	–				L. Day
Friend, by Mr. G. Hodson	–	–	–				Do
Friend, by Rev. D. Nicol	1	0	0	–	–	–	
Friend, by Rev. S. Hacket	1	0	0	–	–	–	
Frost, Mrs. Great Portland-street	–	–	–	1	1	0	Do
Fryett, Mr. S. Whitecross-street	–	–	–	1	1	0	Do
Fyffe, Mr. H. Holborn	–	–	–	1	1	0	Xmas
F. S.	–	–	–	1	1	0	L. Day
Gabriels, Messrs. Banner-street	–	–	–	2	2	0	Mich
Gainsborough, Mr. Friday-street..........	–	–	–	2	2	0	Mid
Gaitskell, Mr. Rotherhithe.........1801	10	0	0	–	–	–	
Gale, Mrs. Old Bailey	1	0	0	–	–	–	
Gamon, Mr. Somerset-str. Portman-sqr.	–	–	–	1	1	0	L. Day
Gann, Mr. Gracechurch-street............	–	–	–	1	1	0	Do
Gant, Mr. J. Hackney grove	–	–	–	2	2	0	Do
Garling, Mr. King-street, Holborn......	–	–	–	1	1	0	Mich
Garrett, Mr. S. Copthall-court............	–	–	–	1	1	0	Xmas
Garwood, Mr. Mansel-street..............	–	–	–	1	1	0	L. Day
Gatfield, Mr. St. Paul's Church-y. 1800	21	0	0	–	–	–	
Gaviller, Mr. Clapton 1796	10	10	0	–	–	–	
Ditto 1800	50	0	0	2	2	0	Do
Geary, Rev. C. Palace-row, New-road...	–	–	–	1	1	0	L. Day

	Donations.			Annual Subscriptions.			
	£	s.	d.	£	s.	d.	
George, Mr. Holywell-street	–	–	–	1	1	0	Mid
George, Mrs. Ditto.........................	–	–	–	1	1	0	Do
Gibbs, Mr. J. Castle-street, Falcon-sqr.	–	–	–	0	10	6	Do
Gibson, Mr. Theobald's-road	–	–	–	1	1	0	L. Day
Gibson, Mr. Wardrobe-place..............	–	–	–	1	1	0	Do
Giles, Mr. Water-lane	–	–	–	2	2	0	Mid
Giles, Mrs. Clapham-road	–	–	–	1	1	0	L. Day
Gillespie, Mr. Stockwell....................	–	–	–	1	1	0	Do
Gillespie, Mr. Crutched-friars	–	–	–	1	1	0	Do
Glascott, Rev. Mr. per Mr. Butcher ...	–	–	–	1	1	0	Do
Godbold, Mr. Tottenham-court-road ...	–	–	–	1	1	0	Mid
Goode, Rev. Mr. Islington	–	–	–	1	1	0	L. Day
Goodhart, Mr. Hackney	–	–	–	1	1	0	Do
Gordon, Mr. A. Broad-street 1816	10	10	0				
Gore, Rev. Mr. Bache's-row, Hoxton ...	–	–	–	1	1	0	Do
Gosling, Mr. R. Fenchurch-street 1796	25	0	0				
Ditto 1800	10	10	0				
Gough, Mrs. Camberwell-green	–	–	–	1	1	0	Do
Gouger, Mr. 47, Aldermanbury 1796	20	0	0	–	–	–	
Gouldsmith, Mr. E. Highbury ...1802	10	0	0				
Ditto 1807	10	10	0	1	1	0	Do
Ditto 1817	10	10	0	–	–	–	
Grange, Mr. Covent-garden	–	–	–	0	10	6	Xmas
Grange, Mrs. Piccadilly.....................	–	–	–	1	1	0	Do
Greaves,Wood,&Co.Messrs.Boro' 1800	10	10	0	–	–	–	
Green, Mr. G. Blackwall............1813	21	0	0	–	–	–	
Green, Mr. T. Miles's-lane	–	–	–	2	2	0	Mid
Greig, Rev. G. Hampstead-road	–	–	–	2	2	0	L. Day
Gribble, Mr. Camberwell	–	–	–			0	Do
Gribble, Mr. J. B. Old Jewry	–	–	–			0	Do
Grieve, Mr. Bethnal-green	–	–	–			0	Mich
Griffith, Mr. Oxford-street	–	–	–			0	L. Day
Groome, Mr. Brompton-row..............	–	–	–	1	1	0	Do
Grove, Mr. Charing-cross	–	–	–	3	3	0	Do
Gwillim, Mr. per Mr. Palmer, Piccadilly	–	–	–	1	1	0	L. Day
Gwilt, Mrs. Paragon ....:...........	10	10	0	–	–	–	
G. G....................................	1	0	0	–	–	–	
Hadland, Mr. Holborn-hill	–	–	–	1	1	0	Mich
Hale, Mr. Wood-street, Spitalfields ...	–	–	–	1	1	0	L. Day
Hale, Mrs. Burton-crescent	–	–	–	1	1	0	Do
Halford, Miss, New Broad-street-build.	–	–	–	1	1	0	Xmas
Halford, Mr. Ditto 1796	20	0	0	–	–	–	
Hammond, Mr. Whitechapel	–	–	–	1	1	0	Mid
Hankey, Mr.W.A. Fenchurch-st. 1796	10	10	0	10	0	0	Do
Hankey, Mr. T. Ditto..............1817	10	0	0	–	–	–	
Hanson, Mr. Hammersmith 1796	10	0	0	–	–	–	
Hardcastle, Reyner, and Corsbie,							
Messrs. 1796	300	0	0	–	–	–	
Hardcastle, Mr. J. Hatcham 1800	100	0	0	21	0	0	Xmas
Hardcastle, Mr. J. Jun. Ditto............	–	–	–	2	2	0	Do
Hardcastle, Mr. A. Ditto	–	–	–	2	2	0	Do
Harford, Mr. Shoreditch	–	–	–	1	1	0	L. Day
Harper, Rev. Mr. East-lane, Walworth	–	–	–	1	1	0	Do
Harper, Mr. Jerusalem Coffee-house ...	–	–	–	1	1	0	Do
Harris, Rev. Mr. Islington	–	–	–	1	1	0	Mich
Harvey, Mr. Charlotte-street	–	–	–	1	1	0	L. Day
Hasloch, Rev. Mr. Kentish-town.........	–	–	–	1	1	0	Do
Hawksley, Rev. Mr. Charles-square ...	–	–	–	1	1	0	Mich
Hayes, Mrs. John-st.Tottenham-court-r.	–	–	–	1	1	0	L. Day
Hayes, Mrs. Bartlett's-buildings	–	–	–	1	1	0	Mid
Hayter Mr. T. Brixton 1814	100	0	0	–	–	–	
Hayward, Captain Peter, Highgate......	–	–	–	1	1	0	Mich
Heberts, Mr. Newington-green	–	–	–	2	2	0	Mid

	Donations.			Annual Subscriptions.			
	£	s.	d.	£	s.	d.	
Henderson, Mr. Old Broad-street	–	–	–	1	1	0	L. Day
Hepburn, Mr. Long-lane, Southwark	–	–	–	1	1	0	Do
Herbert, Mr. Wood-street	–	–	–	2	2	0	Xmas
Herne, Mr. Bank	–	–	–	1	1	0	Do
Herne, Mr. E. Hoxton-square	–	–	–	1	1	0	Do
Herne, Mrs. Ditto	–	–	–	1	1	0	Do
Hersant, Mr. Broker's-row	–	–	–	1	1	0	Mid
Hesketh, Mr. J. per Mr. J. Fenn	–	–	–	1	1	0	L. Day
Hewlings, Mr. Chad's-row, Gray's-inn-l.	–	–	–	1	1	0	Do
Heygate, Mr. J. Bridge-street ...1796	10	0	0	–	–	–	
Hibberdine, Mr. Wilderness-row	–	–	–	1	1	0	Do
Hickson, Mr. Wandsworth	–	–	–	1	1	0	Xmas
Hill, Rev. Rowland, Surrey-road	–	–	–	2	2	0	L. Day
Hill, Mr. Castle-court, Birchin-lane	–	–	–	1	1	0	Mid
Hill, Mrs. Fore-street	–	–	–	1	1	0	L. Day
Hobart, Mr. Cannon-street	–	–	–	1	1	0	Do
Hockley, Rev. Mr. Windmill-st. Finsb.	–	–	–	1	1	0	Do
Holehouse, Mr. Borough	–	–	–	2	2	0	Do
Holland, Mr. Edmund, St. Pancras	–	–	–	1	1	0	Do
Holloway, Mr. J. City-road...1796	10	0	0	–	–	–	
Holman, Mr. Lower Thames-str. 1802	15	0	0	0	10	6	Do
Honyman, Mr. Church-str. Spitalfields	–	–	–	1	1	0	Do
Honyman, Mrs. Ditto	–	–	–	1	1	0	Do
Hoppe, Mrs. Islington	–	–	–	2	2	0	Do
Hoppe, Miss, Ditto	–	–	–	1	1	0	Do
Horton, Miss, Lower-street, Islington	–	–	–	2	2	0	Do
Hough, Mr. Tavistock-street	–	–	–	1	1	0	Do
Houston, Mr. Great St. Helen's	10	10	0	–	–	–	
Howard, Mr. R. Stamford-hill ...1799	10	0	0	–	–	–	
Howard, Mr. Fetter-lane	–	–	–	1	1	0	L. Day
Howell, Mr. J. Wood-street, Cheapside	–	–	–	1	1	0	Do
Hughes, Rev. J. Battersea...1812	10	10	0	–	–	–	
Humphrys, Rev. Mr. Canterbury-row	–	–	–	1	1	0	Do
Hunt, Mr. Owen's-row, Islington	–	–	–	1	1	0	Xmas
Hunter, Mr. Broker's-row	–	–	–	1	1	0	Mid
H. Y. by Mr. Battens, Clapham	–	–	–	1	1	0	L. Day
Jack, Mr. Sloane-street	–	–	–	1	1	0	L. Day
Jackson, Rev. Mr. Stockwell	–	–	–	1	1	0	Do
Jackson, Mr. Hackney	–	–	–	1	1	0	Do
Jacob, Mr. Lambeth	–	–	–	1	1	0	Do
Jaques, Mr. Leather-lane	–	–	–	1	1	0	Do
James, Mrs. Hackney	–	–	–	1	1	0	Do
James, Mr. Great Queen-street	–	–	–	1	1	0	Xmas
James, Rev. T. Little Moorfields	–	–	–	1	1	0	Mid
Jarvis, Mr. Kingsland	–	–	–	1	1	0	L. Day
Jennings, Mrs. Warwick-lane	–	–	–	1	1	0	Do
Johnson, Mr. Whitecross-street	–	–	–	1	1	0	Do
Johnson, Mr. Lant-street	–	–	–	1	1	0	Do
Johnson, Mr. J. Bishopsgate-street	–	–	–	1	1	0	Do
Johnson, Mr. by Mr. Cole	–	–	–	0	10	6	L. Day
Jones, Rev. Mr. Islington ...1796	10	10	0	–	–	–	
Jones, Mrs. John-st. Tottenham-ct.-rd.	–	–	–	1	1	0	Do
Jones, Mr. Old Jewry	–	–	–	0	10	6	Xmas
Jordan, Mr. Leadenhall-street	–	–	–	1	1	0	Mid
Jowett, Mr. Camberwell	–	–	–	1	1	0	L. Day
Ireland, Mr. Cannon-street	–	–	–	1	1	0	Do
Irvin, Captain, Sloane-street	–	–	–	1	1	0	Do
Ivatts, Mrs. Peckham	–	–	–	1	1	0	Do
I. C.	5	0	0	–	–	–	
I. E. Finsbury-street, Chiswell-street	–	–	–	2	2	0	Mid
Kello, Rev. Mr. Bethnal-green	–	–	–	1	1	0	L. Day

	Donations.			Annual Subscriptions.		
	£	s.	d.	£	s.	d.
Kemble, Mr. E. Watling-street	–	–	–	1	1	0 L. Day
Kemble, Mr. H. Ditto	–	–	–	1	1	0 Do
Kennerley, Mr. T. Bedford-court	–	–	–	1	1	0 Do
Kent Mr. W. Clapton.............1818	10	10	0	–	–	–
Kent, Mr. S. L. Carpenters' Hall.........	–	–	–	1	1	0 Mid
Kidd, Rev. Mr. Clapton	–	–	–	1	1	0 Do
Kilby, Mr. Oxford-street	–	–	–	1	1	0 Mich
King, Mr. J. Islington-road	–	–	–	1	1	0 L. Day
King, Mr. Broad-street Buildings	–	–	–	1	1	0 Mid
King, Mrs. ditto	–	–	–	1	1	0 Do
King, Mr. W. Little Tower Hill.........	–	–	–	1	1	0 Xmas
Kinnaird, Mr. Redcross-street	–	–	–	1	1	0 L. Day
Knight, Mr. Strand	–	–	–	2	2	0 Do
Knight, Mrs. ditto	–	–	–	1	1	0 Do
Knight, Mr. King-street, Clerkenwell...	–	–	–	1	1	0 Do
Knight, Mr. W. Gainsford-street.........	–	–	–	1	1	0 Mich
Knight, Mr. H. Jun. Stepney-causeway	–	–	–	1	1	0 L. Day
Knowles, Mrs. Palace-row, New-road...	–	–	–	0	12	0 Do
Lack, Mr. Sen. Wormwood-street	–	–	–	1	1	0 Xmas
Lack, Mr. J. ditto	–	–	–	1	1	0 Do
Langton, Mr. D. Dalston 1817	10	10	0	–	–	–
Ditto	2	0	0	–	–	–
Latham, Mr. Walworth.....................	–	–	–	1	1	0 Do
Law, Miss, by Mrs. Rowland Hill	–	–	–	1	1	0 L. Day
Lawson, Mr. E. Brown's-lane......1810	10	10	0	–	–	–
Lea, Mr. Old Jewry	–	–	–	1	1	0 Do
Lees, Mr. Queen's-row, Camberwell ...	–	–	–	1	1	0 Do
Lees, Mr. W. Tower	–	–	–	1	1	0 Do
Legg, Mr. S. Fleet-street	–	–	–	1	1	0 Do
Lemage, Mr. Upper Smith-st. North-ampton-square	–	–	–	1	1	0 Do
Leslie, Mr. Conduit-street..................	–	–	–	1	1	0 Mid
Lightfoot, Mr. Holles-street...............	–	–	–	1	1	0 L. Day
Lister, Mr D. Hackney 1816	10	10	0	–	–	–
Ditto 1818	10	0	0	–	–	–
Livesey, Mr. T. Wood-street	–	–	–	1	1	0 Xmas.
Lloyd, Mr. J. Great Eastcheap............	–	–	–	1	1	Do
Lloyd, Mr W. F. Masons' Hall	–	–	–	1	1	0 Do
Lonsdale, Mr. Great Marlborough-str.	–	–	–	1	1	0 L. Day
Lotherington, Captain, by Rev. Mr. Vautin	–	–	–	1	1	0 Do
Lucas, Mr. Wandsworth Road.............	–	–	–	2	2	0 Xmas
Lush, Mr. C. per Rev. Mr. Platt.........	–	–	–	1	0	0 Mich
Maberly, Mr. St. Martin's-lane	–	–	–	1	1	0 L. Day
Maberly, Mrs Welbeck-street.............	–	–	–	1	1	0 Do
M'Dowall, Mr. S. Leadenhall-street ...	–	–	–	2	2	0 Do
M'Whinnie, Mr. Strand	–	–	–	1	1	0 Mid
Madgwick, Mr. St. John's-lane............	–	–	–	1	1	0 L. Day
Maitland, Mrs. Walworth.................	–	–	–	1	1	0 Do
Manuel, Rev. Dr. Charles-str North-ampton-square	–	–	–	1	1	0 Mid
Marten, Mr. America-square......1796	10	10	0	–	–	–
Mason, Mr. Camden-town..................	–	–	–	1	1	0 Do
Mason, Mr. High Holborn	–	–	–	1	1	0 L. Day
Mather, Mr. King-street, Golden-sq. ...	–	–	–	1	1	0 Do
Mead, Mr. Wood-street.....................	–	–	–	1	1	0 Do
Medlycott, Mr. Southwark	–	–	–	2	2	0 Do
Medlycott, Mrs. Ditto	–	–	–	1	1	0 Do
Metcalf, Mr. Camberwell	–	–	–	1	1	0 Xmas
Meriton, Mrs. Peckham.....................	–	–	–	1	1	0 L. Day
Meyer, Mr. Leadenhall-street ...1796	25	0	0	–	–	–

	Donations.			Annual Subscriptions.		
	£	s.	d.	£	s.	d.
Meyer, Mr. Leadenhall-street ...1800	25	0	0	5	5	0 Mich .
Meyer, Mr. G. Salvador-house ...1809	20	0	0	–	–	–
Meymott, Mr. T. Moorfields	–	–	–	2	2	0 L. Day,
Meymott, Mr. W. by Mr. T. Meymott 1796	10	10	0	2	2	0 Do
Mickle, Mr. Dalston-terrace	–	–	–	1	1	0 Mich
Middlemiss, Mr. Hoxton-fields	–	–	–	1	1	0 L. Day
Middleton, Mr. St Martin's-lane	–	–	–	2	2	0 Do
Millar, Mr. Bethnal-green	–	–	–	1	1	0 Mich
Miller, Mr. E. Regent-street, Kenning.	–	–	–	1	1	0 L. Day
Mills, Mr. S. Finsbury-place......1796	10	10	0	–	–	–
Ditto 1811	10	0	0	–	–	–
Mills, Mrs. Islington 1796	50	0	0	–	–	–
Mills, Mrs. Tyndale-place	–	–	–	3	3	0 L. Day
Mitchell, Mr. Kentish-town...............	–	–	–	1	1	0 Do
Mitchell, Mr. Holborn	–	–	–	1	1	0 Do
Mitchell, Mr. Whitechapel	–	–	–	1	1	0 Do
Mitton, Mrs. Tavistock-place	–	–	–	1	1	0 Mid
Moginie, Mr. S. Prince's-row, Pimlico	–	–	–	1	1	0 L. Day
Monds, Mr. T. W. Langley-place	–	–	–	1	1	0 Xmas
Money, Mr. Hampstead-road	–	–	–	1	1	0 L. Day
Moore, Mr. St. Martin's-court............	–	–	–	1	1	0 Do
Moore, Mr. Great Queen-street	–	–	–	1	1	0 Do
Moore, Mrs. Camberwell-green	–	–	–	1	1	0 Do
Moore, Rev. H. Vauxhall....................	–	–	–	1	1	0 Mid
Moore, Miss, St. James's-place	–	–	–	1	1	0 L. Day
Moreland, Mrs. Old-street	–	–	–	1	1	0 Do
Moreland, Mr. Ditto	–	–	–	1	1	0 Do
Moreland, Mrs. Clapton	–	–	–	2	2	0 Do
Morgan, Mrs. Wellington-place	–	–	–	1	1	0 Xmas
Morris, Mr. T. Camberwell 1800	10	0	0	–	–	–
Morris, Mr. per Mr. Preston	–	–	–	3	3	0 Mid
Mosely, Mr. R. Piccadilly..................	–	–	–	1	1	0 L. Day
Muggeridge, Mr. Up. Thames-st 1813	10	0	0	–	–	–
Mum, Mr. per Mrs. Martin,Whitechap.	–	–	–	2	2	0 Do
Murray, Lady A. by Mrs. Rowland Hill	–	–	–	5	0	0 Do
Murray, Mr. Prince's-str. Leicester-sqr.	–	–	–	1	1	0 Do
Murray, Mr. Exeter-street, Sloane-str.	–	–	–	0	10	6 Do
Muston, Mr. Hatton-garden	–	–	–	1	1	0 Do
M. S. by Mr. Cecil, Thames-street	–	–	–	1	1	0 Mich
Nash, Mr. Maiden-lane, Battle-bridge	–	–	–	1	1	0 Do
Nash, Mr. Angel-place, Bishopsgate-st.	–	–	–	1	1	0 Do .
Nattrass, Mr. Colchester-street	–	–	–	1	1	0 Mid
Neale, Mr. Rosoman-street	–	–	–	1	1	0 L. Day
Neale,Mr. C. Devonshire-pl. Paddington	–	–	–	1	1	0 Mich
Neele, Mr. G. Judd-place, Somer's-town	10	10	0	–	–	–
Nelson, Mrs. E. Kentish-town.............	–	–	–	1	0	0 Do
Nesham, Mr. Garlick-hill	–	–	–	1	1	0 Do
Nesham, Mrs. Ditto	–	–	–	0	10	6 Do
Nicol, Rev. Dr. Hans-place	–	–	–	1	1	0 L. Day
Nisbet, Mr. Castle-st. Oxford-st. 1817	10	10	0	–	–	–
Niven, Mr. King-street, Soho ...1815	10	10	0	–	–	–
Nodes, Mr. Great Chapel-street	–	–	–	1	1	0 Do
Noeth, Mr. Cambridge-heath	–	–	–	1	1	0 Do
Nokes, Mr. Rodney-buildings	–	–	–	1	1	0 Do
Norman, Mr. Gloucester-st. Hackney-r.	–	–	–	1	1	0 Do
Nutter, Mr. Jun. Gun-str. Spitalfields	–	–	–	1	1	0 Xmas
N. C...	0	12	0	–	–	–
Oates, Rev. Mr. Islington..................	–	–	–	1	1	0 L Day
Ody, Mr. Kentish-town.....................	–	–	–	2	2	0 Do
Ogborn, Mr. Bishopsgate-street	–	–	–	2	2	0 Do

C

	Donations.			Annual Subscriptions.		
	£	s.	d.	£	s.	d.
Ogden, Mr. Walworth	–	–	–	1	1	0 Do
Ogdin, Mr. Upper Thames-street	–	–	–	2	2	0 L. Day
Oldfield, Mr. Peckham	–	–	–	5	5	0 Do
Oldham, Mr. O. Montague-place........	–	–	–	5	5	0 Do
Oldham, Mr. J. Jun. Holborn.............	–	–	–	1	1	0 Do
Omer, Mr. Lower-street, Islington......	–	–	–	0	10	6 Do
Owen, Mrs. Shoreditch	–	–	–	1	1	0 Do
Pain, Mr. Wilsted-street, Somer's-town	–	–	–	1	1	0 Do
Pantin, Mr. Smithfield	–	–	–	1	1	0 Do
Parker, Mr. King's-mews	–	–	–	1	1	0 Do
Parkes, Mrs. Palace-row, New-road ...	–	–	–	1	1	0 Do
Parkinson, Mr. Bank	–	–	–	1	1	0 Do
Parkinson, Mr. T. Oxford-street	–	–	–	1	1	0 Xmas
Parkinson, Mrs. Clapton	–	–	–	1	1	0 Mid
Parks, Mr. Kingsland....................	–	–	–	1	1	0 L. Day
Parnell, Mr. W. Botolph-lane	–	–	–	1	1	0 Do
Parnell, Rev. J. per Mr. W. Parnell ...	–	–	–	1	1	0 Do
Parry, Mr. Leather-lane	–	–	–	1	1	0 Xmas
Patterson, Mr. G. Bishopsgate-st. 1796	10	0	0	–	–	–
Pattison, Mr. Cross-st. Islington 1816	10	10	0	–	–	–
Paynter,Messrs.F&Co.Coleman-st 1810	10	0	0	–	–	–
Pearson, Mr. Upper Homerton	–	–	–	5	5	0 L. Day
Pearson, Mrs. Ditto	–	–	–	1	1	0 Do
Pellatt, Mr. T. Fenchurch-street.........	–	–	–	1	1	0 Do
Pellatt, Mr. A. St. Paul's Church-yard	–	–	–	1	1	0 Do
Pellatt, Mr. A. Jun. Ditto	–	–	–	1	1	0 Mid
Pemberton, Mr. R Kingsland-road......	–	–	–	1	1	0 Do
Pettet, Mr. Vauxhall......................	–	–	–	1	1	0 Do
Perry, Miss H. Crescent, Minories......	–	–	–	1	1	0 L. Day
Perry, Miss S. Ditto	–	–	–	1	1	0 Do
Petch, Mrs. North-st. Finsbury...1796	10	0	0	1	1	0 Do
Pettingell&Andrews,Messrs.Berkley-sq.	–	–	–	1	1	0 Do
Phelps, Mr. Ely-place	–	–	–	1	1	0 Mid
Phillips, Rev. Mr. Mill-hill	–	–	–	1	1	0 L. Day
Phillips, Mr. Sen. Holborn	–	–	–	1	1	0 Mid
Phillips, Mr. Jun. Ditto	–	–	–	1	1	0 Xmas
Phillips,Capt.'per Mr.Bayley, Crooked-l.	–	–	–	1	1	0 Mid
Pink, Mr. Hackney-terrace	–	–	–	1	1	0 L. Day
Piper, Mr T. Little Eastcheap...1818	10	10	0	–	–	–
Pirie, Mr. J. Camberwell 1814	10	10	0	–	–	–
Platt, Rev. Mr. Wilmot-square...1800	10	0	0	1	1	0 Do
Platt, Mrs. Ditto.........................	–	–	–	1	1	0 Do
Platt, Mr. Stamford-street 1800	10	10	0	2	2	0 Do
Plummer, Mr. T. Camberwell ...1796	21	0	0	–	–	–
Ditto 1800	20	0	0	–	–	–
Pomeroy, Mr. Moore-place, Lambeth	–	–	–	1	1	0 Do
Pontin, Mr. 2, Perceval-street............	–	–	–	2	2	0 Do
Pousset, Mr. Hackney 1796	10	0	0	–	–	–
Powell,Mr. G. York-buildings, Islington	–	–	–	1	1	0 Do
Pratt, Rev. Mr. Doughty-street	–	–	–	1	1	0 Mich
Preston, Mr. Miles's-lane 1800	10	0	0	1	1	0 L. Day
Pretty, Mr. Hoxton	–	–	–	1	1	0 Do
Price, Mr. Steel-yard....................	–	–	–	1	1	0 Xmas
Price, Mr. Haymarket	–	–	–	1	1	0 Do
Pringle, Mrs. per Mr. Beams	–	–	–	1	1	0 Mid
Pritt, Mr. Wood-street	–	–	–	1	1	0 Xmas
Procter & Brownlow, Messrs. Fleet-str.	–	–	–	4	4	0 Mich
Procter, Mrs. Islington	–	–	–	1	1	0 L. Day
Puget, Mrs. Sackville-street 1812	10	10	0	–	–	–
Ditto 1813	25	0	0	–	–	–
Ditto, per Mr. T. Smith, Moorfields ...	–	–	–	5	5	0 Xmas
Radcliffe, Mr. Pimlico	–	–	–	1	1	0 Mich

	Donations.			Annual Subscriptions.		
	£	s.	d.	£	s.	d.
Radley, Mr. J. Fleet-street	-	-	-	2	2	0 Xmas
Ralph, Mr. J. Cheapside	-	-	-	1	1	0 L. Day
Randoll, Mr. Owen's-pl. Goswell-road...	-	-	-	2	2	0 Do
Ranier, Mr. Daniel	5	0	0	-	-	-
Rattray, Mr. Piccadilly....................	-	-	-	2	2	0 Xmas
Reid, Mr. Old Compton-street............	-	-	-	1	1	0 L. Day
Reid, Mr. W. Minories....................	-	-	-	1	1	0 Xmas
Reyner, Mr. Mark-lane 1797	10	10	0	-	-	-
Ditto 1800	100	0	0	5	5	0 Do
Richards, Rev. J. J. Camden-town	-	-	-	1	1	0 Xmas
Richardson, Mr. LittleTower-street, per						
Mr. Reyner.............................	-	-	-	1	0	0 Mid
Riddell, Mr. A. Queen-street ...1813	35	10	0	5	5	0 Xmas
Roberts, Mr. G. Fore-street 1796	10	10	0	-	-	-
Roberts, Mr. T. Lambeth 1815	10	10	0	-	-	-
Roberts, Mr. Josiah, Gould-square......	-	-	-	2	2	0 L. Day
Roberts, Mr. Little Eastcheap............	-	-	-	1	1	0 Xmas
Robertson, Mr. Kennington-cross	1	0	0	-	-	-
Robinson, Mr. S. Albion-place ...1796	10	0	0	1	1	0 L. Day
Rohrs, Mr. J. Prince's-pl. Cable-street	-	-	-	1	1	0 Xmas
Rothwell, Mr. R. King-street......1800	21	0	0	-	-	-
Ditto 1814	10	10	0	-	-	-
Ruffles, Miss, Rotherhithe	-	-	-	1	1	0 L. Day
Rusby, Mr. Bermondsey-square	-	-	-	2	2	0 Do
Rutt, Miss, Hackney.....................	-	-	-	1	1	0 Do
R. S. G.	-	-	-	1	1	0 Do
Sabine, Mr. W. Islington 1797	10	0	0	-	-	-
Salter, Mr. Camden-town	-	-	-	0	10	6 Xmas
Sard, Mr. St Martin's-lane	-	-	-	1	1	0 Do
Sargeant, Mrs. Old Gravel-lane	-	-	-	1	1	0 Do
Sergeant, Mr. Camberwell	-	-	-	1	1	0 L. Day
Saunders, Mr.J.E.LawrencePountney-l.	-	-	-	1	1	0 Do
Scott, Mr. Whitehead's-grove, Chelsea	-	-	-	1	1	0 Do
Season, Mrs. Minories	-	-	-	1	1	0 Do
Sells, Mr. Bankside	-	-	-	1	1	0 Do
Selwyn, Mr. Northampton-street	-	-	-	1	1	0 Do
Sergrove, Mr. Charles-square	-	-	-	1	1	0 Xmas
Sewell, Mr. Albion-ter. Commercial-rd.	-	-	-	1	1	0 L. Day
Shackleton, Mr. C. Little Suffolk-street	-	-	-	1	1	0 Do
Sharp, Mr. Threadneedle-street...1800	21	0	0	-	-	-
Sharp, Mr. Cannon-street	-	-	-	1	1	0 Mich
Shaw, Mr. Mark-lane.....................	-	-	-	1	1	0 Xmas
Shepherd, Mr. Bishopsgate-street	-	-	-	1	1	0 Do
Sherrings, Mr. John, Borough ...1796	10	10	0	-	-	-
Shewell, Mr. E. Clapham-road ...1815	52	10	0	-	-	-
Ditto 1816	52	10	0	-	-	-
Shireff, Mr. Grafton-street	-	-	-	1	1	0 L. Day
Shields, Capt. Rodney-buildings	-	-	-	1	1	0 Mid
Shorland, Mrs. Manor-place, Chelsea...	-	-	-	1	1	0 Xmas
Short, Mr. J. R. Kingsland	-	-	-	1	1	0 Mid
Shout, Mr. R. Holborn	-	-	-	1	1	0 Xmas
Shrubsole,Mr.W.Bank of England 1796	20	0	0	-	-	-
Ditto 1800	10	0	0	1	1	0 L. Day
Sims, Messrs. Sun Tavern-fields	-	-	1	5	5	0 Do
Simpson, Mr. J. G. Bush-lane ...1814	10	10	0	3	3	0 Mich
Simpson, Rev. Dr. Hoxton College......	-	-	-	1	1	0 Do
Simpson, Mr. Newgate-street	-	-	-	1	1	0 L. Day
Simpson, Mr. R. Hoxton	-	-	-	1	1	0 Do
Slack, Mr. Bank	-	-	-	1	1	0 Do
Slark, Mr. W. Clapton..............1816	50	0	0	-	-	-
Slatter, Mr. Jun. Audit Office............	-	-	-	1	1	0 Mid
Sleape, Mr. Fish-street-hill	-	-	-	1	1	0 Do

	Donations.			Annual Subscriptions.		
	£	s.	d.	£	s.	d
Slingsby, Mrs. Old-street	–	–	–	1	1	0 Xmas
Sloper, Rev. N. E. Hemas-ter. Chelsea	–	–	–	1	1	L. Day
Smart, Mr. T. Hackney	–	–	–	1	1	Mich
Smith, Rev. Dr. Hackney-terrace	–	–	–	1	1	L. Day
Smith, Mrs. Ditto	–	–	–	1	1	Do
Smith, Rev. Mr. Spa-fields	–	–	–	2	2	Do
Smith, Mr. Surrey-road....................	–	–	–	1	1	Do
Smith, Mr. Cateaton-street.	–	–	–	1	1	D
Smith, Mr. Beech-street	–	–	–	1	1	Do
Smith, Mr. Gutter-lane....................	–	–	–	1	1	Do
Smith, Mrs. Colchester-street	–	–	–	1	1	Xmas
Smith, Mr. Red-lion-street	–	–	–	1	1	Mid
Smith, Mr. Royal Exchange	–	–	–	1	1	Do
Snelgar, Mr. H. Charles-sq. Hoxton ...,	–	–	–	1	1	Xmas
Snow, Mrs. per Messrs. Procter & Co...	–	–	–	3	0	Mich
Soames, Mr. Newington-green............	–	–	–	1	1	L. Day
Sowerby, Mr. G. Mead-place, Lambeth	–	–	–	1	1	Mid
Spragg, Mr. Kingsland-crescent	–	–	–	1	1	L. Day
Spark, Mr. Shoe-lane	–	–	–	2	2	Do
Stafford, Mr. Borough-market	–	–	–	0	10	Do
Steell, Mr. R. G. Islington.........1800	10	0	0	1	1	Do
Steinkopff, Rev. Dr. Savoy 1813	10	0	0	1	1	Xmas
Stephenson, Mr. William-st. Blackfriars	–	–	–	1	1	L. Day
Stephenson, Mrs. Ditto	–	–	–	1	1	Do
Steven, Mr. Robert, Shacklewell.........	–	–	–	1	1	Do
Steven, Mr. R. Jun. Upper Thames-st.	–	–	–	1	1	Mich
Stiff, Mr. New-st. Covent-garden, 1796	20	0	0	2	2	L. Day
Stimson, Mrs. Prospect-place, Lambeth	–	–	–	1	1	Do
Stobart, Mr. Cannon-street	–	–	–	1	1	Do
Stokes, Mr. Peckham......................	–	–	–	1	1	Do
Stonard, Mr. J. Stamford-hill	–	–	–	5	5	Xmas
Strange, Messrs. J. Bishopsgate-st. 1796	10	0	0	–	–	–
Strange, Mr. J. Ditto	–	–	–	5	0	L. Day
Strange, Mr. J. Hatton-garden	–	–	–	1	1	D
Streetin, Mr. Islington	–	–	–	2	2	D
Strickland, Mr. Newgate-market.........	–	–	–	1	1	D
Strongitharm, Mr. Pall-mall..............	–	–	–	1	1	Do
Struthers, Mr. W. Scotland-yard...1813	10	0	0	–	–	–
Strutt, Rev. Mr. Charles-street, City-r.	–	–	–	1	1	Xmas
Stunt, Mr. Walworth......................	–	–	–	1	1	Mid
Surgey, Mrs. Upper Homerton	–	–	–	1	1	L. Day
Suttaby, Mr. Stationers'-court............	–	–	–	1	1	Do
Summerland, Mr. Upper Thames-street	–	–	–	1	1	Xmas
Summers, Mr. Bond-street	–	–	–	1	1	L. Day
Sundius, Mr. Stoke Newington ...1797	10	10	0	–	–	–
Ditto 1800	21	0	0	–	–	–
Sykes, Mr. J. Red Cross-street	–	–	–	5	0	0 Mid
S. M. by Rev. Mr. Burder	15	0	0	–	–	–
S. N. Aldermanbury	–	–	–	1	1	0 L. Day
Tagg, Mrs. Shacklewell	–	–	–	1	1	0 L. Day
Tarn, Mr. Earl-street, Blackfriars	–	–	–	1	1	0 Xmas
Tarrington, Mr. J. Mile-end	–	–	–	1	1	0 Do
Taylor, Mr. J. Old Broad-street, 1813	10	0	0	–	–	–
Taylor, Mr. Wilderness-row	10	10	0	–	–	–
Taylor, Mr. Kingsland-crescent	–	–	–	1	1	0 L Day
Taylor, Mr. S Poultry	–	–	–	1	1	0 Do
Teape & Jones, Messrs. George-street, Tower-hill	–	–	–	3	3	0 Mich
Thodey, Mr. Poultry......................	–	–	–	1	1	0 L. Day
Thompson, Mr. J. Colebrook-row, 1815	10	10	0	–	–	–
Thompson, Mr. T. Colebrook-row	–	–	–	2	2	0 Do
Thompson, Mr. W. Colebrook-row	–	–	–	1	1	0 Do

	Donations.			Annual Subscriptions.		
	£	s.	d.	£	s	d
Thompson, Mr. P. Frith-street	–	–	–	1	1	0 Do
Thompson, Mrs. Kentish-town............	–	–	–	1	1	0 Do
Thompson, Mr. G. B. Oxford-street ...	–	–	–	1	1	0 Mich
Thorley, Mr. County-terrace	–	–	–	1	1	0 L. Day
Thorn, Mr. Oxford-street..................	–	–	–	1	1	0 Do
Thornton, Mr. R M. P. 1797	10	10	0	–	–	–
Thornton, Mr. S. M. P. King's-arms-y.	–	–	–	5	5	0 Do
Thring, Mrs. John-st. Tottenham-ct-rd.	–	–	–	2	2	0 Do
Thurlborn, Mr. Holborn	–	–	–	1	1	0 Do
Timmings, Mrs. Bethnal-green	–	–	–	1	1	0 Do
Tinsley, Mrs. Hackney	–	–	–	0	10	6 Mid
Tomkins, Mr. W. New Broad-street ...	–	–	–	1	1	0 Mich
Tomlin, Rev. Mr per Mr. Legg	–	–	–	1	1	0 L. Day
Toomer, Mr. E. per Mr. R. Steven ...	–	–	–	1	1	0 Mich
Towle, Mr Walworth	–	–	–	1	1	0 L. Day
Townley, Mrs. Cheyne-walk, Chelsea...	–	–	–	1	1	0 Do
Townley, Rev. Dr. Ditto	–	–	–	1	1	0 Mid
Townsend, Mr. W. Holborn 1815	10	0	0	1	1	0 L. Day
Townsend, Rev. J. Bermondsey	–	–	–	1	1	0 Mid
Tracy, Rev. S. W. Fulham-road	–	–	–	1	1	0 Xmas
Trueman, Mr. Islington	–	–	–	1	1	0 Do
Tucker, Mr B. Kentish-town	–	–	–	2	2	0 L. Day
Tucker, Mr. R. Upper Thames-street...	–	–	–	1	1	0 Do
Tutt, Mr. Royal Exchange 1796	11	11	6	–	–	–
Tyler, Mr. Homerton-terrace	–	–	–	1	1	0 Do
Upton, Rev. Mr. Brunswick-street......	–	–	–	1	1	0 Do
Uwins, Mrs Thavies-inn	–	–	–	2	2	0 Do
Uwins, Mrs. Pentonville	–	–	–	1	1	0 Do
Vanhouse, Mr. James, Tower-street ...	–	–	–	2	2	0 Do
Vaughan, Mr. per Rev. Mr. Platt	–	–	–	1	1	0 Do
Vautin, Rev. Mr. Shadwell	–	–	–	1	1	0 Do
Venables, Mr. Queenhithe	–	–	–	3	3	0 Do
Viney, Mr. St. Paul's Church-yard......	–	–	–	1	1	0 Do
Wackerill, Mr. Hoxton-square............	–	–	–	1	1	0 Do
Waistell, Mr. Kentish-town	–	–	–	2	2	0 Do
Walford, Rev. Mr. Homerton............	–	–	–	1	1	0 Do
Walker, Mr. T. Piccadilly	–	–	–	1	1	0 Do
Walker, Mrs. Ditto	–	–	–	1	1	0 Do
Wallace, Cook, & Co Messrs. Trump-street 1796	10	0	0	–	–	–
Walley, Mr. Hackney	–	–	–	2	2	0 Do
Wallis, Mr. Somer's-town..................	–	–	–	2	2	0 Do
Wallis, Mr. W. Surry-road	–	–	–	1	1	0 Do
Wallington, Mr. Burrows-buildings ...	–	–	–	1	1	0 Xmas
Walton, Mr. Little Britain 1800	10	0	0	1	1	0 L. Day
Wardall, Mr. Manor-place, Walworth	–	–	–	1	1	0 Do
Waring, Mr. F. Paddington 1796	10	0	0	–	–	–
Warmington, Mr. Gracechurch-street	–	–	–	1	1	0 Do
Warren, Mr. Stationers'-court	–	–	–	1	1	0 Mid
Warren, Mrs. Ditto	–	–	–	1	1	0 Do
Waters, Mr. Hackney	–	–	–	1	1	0 L. Day
Waters, Mrs. Ditto	–	–	–	1	1	0 Do
Watson, Dr. Asylum for Deaf & Dumb	–	–	–	1	1	0 Do
Watson, Mr. J. Watling-street	10	10	0	–	–	–
Watts, Mr. J T. Angel-court	–	–	–	2	2	0 Xmas
Waugh, Rev. Dr Salisbury-place	–	–	–	1	1	0 L. Day
Webber, Mr. J. Milk-street 1800	10	10	0	–	–	–
Ditto 1815	50	0	0	–	–	–
Wells, Mr. B. Serjeants' Inn	–	–	–	1	1	0 Do
Wells, Mr. per Mr. Taylor	–	–	–	1	1	0 Do

	Donations.			Annual Subscriptions.		
	£	s.	d.	£	s.	d.
Wells, Mr. J. Arlington-str. Camden-t.	–	–	–	1	1	0 Mid
Wenham, Mr. J. Throgmorton-street...	–	–	–	1	1	0 Mich·
Werninck, Rev. Dr. Camberwell-grove	–	–	–	1	1	0 L. Day
Westley, Mr. Somers-town	–	–	–	2	2	0 Do
Whately and Patton, Messrs. per Mr.						
Reyner 1800	10	10	0	–	–	–
Wilberforce, W. Esq. M.P. 1796	10	10	0	–	–	–
Ditto 1810	10	10	0	–	–	–
Ditto 1812	10	10	0	–	–	–
Ditto 1818	10	0	0	–	–	–
Wilcoxon, Mr. Lombard-street	–	–	–	1	1	0 Do
Wilks, Rev. Matthew, Hoxton ...1800	20	0	0	1	1	0 Mid
Wilks, Rev. Mark, Peckham	–	–	–	1	1	0 Xmas
Williams, Rev. T. Stepney.........1796	10	0	0	–	–	–
Williams, Mr. Hackney	–	–	–	1	1	0 L. Day
Williams, Rev. W. B. M. A. Homerton	–	–	–	1	1	0 Mid
Williams, Rev. Mr. Gate-street	–	–	–	1	1	0 Mich
Wilkinson, Mr. Fenchurch-street 1796	20	0	0	3	3	0 Do
Wilkinson, Mr. Jun. Moorfields	–	–	–	1	1	0 Do
Willis, Mr. Chatham-place	–	–	–	1	1	0 L. Day
Wilson, Lady 1817	21	0	0	–	–	–
Wilson, Mr. J. Islington............1796	100	0	0	5	5	0 Xmas
Wilson, Mr. T. Highbury 1796	100	0	0	–	–	–
Wilson, Mr. Jos. Milk-street......1796	100	0	0	–	–	–
Wilson, Mrs. Camberwell 1809	50	0	0	–	–	–
Wilson, Mr B. Moorfields	–	–	–	1	1	0 L. Day
Wilson, Mr J. Ditto.....................	–	–	–	1	1	0 Do
Wilson, Mr. W. Ditto	–	–	–	1	1	0 Do
Wilson, Mr. J. B. Clapham	–	–	–	5	5	0 Mid
Wilson, Mr. J. Jun. 124, Wood-street	–	–	–	1	1	0 Mich
Winchester, Mr. Cecil-st. Strand, 1800	10	0	0	1	1	0 Do
Witton, Mrs. Chiswell-street	–	–	–	1	1	0 Mid
Wolff, Mr. G. Balham 1798	100	0	0	–	–	–
Ditto 1800	50	0	0	–	–	–
Ditto 1804	20	0	0	–	–	–
Wontner, Mr. J. Minories 1816	10	10	0	–	–	–
Wontner, Mr. Ditto	–	–	–	1	1	0 L. Day
Wood, Mr. Shoe-lane.....................	–	–	–	0	10	6 Do
Wood, Mrs. Commercial-road............	–	–	–	0	10	6 Do
Wood, Mrs. New Norfolk-str. Park-lane	–	–	–	1	1	0 Mid
Woodd, Rev. B. Paddington 1805	10	10	0	–	–	–
Wright, Mr. J. M. Peckham-rye	–	–	–	1	1	0 Xmas
Wright, Mr. Stamford-hill	–	–	–	1	1	0 Mid
Wyatt, Mr. Coleman-street	–	–	–	1	1	0 L. Day
W...........	10	0	0	–	–	–
W. Mrs.	10	0	0	–	–	–
Yates, Mr. Cursitor-street	–	–	–	1	1	0 Do
Yockney, Mr. S. Bedford-street...1800	10	0	0	1	1	0 Do
Young, Captain W. Deptford	–	–	–	1	1	0 Do
Young, Mr. Hampstead-road	–	–	–	1	1	0 Do
Young, Mrs. Ditto............................	–	–	–	1	1	0 Do
Young. Mr. Camden-town	–	–	–	1	1	0 Do
Young, Mr. Poland-street.................	–	–	–	1	1	0 Mid
Zeigalhaupt, Mr. Petticoat-lane	–	–	–	1	1	0 L. Day

AUXILIARY SOCIETIES,
CONGREGATIONAL COLLECTIONS, &c.

From April 1, 1817, to April 1, 1818,

IN LONDON AND ITS VICINITY.

Subscribers of 10s. per Annum, and upwards, only are inserted.

ANNUAL MEETING IN LONDON, 1817.

Collections.

	£	s.	d.
Surrey Chapel	434	16	0
Tabernacle	160	3	4
Spa Fields Chapel	122	18	0
Tottenham Court Chapel	173	0	2
St. Ann's Church, Blackfriars	146	15	0
Sion Chapel	120	0	0
Islington Chapel	62	7	6
Orange Street Chapel	86	5	0
Rev. Mr. Upton's Meeting	42	11	10
	1348	16	10

BETHNAL GREEN AUXILIARY SOCIETY.

Treasurer, Mr. Mead.
Secretaries, Mr. D. Martin—Mr. J. Smith—Mr. J. Hill.

	£	s.	d.		£	s.	d.
Acutt, Rev. J.	1	1	0	Manning, Mr.	0	10	6
Ball, Mr. E.	1	1	0	Matthews, Mr. H.	0	12	0
Bateman, Mr.	0	10	6	Mead, Mr.	1	1	0
Brown, Rev. W.	0	10	6	Pashen, Mr.	0	10	6
Buckingham, Mr.	0	10	6	Piercy, Rev. J. S.	0	10	6
Calladine, Mr.	0	12	0	Page, Mr.	0	10	6
Collett, Mr. W.	0	12	0	Parry, Mr.	0	12	0
Crockford, Mr. S.	0	10	6	Simmons, Mr. J.	0	10	6
Daycock, Mr. J	0	10	6	Smith, Mr. J.	0	10	6
Daycock, Mr. J. C.	0	10	6	Smith, Mr. J.	0	10	6
Dymock, Mr. F.	0	10	6	Stanley, Mr.	0	10	6
Gilbert, Mr. W.	1	1	0	Sysum, Mr.	0	10	6
Gladding, Mr. J.	1	6	0	Thomason, Mr.	0	10	6
Giles, Mrs.	0	10	6	Wood, Mr. B.	0	12	0
Hardenham, Mr.	0	13	0	A Friend, by Mr. Mann	0	12	0
Knight, Mr. W.	0	10	6	Amount of small Subscriptions			
Lincheux, Miss M.	0	13	0	under 10s. per annum	28	10	0
Long, Mr.	0	10	6				
Mann, Mr.	0	12	0		50	0	0

BETHNAL GREEN JUVENILE SOCIETY.

Subscriptions by Miss E. Haye 6 13 0

NEW BROAD STREET FEMALE SOCIETY.

Subscriptions by Miss Wilkinson, *Treasurer* 46 3 0

CAMBERWELL AUXILIARY SOCIETY.

Treasurer, Mr. Josiah Roberts.
Secretary, Rev. John Innes.

	£	s.	d.		£	s.	d.
Barwise, Miss	0	12	0	Bradley, Mrs.	1	0	0
Bowler, Mr.	1	1	0	Browning, Miss	0	10	6
Boyd, Mr.	1	1	0	Buxton, Mr.	1	1	0

	£	s.	d.		£	s.	d.
Clifford, Mr.	1	1	0	Plummer, Mr. W.	5	5	0
Collin, Mr.	1	1	0	Pellatt, Mrs.	0	10	6
Cruikshank, Mr.	1	1	0	Pirie, Mr.	2	2	0
Darley, Mrs.	0	10	0	Rentall, Mr.	1	1	0
Edsall, Mr.	0	10	6	Sadler, Mr.	0	10	6
Edsall, Mrs.	0	10	6	Sadler, Mr. T.	0	10	6
Forbes, Mr. W.	1	1	0	Squires, Mrs.	1	0	0
A Friend	0	12	0	Simms, Mrs.	1	1	0
Ditto	1	1	0	Smith, Mr.	1	0	0
A few Friends	1	6	0	Sherring, Mr.	1	1	0
Greenhough, Mr.	1	1	0	Swain, Miss	0	12	0
Haines, Mr.	0	12	0	Stunt, Mr.	1	1	0
Hughes, Mrs. young Ladies	0	12	0	Thompson, Miss A.	1	8	0
Innes, Rev. J.	1	1	0	Wallington, Mr.	1	0	0
Kemble, Mr. H.	10	10	0	Wastie, Mr.	1	1	0
Kemble, Mr. C.	10	10	0	Whitaker, Mr.	0	10	0
Keith, Sir G.	1	0	0	Whitly, Mr.	1	0	0
Lamb, Captain	0	10	0	Whitly, Mr. W.	0	12	0
Lees, Mr.	1	0	0	Whitly, Miss C	0	12	0
Lees, Mr. W.	1	0	0	Wickson, Mr.	1	1	0
Lloyd, Mr.	1	0	0	Wills, Mr.	0	10	6
Maitland, Mr	0	10	6	Winter, Mr.	0	12	0
Manfield, Mr. W.	10	10	0	Young, Mr.	1	0	0
Manfield, Mrs.	1	1	0	Subscriptions under 10s. per			
Mayhew, Mrs.	1	1	0	annum	10	2	10
Ogden, Mr.	1	1	0				
Paynter, Mr. F.	10	10	0		104	3	10
Paynter, Mrs.	1	1	1				

CHAPEL STREET, SOHO, ASSOCIATION.

Subscriptions by Rev. Mr. Stollery 65 0 0

CHURCH STREET, MILE END.

Contributions in the Rev. G. Evans's Congregation—Mr. G. Evans, jun. and Miss Cock, Secretaries.

	£	s.	d.		£	s.	d.
Two-thirds of the amount collected	30	0	0	Saturday evening at Mr. Evans's Chapel	2	5	6
A few Friends who hold a Meeting for Prayer on a					32	5	6

CLERKENWELL AUXILIARY SOCIETY.

Treasurer, Mr. C. Dudley.

Secretaries, Mr. S. Fuller—Mr. C. Holmes.

	£	s.	d.		£	s.	d.
Aspin, Mrs.	0	12	0	Clarke, Miss	1	1	0
Austin, Mr.	1	1	0	Cleaton, Mr. E.	1	1	0
Ayres, Mr.	0	12	0	Cock, Mrs.	1	0	0
Ayres, Mrs.	0	12	0	Coles, Mr. J.	0	12	0
Baylie, Mr.	1	1	0	Davies, Mr. D.	1	1	0
Baylie, Mr. W.	0	12	0	Douglas, Mr.	0	12	0
Baylie, Mr. E. jun	0	12	0	Dudley, Mr.	1	1	0
Beeby, Mr.	0	10	6	Ellis, Mr.	1	0	0
Bliss, Mr.	0	10	6	Fleetwood, Mr.	0	12	0
Bennington, Mr.	1	6	0	Fuller, Mr.	0	12	0
Boulton, Mr.	1	1	0	Grant, Mr. H.	1	0	0
Bradshaw, Mr. W.	0	10	0	Green, Mr.	0	12	0
Bradshaw, Miss	0	12	0	Grieg, Mr.	0	12	0
Britten, Mr.	1	1	0	Hadlow, Mr.	0	12	0
Britten, Mrs.	0	10	6	Haines, Mr.	1	4	0
Burge, Mr.	1	1	0	Halditch, Mr.	1	1	0
Burn, Mr.	1	1	0	Hodge, Mr.	1	0	0
Bidford, Mr.	0	10	6	Holmes, Mr. C.	0	12	0

	£	s.	d.		£	s.	d.
Holmes, Mr.W.	0	12	0	Selby, Mr.	0	10	6
Hughes, Mr. N	1	0	0	Shipman, Mr.	0	12	0
Immyns, Miss	0	10	6	Sibbald, Mr	0	10	6
Jenkins, Mr.	0	12	0	Simco, Mr.	0	12	0
Jenkins, Mrs.	0	12	0	Simco, Mr & Mrs.	0	13	0
Justins, Mr.	0	12	0	Smith, J. Esq.	1	1	0
Jackson, Messrs. W. & H.	0	10	6	Stringall, Mr. R	0	17	4
Kirkwood, Mr.	0	12	0	Stringall, Mr. T.	0	12	0
Leaver, Mr.	0	10	6	Thorpe, Mr. jun.	0	12	0
Mallett, Mr.	0	12	0	Walker, Mr.	1	0	0
Mallett, Mrs.	0	12	0	Walker, Mr. E.	0	10	6
Marriott, Mr.	0	12	0	Watson, Mr.	0	10	0
Maynard, Mr.	0	10	0	Willmott, Mr.	0	12	0
Neale, Mr.	0	12	0	Wilson, Mr.	0	10	0
Neville, Miss	0	12	0	Also about 280 Subscribers			
Nickolls, Mr.	0	18	0	under 10s. each	133	10	8
Owen, Mr.	1	6	0				
Ricket, Mr.	1	0	0		185	0	0
Roberts, Mr.	1	0	0				

CROWN COURT AUXILIARY MISSIONARY SOCIETY.

MALE BRANCH.

Treasurer—Mr. Young.

Secretary—Mr. Stephenson.

Annual Subscribers.	£	s.	d.		£	s.	d.
				Moore, Mr.	0	10	6
Alexander, Mr G.	0	10	6	Nicholson, Mr.	0	10	6
Alexander, Mr. W.	0	10	0	Parish, Mr.	0	10	0
Anderson, Mr.	0	10	6	Rae, Mr.	0	10	6
Barlace, Mr.	0	10	0	Reid, Mr. W.	0	10	6
Bickerton, Mr.	1	1	0	Reid, Mr. T.	0	10	6
Black, Mr.	1	0	0	Stanners, Mr.	1	1	0
Campbell, Mr.	0	10	0	Stephenson, Mr.	0	10	6
Cowie, Mr	0	10	6	Stirling, Mr.	0	10	6
Crighton, Mr.	1	0	0	Wallace, Mr.	1	1	0
Gibson, Mr.	0	10	6	Young, Mr. Sen.	0	10	6
Grant, Mr.	1	1	0	Young, Mr. Jun.	1	1	0
Hall, Mr.	0	10	6	Young, Mr. G.	0	10	0
Harrison, Mr.	0	10	0	Young, Mr. W.	0	10	0
Hepburn, Mr.	0	10	6	Subscriptions under 10s. ℣ ann.	8	18	8
Johnson, Mr.	1	1	0				
M'Whinnie, Mr.	0	10	6		29	4	2
Mitchell, Mr	0	12	0				

FEMALE BRANCH.

Treasurer—Mrs. Stephenson.

Secretary—Mrs. Johnston.

Annual Subscribers.	£	s.	d.		£	s.	d.
				Gordon, Miss	0	12	0
Andrews, Miss	0	12	0	Harrison, Mrs.	0	10	6
Black, Mrs.	0	10	6	Johnston, Mrs.	0	10	6
Bray, Mrs.	0	10	0	Laing, Mrs.	0	10	0
Bickerton, Mrs.	0	10	0	Langton, Mrs.	0	10	6
Blair, Mrs.	1	0	0	Leeson, Mrs.	1	0	0
Barlace, Mrs.	0	10	0	M'Craw, Mrs.	1	0	0
Biddell, Mrs.	0	10	0	M'Diamed, Mrs.	0	10	6
Cowie, Mrs.	0	10	6	M'Whinnie, Mrs.	0	10	6
Campbell, Mrs.	1	1	0	Morrison, Mrs.	0	10	0
Dermer, Mrs.	1	1	0	Moore, Mrs.	0	10	6
Dermer, Miss	0	10	6	Nicholson, Mrs.	0	10	6
Davie, Mrs.	0	10	6	Rennie, Mrs.	1	0	0
French, Mrs.	1	0	0	Reid, Mrs.	0	10	6
Greig, Mrs.	0	10	6	Reid, Miss	0	10	6
Gibson, Mrs.	0	10	6	Reid, Miss E.	0	10	6

D

	£	s.	d.		£	s.	d.
Reid, Mrs. T.	0	10	6	Webster, Mrs.	0	12	0
Runder, Mrs.	0	10	0	Whisson, Miss	0	10	0
Stanners, Mrs.	0	10	6	Williams, Mrs.	0	10	6
Stanhope, Mrs.	0	10	0	Weatherstone, Mrs	0	10	6
Stephenson, Mrs.	0	10	6	Young, Mrs.	0	10	6
Stirling, Miss	0	10	6	Young, Mrs. J.	1	1	0
Wallace, Mrs.	0	10	6	Small contributions	13	2	0
Wallace, Miss.	0	10	6				
Wallis, Mrs.	0	10	0		42	4	6
Walker, Miss	0	10	6				
Walker, Miss S.	0	10	6				

JUVENILE BRANCH.

Treasurer—Mr. James Stephenson.

Secretary—Mr. Alexander Greig.

Annual Subscribers.

	£	s.	d.		£	s.	d.
Allan, Mr. T.	0	12	0	Reid, Mr. W. Jun.	0	10	6
Baddeley, Mr. C.	0	12	0	Reid, Mr. John	0	10	6
Berry, Mrs. E.	0	12	0	Spayne, Mrs.	0	10	0
Biddell, Mr. T. jun.	0	12	0	Stephenson, Mr. (D)	1	1	0
Carr, Mr. sen.	0	12	0	Stephenson, Mr. J. James	1	0	0
Chalmers, Misses C. and E.	0	12	0	Stephenson, Miss Maria	0	10	0
Chreighton, Miss	0	10	0	Stephenson, Miss Isabella	0	10	0
Clymer, Mr. M.	0	12	0	Walker, Mr. H.	0	12	0
Cooper, Mr. E	0	12	0	Young, Mr. sen.	0	10	0
Farquharson, Mr.	0	10	0	Young Ladies of Mrs. Greig's			
Frazer, Mr. R.	0	12	0	School, and Masters J. and			
Forbes, Miss E.	0	12	0	G. Greig	1	16	0
Friendly Society's School, Fe-				A Friend	1	0	0
male Children of the	1	0	0	Female Children in the Bible			
Gibson, Mr. J.	0	12	0	Class of the Crown Court			
Gibson, Mrs.	0	10	6	Sabbath School	0	8	3
Greig, Mr. A.	1	1	0	And 100 Subscribers under 10s.	3	2	9
Hall, Mr. James	0	10	6				
Hood, Mr T.	0	10	0		26	0	0
Instant, Mr. T.	0	12	0	Female Branch	42	4	6
Morrison, Mr. G.	0	10	0	Male Ditto	29	4	2
Norris, Miss E.	0	12	0				
Reid, Mr. Sen. (D.)	1	1	0		97	8	8

FOUNDERS' HALL—REV. W. STRUTT.

Annual Subscriptions.

	£	s.	d.		£	s.	d.
Barnes, Mrs.	1	6	0	Sundry Subscriptions, Dona-			
Baker, Mr. J.	1	0	0	tions, &c	59	0	1
Morshead, Miss	0	13	0	Sunday School Children	10	15	3
Morshead, Miss H. P.	0	13	0				
Todd, Mr. J.	1	0	0		74	7	4

FETTER LANE AUXILIARY SOCIETY—REV. G. BURDER.

	£	s.	d.
Male Branch, by Mr. J. Muston	35	8	3
Female ditto, by Mrs. Muston	26	6	0
	61	14	3

GATE STREET CHAPEL.

	£	s.	d.
Collection by Rev. G. Williams	20	0	0

HACKNEY DISTRICT AUXILIARY SOCIETY.

General Subscriptions by Mr. W. Pearson, *Treasurer.*

	£	s.	d.		£	s.	d.
Austin, Mr.	1	6	0	Boyd, Mrs.	1	8	0
Austin, Mrs.	0	10	0	Britten, Mr.	1	0	0
Bailey, Miss	0	12	0	Child, Mr. and Family	0	10	6

	£	s.	d.		£	s.	d.
Chambers, Miss	0	12	0	Loddiges, Mr.W.	1	1	0
Clapton Prayer Meeting, by				Mundull, Mr.	0	10	6
the Rev. Mr. Burder	2	1	0	Marillier, Mrs.	0	10	0
Crammond, Mrs.	0	10	0	Mitchel, Rev. Mr.	1	1	0
Fotheringham, Miss	1	5	0	Parker, Mr. and Family	0	10	0
Gaviller, Mr.	1	1	0	Pearson, Mr. and Family	2	16	4
Hale, Mr. and Family	0	12	0	Slark, Mr.	1	1	0
Hankey, Mr. Alers & Family	0	15	6	Terry, Miss	0	10	6
Harper, Mrs.	1	1	0	Wafford, Mr. and Son	0	10	3
Hayward, Mr.	0	10	0	Various sums under 10s.	13	12	4
Hawkins, Mr.	1	0	0				
Horner, Mrs.	1	1	0		37	17	11
Heudebourck, Mr.	1	0	0				

Well Street Chapel.

Contributions by Mr. J. Jackson, Treasurer.

	£	s.	d.		£	s.	d.
Coward, Mr.	1	1	0	Starkey, Mr. and Family	1	6	6
Collison, Rev. George	0	10	0	Shepherd, Mr	0	10	6
C——, Mr.	0	15	0	Todrig, Mrs. and Family	1	1	0
Edmeston, Mr. and Mrs.	0	10	0	Tarling, Mr.	0	12	0
Goodhart, Mr.	1	0	0	From the Girls now in the			
Guillonneau, Mrs. and Miss	0	13	10½	School of Industry, Bohe-			
Hughes, Mrs.	1	0	0	mia-place, from Lady Day			
Hankey, Mr. and Family	0	15	6	to Christmas, 1817.	2	2	6
King, Mr.	0	10	6	From those who have left the			
King, Captain	0	10	6	School, and are at Service	2	17	5¼
Lowe, Mrs.	1	1	0	Sundry Sums under 10s.	13	1	8
Muscutt, Miss and Family	0	12	0				
Pursord, Mr.	0	10	6		31	12	0
Payne, Mr.	0	10	6				

Gravel Pit Meeting—Rev. Dr. Smith's.

FEMALE ASSOCIATION.

	£	s.	d.		£	s.	d.
Aldersey, Mrs.	1	0	0	Morley, Mrs	0	12	0
Aldersey, Mrs A.	1	1	0	Meek, Mrs.	1	0	0
Adam, Mrs	0	10	0	Olding, Mrs.	0	10	0
Boyle, Mrs.	1	0	0	Parker, Mrs.	0	12	0
Copling, Mrs.	1	0	0	Rutt, Miss	0	10	0
Fearn, Mrs.	0	16	0	Rudd, Mrs.	0	16	0
Fotheringham, Miss, & young				Sims, Mrs	0	10	0
Ladies	5	0	0	Trotman, Mrs.	0	10	0
Hovell, Mrs.	0	10	0	Trotman, Miss	0	10	0
Hankey, Thomas	2	0	0	Wenham, Mrs	0	12	0
Hankey, Mrs. A.	0	10	0	Sundry Subscriptions under			
Hankey, Miss A.	0	10	0	10s. per annum	18	5	10
Hale, Mrs.	1	0	0				
Hale, Miss	0	10	0		40	4	10
Hale, Miss M.	0	10	0				

JUVENILE ASSOCIATION.

	£	s.	d.		£	s.	d.
Aldersey, Mr. R.	0	10	0	Rutt, Mr.	0	10	0
Aldersey, Mr. J.	0	10	0	Worsley, Mr.	0	10	0
Eagle House Academy	3	18	0	Sundries, under 10s.	5	12	4
Hale, Mr.	1	6	0				
Meek, Mr G.	0	10	0		13	16	4
Olding, Mr.	0	10	0				

GENERAL ASSOCIATION.

	£	s.	d.		£	s.	d.
Aldersey, Mr. J.	1	0	0	Duncan, Mr.	1	0	0
Aldersey, Mr. W.	1	6	0	Hale, Mr.	1	0	0
Aikin, Mr.	1	1	0	Grey, Mr.	0	10	0
Adam, Mr.	1	0	0	Meyers, Mr.	0	10	0
Conder, Mr.	0	10	0	Parker, Mr	0	12	0

	£	s.	d.
Rutt, Mr.	1	0	0
Shepheard, Mr.	0	10	0
Trotman, Mr.........................	0	10	0
Underhill, Mr.	0	10	0
Wenham, Mr........................	0	10	0

	£	s.	d.
Sundry Subscriptions under			
10s.	1	6	0
	11	15	0

St. Thomas's Square—Rev. H. F. Burder.

Annual Subscriptions.

Addisson, Mr......................	1	1	0
Austen, Mr. and Family	2	0	8
Austen, Miss	0	10	0
Burder, Mr.	1	1	0
Burder, Mrs.	1	1	0
Banger, Mr.	1	0	0
Banger, Mr. jun.	1	0	0
Banger, Mrs.	1	1	0
Bartlett, Mr.	1	1	0
Boult, Mr. James	1	1	0
Boult, Mrs.	1	1	0
Boult, Mr. Thomas	1	1	0
Boult, Mr. P. S..................	1	1	0
Boult, Miss L.	0	10	6
Boult, Miss M. A...............	0	10	6
Bowley, Mrs.	0	10	6
Butler, Misses	0	12	0
Cooper, Mrs.	1	0	0
Child, Mrs.	0	10	6
Childs, Misses	1	0	0
Clause, Miss	0	10	6
Dennis, Mr. and Family	1	11	6
Davis, Mr. J.	0	10	0
Davis, Mr. B.	0	10	0
Duncan, Mrs.	0	10	6
Eyre, Misses	1	4	0
Fox, Mr...........................	0	10	6
Fox, Mrs.	0	10	6
Fox, Mr. G.......................	0	10	6
Fisher, Mrs.......................	0	10	6
Gray, Mr.	1	1	0
Gray, Mrs.	0	10	6
Grout, Mrs........................	1	1	0
Hawkins, Mr.	0	10	6
Hawkins, Mrs.	0	10	6
Hardy, Mr. John	0	10	6
Hunt, Mr.	0	12	0
James, Mr. W.	0	10	6
Jupp, Misses	0	12	0
Kirkpatrick, Mr..................	1	1	0
Kirkpatrick, Mr. J. W..........	1	1	0
Kirkpatrick, Miss R.	0	10	6
Kirkpatrick, Miss J.	0	10	6
Keen, Misses	0	16	0
Lane, Mrs.	0	10	6

Lister, Mr. and Servants	1	12	0
Oakley, Mr.......................	0	10	6
Parker, Mrs.	0	10	0
Parker, Misses...................	1	1	0
Pretlove, Mrs....................	0	10	0
Reed, Mr.	1	1	0
Roberts, Mrs.	1	1	0
Ridge, Mr.	1	1	0
Ridge, Mrs.......................	0	10	6
Surgey, Mr.......................	1	1	0
Toms, Miss	0	10	6
Wafford, Mr.	1	10	6
Wafford, Mr. J.	1	1	0
Wafford, Miss F.	0	10	6
Wafford, Miss A.	0	10	6
Wafford, Miss C.	0	10	0
Wafford, Miss E.	0	10	6
Whitesmith, Misses	0	12	
Wells, Mr.	0	10	
Whitehead, Mrs.	0	10	
Two Servants....................	0	12	
Servants (Mr. Banger's)........	0	18	
A few young Men in the Adult School	1	2	
Sundries	5	4	1
	59	12	

Juvenile.

Ferguson's, Miss, School	4	5	
Swallwell's, Miss, School	3	0	
Sunday School Girls	0	5	
	7	10	11

Donations.

Lewin, Mr.	10	10	
Gray, Mr.	1	1	
A Friend..........................	1	0	
	12	1	

Annual Subscriptions	59	1	
Juvenile	7	10	
Donations	12	1	
	79	13	11

Walthamstow Branch.

Collected by Misses Calrow.

Donation from a Friend	2	0	0
Champion, Mr.	1	0	0
Penny a week subscriptions	12	0	0

Collected by Miss Turner, Leyton.

| Including £7 from the Family of D. Bevan, Esq. .... | 13 | 16 | 4 |

Collected by Miss Clarke, Wanstead.

Briscoe, Mr......................	0	10	
Crow, Mr.	1	1	
Clarke's, Mr. Family............	5	0	
Dubonlay, Mrs.	1	0	
Hewitt, Mrs.	0	15	
Knowles, Mr.	1	0	
Friend	0	10	

	£	s.	d.
Saunders's, Mr. Family	2	16	8
Stratton, Mr.	1	0	0
Wilks, Mr.	1	0	0
A Friend	1	1	0
A Friend	0	10	6
Small Donations, and One Penny per week Subscriptions	3	15	10

	£	s.	d.
Hall, Mr James	1	1	0
Plant, Mr.	2	2	0
	51	19	4

Exclusive of £10, a Donation from Mrs. R. Smith to the Parent Society, by Rev. G. Collison.

Amount by Mr. Pearson	57	17	11
Ditto Well-street Chapel	31	12	0
Ditto Gravel Pit Meeting	50	4	0
Ditto St. Thomas's-square	79	13	11
Ditto Walthamstow	51	19	4

Hackney District......251 7 2

HOLYWELL MOUNT CHAPEL—REV. W. F. PLATT.

Felton, Mr.	1	0	0
Martin, Mr.	0	10	0
Northover, Mr. Sen	2	12	0
Northover, Mr. Jun.	1	6	0
Northover, Mr. J.	0	13	0
Wilkinson, Mrs. Rachel	0	13	0
Wilkinson, Mr. Frederick	0	13	0
Wilkinson, Mr. John	0	13	0

And 90 Subscribers of a Penny per Week, and upwards	16	17	2
Sunday School Children	9	0	0
Poor Children Ditto, Bethnal Green	1	13	0
	35	10	2

HOPE STREET, SPITALFIELDS, AUXILIARY ASSOCIATION.

Subscriptions by Mr. J. Swaine 2 14 6

HORSELYDOWN MEETING—REV. J. BODINGTON.

FEMALE AUXILIARY SOCIETY.

Treasurer—Mrs. Tunno.

Secretaries—Mrs. Warner—Miss Hinton.

Champion, Miss	0	12	0
Clough, Mrs collected by her	1	1	8
Cooper, Mrs.	0	12	0
Fauntleroy, Mrs.	0	12	0
Fauntleroy, Miss	0	10	0
Fauntleroy, Miss S.	0	10	0
Fields, Miss	0	10	0
Gates, Mrs	0	12	0
Hinton, Mrs.	0	10	0
Hinton, Miss S.	0	10	0
Ditto, collected by her	2	2	0
Keen, Mrs.	0	10	0
Mace, Mrs	0	12	0
Mesnard, Mrs.	0	12	0
Natt, Miss	0	12	0

Penney, Miss, collected by her	2	14	3
Scarnell, Mrs.	0	10	0
Strick, Miss, collected by her	1	10	8
Thistlewood, Mrs	0	12	0
Tunno, Mrs	0	10	0
Warner, Mrs.	0	12	0
Webb, Mrs	0	10	0
Wilson, Miss	0	12	0
Wilkinson, Miss, collected by	1	10	4
Yates, Mrs	0	12	0
And about 100 Subscribers under 10s. per annum	15	19	1
	36	0	0

JUVENILE AUXILIARY SOCIETY.

Treasurer—Mr. D. Scott.

Secretaries—Messrs. Wilkinson, Kevan, & P. Kevan

Bates, Mr.	0	12	0
Bodington, Rev. J	1	1	0
Bodington, Miss	0	12	0
Brown, Mr G.	0	12	0
Brown, Mr G collected by him			
Champion, Miss, young Ladies of her School	1	10	0
Cowie, Master E. R	0	10	0

Cowie, Master J.	0	10	0
Cowie, Master F.	0	10	0
Cowie, Master B	0	10	0
Fauntleroy, Mr. T.	1	0	0
Fauntleroy, Mr. R.	0	10	0
Hinton, Mrs. young Ladies of her School	1	9	2
Jesse, Mr. collected by him	2	12	10

	£	s.	d.		£	s.	d.
Kevan, Messrs. N. & P.	0	16	0	Wiggins, Mrs. young Ladies			
Kevan, Mrs. young Ladies of				of her School	1	12	0
her School ....,........	4	15	0	Wilkinson, Mr.	0	12	0
Keen, Misses	0	18	0	Wilson, Mr. collected by him	0	6	0
Newsome, Mr.	0	10	0	And about 250 Subscribers un_			
Peacock, Mr.	0	12	0	der 10s. per annum, mostly			
Pickford, Mr.	0	12	0	of a halfpenny per week ...	33	14	9
Prichit, Miss S. collected by							
her	1	13	3		60	0	0
Sargent, Mr.	0	10	0	Female Auxiliary.........	36	0	0
Scott, Mr.	0	10	0				
Shipton, Mr.	1	0	0		96	0	0

Hoxton Female Auxiliary Society.

Treasurer—Miss Wilson.

	£	s.	d.		£	s.	d.
Anderson, Mrs.	0	12	0	Lack, Miss	0	10	6
Anderson, Miss	0	10	6	Lawrence, Mrs.	0	12	0
Age, Mrs.	0	12	0	May, Mrs.	0	10	6
Anstee, Miss A.	0	10	6	Mason, Miss......................	0	12	0
Arnold, Mrs.	0	10	6	Minns, Mrs...........................	0	12	0
Austin, Mrs.	0	12	0	Mills, Miss	0	12	0
Bibbins, Miss	0	12	0	Maltby, Mrs.	1	1	0
Bunn, Miss	0	12	0	Mason, Miss	0	12	0
Blackall, Mrs.	0	12	0	Needham, Mrs	0	10	6
Brook, Miss...................	0	10	6	Nobbs, Mrs...........................	0	12	0
Brook, Miss H.	0	10	6	Norman, Mrs.......................	0	10	6
Bumstead, Mrs.	1	1	0	Ord, Mrs.		12	0
Blackburn, Mrs.	0	10	6	Pope, Mrs.	0	12	0
Crawford, Miss	0	10	6	Pope, Miss	0	10	6
Crawford, Miss M. A.	0	10	6	Pope, Miss M.......................	0	12	0
Charlton, Miss......................	0	12	0	Pope, Miss H	0	12	0
Cope, Mrs.	0	12	0	Parvin, Mrs	0	12	0
Cunliffe, Mrs.	0	12	0	Parkinson, Miss	0	10	6
Conquest, Miss R.	0	12	0	Pearson, Mrs...........................	0	10	6
Catherwood, Miss	0	10	6	Palmer, Mrs.'	0	10	6
Drane, Mrs........	0	10	6	Richards, Mrs.	0	12	0
Davison, Mrs.	1	0	0	Richards, Mrs. T.	0	12	0
Davy, Mrs.	0	12	0	Robinson, Mrs.	1	0	0
Fisher, Miss...........................	0	12	0	Smith, Miss...........................	0	12	0
Fleureau, Miss	1	1	0	Shrubsole, Miss	0	10	6
Fry, Mrs...............................	0	10	6	Stoner, Mrs	0	10	6
Gleauriau, Miss M................	1	1	0	Spencer, Miss	1	1	0
Gale, Mrs.	0	16	0	Taylor, Mrs.	1	10	0
Gough, Mrs.	1	1	0	Taylor, Mrs. S.	0	12	0
Goddard, Miss....................	0	12	0	Tasker, Miss	0	2	0
Harlow, Miss A....................	0	10	6	Taylor, Mrs. S.	0	1	0
Hall, Mrs.	0	10	0	Tredwell, Mrs.	0	10	0
Hughes, Mrs.	0	12	0	Varco, Miss	0	1	6
Hulme, Miss E.	0	12	0	Wilson, Mrs.	1	0	0
Hardy, Mrs.	0	10	6	Wilson, Miss	1	0	0
Haslewood, Mrs	0	10	6	Wilson, Miss E	0	10	6
Hornby, Miss	0	12	0	Winkworth, Mrs.	0	12	0
Herne, Miss...........................	0	12	0	Winkworth, Miss	0	12	0
Herne, Miss S.	0	12	0	Ward, Mrs...........................	0	10	6
Hadfield, Mrs.......................	1	1	0	Ward, Miss	0	10	6
Jeula, Mrs.	0	12	0	Wait, Mrs.	0	10	6
Jackson, Mrs.	0	10	6	Ward, Mrs...............................	0	12	0
Jackson, Mrs.W.	0	12	0	Walmsley, Mrs.	1	0	0
Jordan, Miss	1	1	0	Sundry small Subscriptions...	76	2	0
Lericheux, Miss	0	10	6				
Larrodere, Mrs.	0	10	6		133	15	0
Lidden, Mrs...........................	0	10	6				

JEWIN STREET ASSOCIATION.

Subscriptions by Rev. Mr. Wood...14 14 8

KINGSLAND AUXILIARY SOCIETY.

President—Rev. John Campbell.

MALE BRANCH.

Secretary—Mr. John Parkinson.

Annual Subscriptions.	£	s.	d.
Barrett, Mr.	1	1	0
Casterton, Mr.	1	1	0
Coles, Mr.	1	1	0
Humphrys, Mr.	1	1	0
Langton, Mr.	1	1	0
Langton, Mr. Joseph	0	10	6
Nattrass, Mr.	1	1	0
Parkinson, Mr.	0	10	6
Parkinson, Mr. John	1	1	0
Rutt, Mr.	1	1	0
Rutt, Mr. William	1	1	0

Collections of One Penny per Week and upwards, by the following Persons:—

	£	s.	d.
Field, Mr. C.	1	5	3
Herbert, Mr.	2	0	4
Hutchins, Mr. Samuel	0	19	5

	£	s.	d.
Jarvis, Mr. jun.	1	7	10
Langton, Mr. Joseph	1	12	7
Marshall, Mr.	0	2	11
Matthews, Mr.	2	6	2
Parks, Mr. S.	0	15	6
Rutt, Mr. Joseph	1	16	1
Theobald, Mr.	0	14	9
Stagg, Mr.	0	9	1
Walley, Mr.	1	19	4
Wood, Mr.	3	11	2
Messrs. Rutt's Men	3	3	5

Donations.

	£	s.	d.
Duby Mr. Casterton	18	0	0
Sundries	5	16	9
A Friend, by Mr. Langton	1	0	0
Sundries	1	5	0
	58	15	7

FEMALE BRANCH.

Treasurer—Miss Rutt.

Secretary—Miss Langton.

Annual Subscriptions.	£	s.	d.
Bumstead, Miss	0	10	6
Casterton, Mrs.	0	10	6
Dowler, Mrs.	0	10	6
Emslie, Miss	0	12	0
Jeffrey, Miss	0	10	0
Langton, Miss	0	12	0
Massey, Miss	0	12	0
Nattrass, Mrs.	0	10	6
Parkinson, Mrs. J.	0	10	6
Rutt, Miss	0	10	0
Rutt, Miss S.	0	10	0
Willats, Mrs.	0	10	6

Sundry small Subscriptions under 10s. collected by

	£	s.	d.
Bonner, Miss	4	2	11
Bower, Miss	7	2	0
Casterton, Miss	0	5	5
Everett, M. A.	0	8	0
Gosling, Miss A.	1	2	7
Hovenden, Miss	1	18	3
Jeffrey, Miss	2	3	0
Parks, Miss.	0	18	10
Parks, Miss S.	3	8	3
Rutt, Miss S.	3	9	5
Tyler, A.	0	16	10
	43	17	6

Donations.

	£	s.	d.
Bagnall, Mr. and Mrs.	10	0	0
Hobson, Mrs	1	0	0
Langton, Miss, a Friend by	0	13	0

Total at Kingsland......102 13 1

LOCK'S FIELDS, WALWORTH.

Collection by Rev. G. Clayton 20 0 0

MULBERRY GARDENS' CHAPEL—REV. R. STODHART.

Sunday School and Friends 19 11 11
A few Friends, by Mr. H. Batger 7 1 6
Mrs. Batger 1 1 0

27 14 5

NORTH LONDON AND ISLINGTON AUXILIARY SOCIETY.

Treasurer—Mr. Trueman.

Secretaries—Rev. J. Yockney—Mr. Lemon.

UNION CHAPEL AUXILIARY.

	£	s.	d.
A. H. by Mrs. Blasson	0	10	6
Adams, Miss	1	0	0
Allnutt, Mrs.	0	10	6
Ashton, Mrs.	0	10	6
A Well-wisher to the Cause of Christ	1	1	0
Bartlett, Miss	0	10	6
Bamford, Mrs. and the young Ladies of her School	1	11	6
Bevan, Mr.	0	10	6
Billing, Mr.	1	1	0
Bleachley, Miss	0	10	6
Blackett, Mrs	1	1	0
Blackett, Mr. John, Jun.	1	1	0
Bolton, Mr.	1	1	0
Bradshaw, Mrs	0	10	6
Browne, Mr.	1	1	0
Browning, Miss	1	1	0
Bradley, Mr.	1	10	6
Burgess, Miss	0	10	0
Campion, Miss	1	1	0
Campion, Mr. John	1	1	0
Campion, Mr. James	0	10	6
Catechumens, a few at Union Chapel, their mites	3	11	0
Child, Mrs.	1	6	0
Chadwick, Mr	0	10	6
Chapman, Mr.	1	1	0
Cork, Master G. collected by	2	14	7
Cordell, Mr.	1	1	0
Collingridge, Mrs collected by her	7	3	1
Cooper, Mr.	1	1	0
Cooper, Miss	0	10	6
Cowland, Miss Henrietta, collected by her	4	16	0
Duthoit, Mr.	1	1	0
Eddis, Mr.	1	0	0
Eddis, Miss	1	1	0
Field, Mr.	1	1	0
Fearne, Mr.	1	1	0
Friend, a, by Mr. Lewis	5	0	0
Friends, a few, by Mr. Lewis	4	4	0
Friend, a, inclosed in a letter to Mr. Lewis	0	10	0
Friend, a	0	10	0
Fryer, Mr.	1	1	0
Gouldsmith, Mr	1	1	0
Gordon, Mrs.	1	1	0
Grace, Mr.	1	1	0
Grace, Mrs	1	1	0
Halson, Mr.	1	1	0
Habgood, Mr.	1	1	0
Hebert, Mr.	1	1	0
I. N. Mr. in aid of Missions	1	0	0
Keymer, Mr	0	10	6
Keymer, Miss, collected by her	3	11	6

	£	s.	d.
Kent, Mrs.	0	10	6
King, Mrs. Highbury	0	10	6
Kirkman, Miss, collected by	2	14	0
Langham, Miss	0	10	6
Lewis, Rev. Thomas	1	1	0
From the young Gentlemen belonging to Mr. Lemon's Academy, *viz.*			
Sundries	1	19	9½

Collected by

	£	s.	d.
Thompson, Master W.	0	8	1½
Moss, Master J.	0	9	10
Taylor, Master S.	2	0	4½
Clarke, Master	0	12	2½
Spalding, Master	0	15	5
Wilkinson, Master	0	16	7½
Gabay, Master	0	2	7½
King, Master	1	9	0
Slater, Master	0	6	0
	9	0	0

	£	s.	d.
Mackenzie, Mrs	0	10	6
Marsom, Mrs.	0	10	6
Mills, Mrs.	1	0	0
Painter, Mr.	0	10	6
Payne, Mrs.	0	10	6
Parkhurst, Elizabeth	0	10	6
Plumbly, Miss	0	10	6
Poole, Mr.	2	2	0
Purdy, Mrs	0	10	0
Phillips, Miss, collected by her	2	18	0
Priestley, Misses, & the young Ladies belonging to their School	3	3	0
Radford, Mrs.	0	10	6
Sargent, Mr.	1	1	0
Schilling, Mr. and the young Gentlemen belonging to his School	1	4	0
School of Industry, Union Chapel, the Girls belonging to it	3	0	0
Ditto, the Boys	5	0	0
Smith, Miss, collected by her	2	5	3
Smyth, Mrs, by Mr. Lewis	6	6	0
Smithyman, Mr.	1	1	0
Springall, Mr.	1	1	0
Springall, Miss, collected by her	2	0	0
Steell, Mr. Robert George	0	10	6
Steell, Mrs.	0	10	6
Steell, Miss E. collected by	2	2	2
Steell, Mrs. Canonbury	0	10	6
Starey, Mr.	1	1	0
Street, Misses, and the young Ladies belonging to their School	2	1	9

	£	s.	d.
Streetin, Mr.	1	1	0
Streetin, Mr. collected by him	2	17	6
Streetin, Miss M. A.	0	10	6
Sundry small Subscriptions under 10s.	4	3	0
Teulons, Miss	1	1	0
Trueman, Mr.	10	10	0
Trueman, Master J.	0	10	6
Trueman, Miss	0	10	6
Thorne, Mr.	2	2	0
Villette, Mrs. and the young Ladies belonging to her Sch	2	15	6

	£	s.	d.
Waters, Mr.	0	10	6
Wilkinson, Miss, collected by her	3	10	2
Wilkins, Mrs. and Daughters	0	18	0
Wood, Mr.	3	1	0
Wright, Mr.	1	1	0
Wyatt, Mrs	1	1	0
Wyatt, Mr. R. B.	1	1	0
Yallop, Mr.	1	1	0
	166	10	6

LOWER STREET AUXILIARY SOCIETY—By Rev. J. Yockney.

	£	s.	d.
Bradshaw, Miss	0	10	0
Braithwait, Mrs.	1	1	0
Field, Miss	1	1	0
Freebairn, Miss, collected by her	2	1	6
Frost, Hannah	0	8	0
Garland, Mrs.	1	0	0
Glanville, Mr.	1	1	0
Gozzards, Misses	0	10	0
Hearn, Mr.	1	0	0
Highley, Mr.	1	0	0
Howells, Misses	1	1	0
Jennings, Misses	0	10	6
Lewin, Mr.	1	0	0

	£	s.	d.
Lister, Mrs.	0	10	6
Milward, Mrs.	0	10	0
Nock, Miss, collected by her	0	16	6
Thornthwait, Mr.	0	10	0
Wilkinson, Miss	1	0	0
Williamson, Mrs.	1	0	0
Worsley, Mrs.	1	0	0
Worsley, Mrs	1	0	0
Worsley, Miss	1	0	0
Yockney, Rev. J	1	1	0
	20	12	0

TONBRIDGE CHAPEL ASSOCIATION.
Subscriptions and Donations, by Rev. B. Rayson ... 114 19 10

HOLLOWAY ASSOCIATION.
Subscriptions and Donations, by Rev. R. Bowden 20 0 0

HIGHGATE CHAPEL ASSOCIATION.
Subscriptions and Donations, by Rev. M. Thomas 12 0 0

ISLINGTON CHAPEL.
Collection at the Formation of the Society 55 11 6

389 13 10

NEW ROAD, ST. GEORGE'S IN THE EAST—REV. ANDREW REED.
JUVENILE FEMALE MISSIONARY SOCIETY.

Subscriptions.

	£	s.	d.
Adams, Mr.	0	10	6
Brooks, Mr.	1	1	0
Brooks, Mrs.	0	10	6
Brooks, Miss	0	10	6
Bromley, Mr.	1	1	0
Bridgman, Mrs.	1	1	0
Ellis, Mr.	1	1	0
French, Mr.	1	1	0
Hannaman, Mr.	0	12	0
Hawkins, Mr.	0	12	0
Hubbock, Mr.	1	1	0
Hubbock, Mrs.	1	1	0
Kilday, Mr.	1	1	0
Parker, Mrs.	1	1	0
Pouncy, Mr.	1	1	0
Reed, Rev. A.	1	1	0

	£	s.	d.
Ring, Mr.	1	1	0
Turner, Mr.	1	1	0
Wright, Mr.	0	12	0
West, Mr.	1	0	0

By Card.

	£	s.	d.
Absolom, Miss	3	18	0
Bourne, Mrs.	1	8	0
Barker, Master	1	14	8
Curtis, Miss	4	13	4
Duncan, Mrs.	4	8	0
Draper, Miss	1	3	1
Edwards, Miss	3	18	5
Humphreys, Miss	2	13	0
Hughes, Miss	4	13	8
Hilder, Miss	1	2	8
Jager, Miss	4	9	6
Moseley, Miss M.	2	3	0

E

	£	s.	d.		£.	s.	d.
Maxwell, Miss	0	16	6	Tickell, Miss	10	15	8
Newell, Miss	3	12	2				
Reed, Miss	10	6	0		81	18	2
Scarr, Master	1	2	6				

ORANGE STREET CHAPEL.

(Branch of the West London Auxiliary Missionary Society.)

Treasurer—Mr. W. Byfield.
Secretary—Mr. G. Brookes.

Subscriptions.

	£	s.	d.		£	s.	d.
Adeney, Mr.	1	1	0	Monk, Mr.	0	10	6
Arundale, Mrs.	0	12	0	Miller, Mr.	0	10	6
Byfield, Mr.	1	0	0	Naylor, Mr.	1	1	0
Buck, Mr.	0	10	6	Nicholls, Mr.	0	10	6
Brookes, Mr.	0	12	0	Odell, Mr.	1	1	0
Burrowes, Mr.	1	1	0	Powell, Mr Richard	1	1	0
Bishop, Mr.	1	0	0	Parker, Mr.	1	1	0
Blazdell, Mr.	1	1	0	Palmer, Mr.	0	12	0
Beazley, Mr.	1	0	0	Price, Mrs.	0	12	0
Bryceson, Mr.	1	1	0	Price, Mr. T.	0	12	0
Bray, Mr.	0	10	6	Robinson, Mr.	1	1	0
Chamberlain, Mr.	0	12	0	Reid, Mrs.	0	10	0
Callard, Miss	0	10	0	Simson, Mr.	1	1	0
Creed, Mrs.	0	10	0	Strongitharm, Mr.	1	1	0
Crozier, Mr.	1	1	0	Smith, Mr. C.	1	1	0
Colwell, Mrs.	0	12	0	Say, Mr.	1	1	0
Chappell, Mr. J.	0	12	0	Sellman, Mr.	1	1	0
Davidson, Mr.	1	1	0	Strachan, Mr.	1	1	0
Freeman, Mrs.	0	12	0	Shackelton, Mr.	1	1	0
Goodchild, Mrs.	0	10	6	Shackelton, Mr. C.	1	1	0
Guy, Mr.	1	0	0	Smith, Mr.	0	10	6
Gill, Mrs.	1	1	0	Symons, Mr.	0	10	0
Goodwin, Mrs.	1	1	0	Sawyer, Mr. Henry	0	10	0
Green, Miss S.	1	0	0	Swaine, Mr. jun	0	10	0
Green, Miss.	1	0	0	Tookey, Mr.	1	1	0
Graham, Mr.	0	10	6	Tiercelin, Mr.	0	12	0
Hirst, Mrs	0	10	6	Thompson, Mr.	1	1	0
Hirst, Miss	0	10	6	Taylor, Mrs. M.	0	10	0
Hough, Mr.	1	0	0	Thomas, Mr.	0	12	0
Hinson, Mr.	0	12	0	Whitham, Miss	0	10	6
Jones, Mr. John	1	1	0	Whitham, Miss A.	0	10	6
Jenkins, Mr. H.	0	10	0	Walker, Mr	1	1	0
Jones, Mr. R.	0	12	0	Walker, Mrs.	1	1	0
Jones, Mr. T.	0	12	0	Walker, Mrs S.	1	1	0
Klyne, Mr.	1	1	0	Wall, Mr	1	0	0
Kemp, Miss.	1	1	0	Wolfe, Mr.	0	10	6
Lanman Mrs	1	1	0	Sundry small sums	6	6	3
Lawrence, Mrs.	0	10	0				
Maberly, Mr.	1	1	0		66	11	9

PELL STREET MEETING—REV. T. CLOUTT.

Collectors—J. Printup—R. Anderson.

	£	s.	d.		£	s.	d.
Anderson, Mr. Robert	0	12	0	son, Thomson, M. A. Phillips, and M. M'Donald, up to June 30, 1817	0	10	0
Cloutt, Rev. Mr. Thomas	1	1	0				
Copeland, Miss	0	8	0				
Drysdale, Mrs.	0	12	0	Phillips, Miss, Card to Sept. 1817	0	10	0
Gillespy, Mr. Thomas	0	12	0				
Knox, Mr.	0	12	0	Ditto, ditto, to Dec. 1817	0	10	0
Printup, Mr.	0	12	0	Ditto, ditto, to March, 1818	0	9	6
Phillips, Mrs.	0	12	0				
Phillips, Miss M. A. collected by Card from Misses Mallin-					7	0	6

QUEEN STREET CHAPEL, RATCLIFF—REV. J. VAUTIN.

Collection 2 9 8

YOUNG LADIES' SOCIETY.

	£	s.	d.		£	s.	d.
Bond, Miss C.	1	0	0	Vautin, Miss E.	1	19	6
Hooper, Miss H.	1	2	6	Vautin, Miss M.	1	3	0
Muller, Miss E.	2	19	0	Walker, Miss H.	2	5	6
Neale, Miss M.	1	4	0				
Rutledge, Miss J.	0	12	0		12	9	6
Trappitt, Miss A.	0	4	0				

ROSE LANE, RATCLIFF—REV. T. WILLIAMS.

	£	s.	d.		£	s.	d.
Braine, Mr.	1	1	0	Wharton, Mr.	1	1	0
Hebditch, Mr.	1	1	0	Whitehead, Mr.	0	10	0
Hunt, Mrs.	0	10	0	Whitehead, Mr J. & Friends	2	12	0
Patrick Mr	1	1	0	Wohlgemeth, Mr. C.	0	12	0
Poyton, Mr. and Friends	5	17	7	Rose-lane Sunday School, 8s.;			
Robinson, Mr	1	1	0	Mr. Brown, 8s.; Miss Talbot, 5s. 10d.	1	1	10
Stevens, Mr. 10s. 6d. Children, 5s.	0	15	6		20	6	11
Tyndale, Mr.	2	2	0				
Williams, Rev. Thomas	1	1	0				

SHADWELL.

Rev. C. Hyatt and Congregation 20 0 0

SHEPHERD'S MARKET—REV. S. HACKETT.

Subscriptions 18 2 11
Sunday School Children 2 1 5

                                 20 4 4

SHOE LANE AUXILIARY SOCIETY.

Subscriptions 15 1 9

SILVER STREET AND ISLINGTON CHAPELS—REV. E. J. JONES.

	£	s.	d.		£	s.	d.
Teachers and Scholars of Silver Street Sunday School	31	14	9	B. Mr.	0	4	0
Ditto Ditto of Farringdon Ditto	3	5	0	Donations	0	10	10
Penny a Week Subscriptions of a few Teachers of Silver St. Boys' School	5	3	10	Teachers and Scholars of Islington Chapel Sun. Sch.	20	15	6
Silver Street Chapel Penny Society	25	9	2	Islington Chapel Penny Soc.	15	16	4
Ditto Praying Society	3	13	4	A few Boys at Mr. Innes's Academy	2	7	0
Collected by Honoria	10	0	0	A few Girls at Mrs Innes's Sch	1	10	0
					120	9	9

SOUTHWARK AUXILIARY SOCIETY.

Balance, by Mr. S Robinson 31 1 3

STEPNEY AUXILIARY MISSIONARY SOCIETY.

MALE BRANCH.
Treasurer—Mr. Monds.

Subscriptions.	£	s.	d.		£	s.	d.
Clayton, Mrs. J.	0	10	6	Edmeston, Mr.	0	16	3
Chowne, Mrs.	0	10	0	Edmeston, Mr. J.	0	10	0
Davis, Mrs.	0	12	0	Ford, Mrs.	0	10	0
Dousberry, Mrs.	1	12	0	Geikie, Mr.	1	1	0
				Hardy, Mr.	0	10	0

	£	s.	d.		£	s.	d.
Hardy, Mrs.	0	10	0	Smith, Miss	0	10	0
Hardy, Miss	0	10	0	Thompson, Miss	1	1	0
Hardy, Mr. J.	0	10	0	Tuckwell, Miss	0	10	0
Hood, Miss	0	12	0	Trenchard, Mrs.	0	10	0
Hankey, Mrs. Alers	0	10	0	Williams, Mrs.	0	12	0
Hankey, Miss Alers	0	10	0	Young, Mrs.	0	10	0
Lawson, Miss	1	1	0	Young Ladies at Miss Olding's			
Marten, Mrs.	0	10	0	School	1	0	0
Manby, Mrs.	0	12	0	Young Ladies at Mrs. Webb's			
Mudge, Miss	0	10	0	School	1	19	6
Nutter, Mrs.	0	10	0	Small subscriptions under 10s.			
Nutter, Mr. Oct.	0	10	0	per annum	38	11	8
Payne, Mr. W.	0	10	0				
Peacock, Mr.	1	1	0		56	14	8
Renshaw, Mrs.	0	12	0				
Sime, Captain	1	1	0				

FEMALE BRANCH.
Treasurer—Miss Hankey.

	£	s.	d.		£	s.	d.
Brown, Mr. James	1	0	0	Robinson, Mr. T. jun.	1	1	0
Ford, Rev. George	1	0	0	Subscrip. under 10s. per an	16	4	4
Heudebourck, Mr.	0	10	0				
Howard, Misses	1	4	0		23	10	10
Masters, Mr.	0	10	6				
Orchard, Mr. J.	1	0	0		80	5	6
Robinson, Mr. T. sen.	1	1	0				

STOCKWELL ASSOCIATION.

Subscriptions and Donations, by Mr. T. Hayter, *Treasurer* 100 0 0

SURREY CHAPEL.

FEMALE ASSOCIATION.
Treasurer—Mrs. B. Neale.

Subscriptions.	£	s.	d.		£	s.	d.
Arnold, Mrs.	0	10	6	Perkins, Mrs.	0	10	6
Barnard, Mrs.	1	1	0	Platt, Mrs.	1	1	0
Bates, Mrs.	0	10	6	Potter, Mrs.	0	10	6
Brown, Mrs.	0	10	6	Southgate, Mrs.	0	10	6
Browne, Miss	0	10	6	Smith, Mrs.	0	10	6
Challenor, Mrs.	0	11	0	Smith, Mrs.	0	10	6
Ching, Mrs	0	10	6	Stevens, Mrs.	0	12	0
Clark, Mrs.	1	1	0	Thurlborn, Mrs.	1	1	0
Darby, Mrs.	0	10	6	Tomlinson, Miss	0	10	6
Darby, Miss	0	10	6	Tomlinson, Miss M.	0	10	6
Davies, Mrs. a Friend	1	0	0	Turner, Mrs.	0	12	0
Forsters, Misses	1	1	0	Turner, Mrs.	0	10	0
Fuce, Mrs.	0	10	6	Walton, Mrs.	0	10	6
Fuce, Miss	0	10	6	Webber, Mrs.	1	1	0
G. T. by Mrs. Davies	0	1	6				
Green, Mrs.	1	1	0	*Collected by*			
Hill, Mrs.	1	1	0	Ackrey, Mrs.	3	14	0
Howell, Miss	0	12	0	Allman, Mrs.	3	14	0
Kenyon, Mrs.	1	1	0	Burford, Miss	6	0	4
Law, Miss	1	1	0	Carter, Miss	3	12	3
Long, Mrs.	1	1	0	Cooper, Miss	4	0	4
Ditto, a Friend	0	10	6	Davies, Mrs.	11	3	5
Main, Mrs.	0	10	6	Davis, Miss	6	8	7
Neale, Mrs.	1	1	0	Eaton, Mrs.	6	7	4
Neale, Mrs B.	1	1	0	Hadland, Miss	2	15	5
Nottage, Mrs.	0	10	6	Jones, Mrs.	11	1	7
Nottage, Miss	0	10	6	Lucey, Miss	2	14	8
Page, Mrs.	0	1	6	Peterson, Miss	4	17	4
				Taylor, Miss	6	9	4

	£	s.	d.
Thatcher, Mrs.	4	15	5
Williams, Miss	11	9	4
Ditto, by a Missionary Castle	1	7	6
Williams, Miss H.	0	18	5

	£	s.	d.
By six young Ladies of Miss Cooper's School	15	9	5
	136	10	2

JUVENILE SOCIETY.

Treasurer—Mr. F. Smith.

Secretaries—Mr. Beams—Mr. Upjohn.

Name	£	s.	d.	Name	£	s.	d.
Armstrong, Mr.	0	10	6	Munday, Mr.	1	0	0
Beams, Mr.	0	18	0	Mackie, Mr	0	10	6
Bates, Mr.	1	1	0	Matthews, Mr.	0	12	0
Carter, Mr D.	0	10	0	Newsome, Mr	1	1	0
Careless, Mr.	0	10	6	Nottage, Mr.	1	1	0
Churchill, Mr. W.	0	10	6	Parr, Mr.	0	12	0
Dix, Mr. T.	0	10	0	Russell, Mr.	0	10	0
Dix, Mr. R.	0	10	0	Southgate, Mr.	1	0	0
Davis, Mr.	0	10	6	Stone, Mr.	0	10	0
Davis, Mr. A. H.	0	10	6	Vials, Mr.	0	10	0
Dawson, Mr. Roger	1	1	0	Upjohn, Mr.	0	10	0
Hadland, Mr.	0	10	6	Wass, Mr.	0	10	0
Hill, Mr.	0	12	0	Williams, Mr.	0	10	0
Holwell, Mr.	0	10	6	Subscriptions under 10s. ℣ an	29	5	0
Jones, Mr.	0	10	6				
Kenyon, Mr.	1	1	0		50	0	0
Lines, Mr.	1	11	6				

TABERNACLE AUXILIARY SOCIETY.

Treasurer—Rev. Matthew Wilks

Secretary—Mr. G. Pearce.

Subscribers.

Name	£	s.	d.	Name	£	s.	d.
Ashley, Mr. H.	1	1	0	Baker, Mr.	0	12	0
Armsby, Mr. and Mrs.	1	1	0	Broyden, Mr.	0	12	0
Arnold, Mr. B.	1	1	0	Brass, Mr.	0	10	6
Adams, Miss, and Family	1	1	0	Bick, Mr.	0	10	0
Ashby, Mr. E.	1	1	0	Bolter, Mr.	0	12	0
Ambler, Mr.	0	10	0	Boggis, Mrs	0	10	6
Allen, Mr.	0	10	0	Blayney, Mr.	0	12	0
Arnold, Mr. E.	0	10	6	Badcock, Mr.	0	10	0
Austin, Mr.	0	10	0	Bibbens, Mrs.	0	10	6
Atkins, Mr.	0	10	0	Bolton, Mrs.	0	10	0
Astor, Mrs.	0	10	6	Bright, Mrs.	0	10	0
Austen, Mrs.	0	10	6	Clark, Mr. C. and Family	3	0	0
Allen, Mr.	0	10	0	Coast, Mrs. and Miss	1	4	0
Bobbitt, Mr. and Mrs.	2	3	9	Clark, Mr. G. and Family	2	0	0
Browning, Mr.	1	1	0	Claybrook, Mrs.	0	10	0
Bartholomew, Mr.	1	1	0	Chawner, Miss	0	12	0
Bateman, Mr. W.	1	1	0	Child, Mr.	0	10	0
Body, Mr.	1	1	0	Crange, Miss	0	10	0
Burles, Mr. and Mrs.	1	11	6	Congdon, Mr.	0	10	6
Box, Miss	1	12	0	Creig, Mr.	0	12	0
Baxter, Mrs.	1	0	0	Cross, Miss	0	10	0
Bashfoot, Miss	1	0	0	Chinn, Mr.	0	13	0
Bowles, Mrs.	0	10	6	Chaplin, Miss	0	10	0
Brown, Mr. E.	0	10	6	Colwell, Mr.	0	10	0
Bolton, Mr. and Family	0	13	8	Clements, Mr. and Mrs.	0	12	0
Brown, Mr.	0	10	0	Dickens, Mr.	1	4	0
Burn, Mr. Sen.	0	10	0	Dale, Mr. Jun.	1	1	0
Brown, Mr.	0	12	0	Duncombe, Mr. and Mrs.	1	1	0
Brand, Mr.	0	10	0	Dale, Mr.	0	12	0
Barrett, Mr. and Family	0	17	4	Devo, Miss	0	12	0
Brittain, Mrs.	0	12	0	Doherty, Mrs.	0	12	0
				Deedy, Miss, and Family	0	18	0

	£	s.	d.
Dainty, Mr.	0	10	0
Davis, Mr.	0	10	0
Dee, Mr. and Mrs.	0	12	0
Edmonds, Mr.	1	0	0
Ewen, Mr.	0	10	6
Eldridge, Mr.	0	12	0
Evans, Mr.	0	10	0
Eaton, Mr.	0	12	0
Edis, Mr.	0	10	0
Flower, Mr.	0	10	6
Fussell, Mr	0	13	0
Feild, Mrs.	1	0	0
Friend, by Mr. Wilks	1	1	0
Family and Brothers, by S. Forsaith	5	5	0
Friends, by Mr. Green, at Pear Tree Street Prayer Meeting	2	7	0
Friends, by Mrs. Petch	1	13	0
Friends, by Mr. Sydenham	1	14	0
Fox, Miss, and Family	0	18	8
Freeman, Mrs. and Miss	0	18	0
Fellows, Miss	0	10	6
Fisher, Miss	0	11	0
Fleeming, Mr.	0	12	0
Frith, Mr.	0	12	0
Feild, Mr. and Miss	0	14	0
Fleetwood, Mrs	0	12	0
Friends, by E. Selby	27	5	0
Greenwood, Mr. and Family	2	12	6
Gilbert, Mr. and Mrs.	1	6	0
Gardiner, Mr.	1	1	0
Gravat, Mr. Sen.	1	1	0
Gaylor, Miss	0	10	6
Gibson, Mr.	0	12	0
Gale, Mr.	0	12	0
Goodluck, Mr	0	12	0
Goudge, Miss, and Family	0	18	0
Hughes, Mr.	0	12	0
Harrison, Misses	1	0	0
Harper, Mr. A.	1	1	0
Houseman, Mr. and Family	1	8	0
Holmes, Mr.	1	0	0
Henderson, Mr. and Family	1	14	0
Holloway, Mr. and Family	1	10	0
Harris, Mrs. and Band	3	0	0
Heudebourck, Mr. and Mrs.	1	0	0
Holmes, Mr.	0	10	0
Hawke, Mr.	0	10	6
Harraden, Mr. and Mrs.	0	12	0
Hudson, Mr. and Mrs.	0	18	0
Hayman, Mrs.	0	12	0
Harris, Mr.	0	12	0
Harrison, Mrs.	0	12	0
Hardwich, Mr.	0	10	6
Jukes, Mr.	1	1	0
Jackson, Mr. and Mrs.	1	11	6
Jerome, Mr.	0	12	0
Jones, Mr.	0	12	0
Knight, Mrs.	0	10	6
King, Mr. and Mrs.	1	0	0
Labrum, Mr. and Family	1	12	0
Lemage, Mr.	1	1	0
Luxford, Miss	0	10	0

	£	s.	d.
Loy, Mr	0	12	0
Lullman, Mrs.	1	1	0
Lefevre, Mr and Family	2	7	0
Langdon, Mrs and Family	1	12	0
Lindley, Mr. and Family	1	11	6
Lambert, Mr.	1	2	0
Lawford, Mrs.	0	12	0
Miller, Mr.	1	0	0
Marshall, Mrs.	1	0	0
Mitchell, Mrs.	0	12	0
Moody, Mr.	0	12	0
Mathews, Mr.	0	12	0
Moss, Mr.	0	12	0
Mitchell, Mr.	0	12	0
Medcalf, Mr.	0	10	0
Nobbs Mr.	0	12	0
Newton, Mr. Sen	0	13	0
Nicklins, Misses	1	1	0
Neave, Mr.	1	1	0
Nicholson, Mr.	0	10	6
Oram, Mr.	0	10	6
Owen, Mr.	0	10	6
Oakey, Miss.	0	10	0
Overton, Mrs	0	12	0
Preston, Misses	1	4	0
Phillips, Mr.	1	1	0
Paynter, Mr.	1	1	0
Perkins, Mrs	1	0	0
Pearce, Mr. and Mrs.	1	1	0
Pearce, Mr and Mrs	0	12	0
Pattison, Mr.	1	1	0
Pattison, Mr Jun	0	10	6
Parquet, Mr.	1	0	0
Paice, Mr.	0	12	0
Paton, Miss	1	1	0
Phillips, Mr.	0	12	0
Peto, Mr	0	12	0
Pain, Mrs	0	13	0
Paley, Mr.	0	12	0
Underton, Mr. and Mrs.	0	12	0
Roberts, Mr. Sen.	1	1	0
Roberts, Mr. E.	0	13	0
Roberts, Mr. J.	0	10	6
Roberts, Mr. L.	0	10	0
Robinson, Mr.	0	10	0
Roates, Mr.	0	10	0
Roberts, Mr.	1	2	0
Rodgers, Mr.	0	14	0
Roberts, Miss	0	10	0
Sowter, Mr.	1	1	0
Sarson, Mr and Mrs	1	1	0
Smart, Mr. W.	2	2	0
Smart, Mr. J.	1	1	0
Scott, Mr.	1	1	0
Swindle, Mr. and Mrs.	1	1	0
Sharp, Mr	1	1	0
Smith, Mr. W.	1	1	0
Selby, Mr. E.	1	1	0
Samuel, Miss	0	10	0
Stelling, Mr.	0	10	6
Selby, Mr. G.	0	10	6
Smith, Mr.	0	10	6
Simons, Mr.	0	10	0
Seaman, Mr.	0	10	6

	£	s.	d.
Tabernacle Charity Sch. Children, by Mr. Child	20	4	6
Tabernacle Sunday Catechetical Sch by Mr J. Barrett	17	14	0
Tomlinson, Mr.	0	12	0
Taylor, Mr.	1	1	0
Tomkin, Mr. and Mrs.	0	18	8
Thompson, Misses	0	16	0
Thatcher, Mrs	0	12	0
Thorman, Mr. and Miss	1	0	0
Throsby, Mr. and Family	1	4	0
Taylor, Miss	0	13	0
Taylor, Mr. W.	0	13	0
True, Mrs. and Family	0	16	0
Titterton, Mrs.	0	12	0
Thompson, Misses	0	18	0
Townsend, Mr. W.	1	1	0
Thorogood, Mrs.	0	10	6
Vidler, Mr.	1	1	0
Windale, Mr.	1	1	0
Witling, Mr.	1	1	0
Wallis, Mr.	1	1	0
Wasmaar, Mr.	0	12	0
Wilkinson, Mr. and Mrs.	1	0	0
Walmsley, Mr.	0	12	0
Wilks, Rev. M.	1	1	0
Williams, Mrs.	0	10	0
Williams, Miss E.	0	10	0
Williams, Miss C	0	10	0
Williams, Mrs.	0	10	0
Waudby, Mrs	0	10	0
Wilder, Mr.	1	1	0
Ward, Mr. and Miss	0	17	2
Wilson, Miss	1	1	0
West, Mr.	0	10	6
Whitting, Mr.	0	10	0
Walker, Mr.	0	10	0
Webber, Mrs.	0	12	0
Wincheap, Mrs.	0	13	0
And about 500 under 10s. per annum.			

	£	s.	d.
Collected by			
Adams, Mr. J.	20	3	9
Appleby, Mr. J.	4	5	10
Ashley, Mr. N.	6	16	4
Bell, Mr.	4	2	6
Brown, Mr. E	4	7	6
Greenhow, Mr. R.	11	16	9
Goldney, Mr J	6	3	3
Greenwood, Mr J.	24	13	10
Harraden, Mr. J. B.	10	16	6
Jukes, Mr H.	6	10	0
Joslin, Mr. J.	8	17	10
King, Mr. T.	16	3	3
Pearce, Mr. R.	12	2	9
Pearce, Mr. G.	25	5	10
Rolfe, Mr. D.	11	19	7
Rodgers, Mr. J.	6	9	6
Roberts, Mr. L.	30	12	6
Roberts, Mr. E. M.	14	0	3
Saunders, Mr. J	4	11	3
Throsby, Mr. G.	2	2	0
Donations and Fragments	49	10	2¾
Collected by Female Committee.			
Box, Miss	7	9	0
Daniels, Miss	9	16	11
Dee, Mrs.	3	19	7
Goulden, Mrs.	2	19	2
Holloway, Mrs.	3	9	6
Harraden, Mrs.	7	5	3
Langdon, Miss.	1	0	2
Nicholls, Mrs	2	6	6
Pearce, Mrs. S.	17	11	0½
Radnall, Mrs.	5	1	7
Rose, Miss	4	7	10
Stutter, Miss	2	5	10
Williams, Miss E.	4	14	6
A few Friends, in aid of the Tabernacle Auxiliary	27		0
Mrs. Harris and Friends	2	10	0
	396	6	7

TOTTENHAM COURT CHAPEL AUXILIARY SOCIETY.
MALE BRANCH.
Treasurer—Mr. W. Strudwicke.

Secretaries—Mr. O. Nodes—Mr. H. Shrimpton.

Subscriptions.	£	s.	d.
Adams, Mr.	0	10	6
Andrews, Mr.	1	8	0
Arnold, Mr.	0	10	0
Ashton, Mr. W.	1	1	0
Baddeley, Mr. J.	1	1	0
Baker, Mr.	0	12	0
Baker, Mr. S.	0	12	0
Blackman, Mr.	0	12	0
Broom, Mrs.	0	12	0
Brown, Mr.	0	12	0
Brown, Mr.	0	12	0
Buck, Mr.	0	13	0
Butter, Mr.	0	10	6
Bushnall, Mr.	0	10	6

	£	s.	d.
Cook, Mr	0	12	0
Cowley, Mr.	1	8	0
Crane, Mr. G.	0	12	0
Cree, Mr. T.	1	1	0
Y. C.	1	0	0
Davidson, Mr. G.	0	10	0
Dickenson, Mr. W	0	10	6
Dickenson, Mr. J.	0	12	0
Ditch, Mr. J.	0	10	0
Dixon, Mr.	1	1	0
Draper, Mr.	0	10	0
Evans, Mr. S.	1	0	0
Foulkes, Mr. C.	0	18	0
French, Mr.	1	1	0
Friend	1	0	0

	£.	s.	d.		£.	s.	d.
Gibson, Mr. John	0	10	6	Prier, Mr.	1	0	0
Gilbee, Captain	1	0	0	Puckett, Mr.	0	12	0
Godart, Mr. P.	0	10	0	Puckett, Mr. J. jun.	0	12	0
Gruby, Mr.	0	12	0	Puckett, Mr. Joseph	0	10	6
G. W.	1	0	0	Rainey, Mr	0	10	6
Habershon, Mr.	1	0	0	Reid, Mr. W.	0	12	0
Habershon, Mr. Joseph	1	0	0	Roberts, Mr J.	0	10	6
Hall, Mr. J.	0	10	6	Rose, Mr. J.	0	10	6
Hay, Mr.	0	12	0	Ross, Mr.	1	1	0
Holt, Mr.	0	10	0	Sams, Mr. G.	1	1	0
Hopper, Mr.	0	12	0	Shrimpton, Mr.	0	12	0
Ince, Mr.	0	10	6	Shrimpton, Mr H	0	12	0
Jay, Mr. James	1	1	0	Skell, Mr.	0	10	0
Johnson, Mr.	1	1	0	Spring, Mr.	0	12	0
Jones, Mr. John	1	0	0	Stewart, Mr.	1	0	0
Jopling, Mr. C.	1	0	0	Stocker, Mr.	0	12	0
Jopling, Mr. Joshua	1	0	0	Strudwicke, Mr.	1	0	0
Kelsall, Mr.	1	0	0	Sweetland, Mr.	0	10	6
Kilby, Mr.	1	1	0	S Y	0	12	0
Lander, Mr.	0	12	0	Taylor, Mr.	0	12	0
Lay, Mr.	0	12	0	Temple, Mr.	0	12	0
Leatt, Mr. H.	0	12	0	Ward, Mr. J.	1	1	0
Lockyer, Mr.	0	10	0	Walker, Mr.	0	10	0
Lyus, Mr.	1	0	0	Wellby, Mr.	0	12	0
Mackig, Mr.	0	12	0	Wellby, Mr. D.	0	12	0
Machin, Mr.	0	12	0	Westall, Mr.	0	10	6
Mann, Mr.	1	1	0	Whitefield, Mr.	0	12	0
May, Mr.	1	1	0	Wickendon, Mr.	0	12	0
Menzies, Mr.	0	13	0	Willey, Mr	0	10	0
Miller, Mr.	0	10	6	Wilson, Mr.	0	10	6
Mills, Mr.	1	1	0	Wright, Mr.	0	12	0
Mitchell, Mr.	0	12	0	Yielder, Mr.	1	1	0
Morgan, Mr.	1	0	0	Young, Mr.	0	12	0
Nodes, Mr. Oliver	1	1	0	Young, Mrs.	0	12	0
Northing, Mr. R.	0	10	0	Union School Boys, 3 quarters	1	8	4
Parkes, Mr.	0	12	0	Union School Girls, ditto	1	2	4½
Parry, Mr.	0	10	0	About 16 under 10s. per ann.			
Peregrine, Mr. O.	0	12	0				
Posselwhite, Mr.	1	1	0		120	0	0
Posselwhite, Mr. G.	1	1	0				

FEMALE BRANCH.

Treasurer—Mrs. Smith.

	£.	s.	d.
Subscriptions and Donations	217	16	3
A few Friends belonging to Tottenham Court Chapel	16	0	0
	353	16	3

UNION STREET MEETING, SOUTHWARK—REV. J. HUMPHRYS.

Subscriptions.

	£.	s.	d.		£.	s.	d.
Bateman, Mr. John	0	10	0	Izod, Mr. William	0	10	0
Blacket, Mr.	1	1	0	Kitching, Mr.	0	10	0
Bousfield, Mr.	1	1	0	Leete, Mr. S.	1	1	0
Coles, Mr. Benjamin, jun.	0	10	6	Maynard, Mr. W. and Family	5	0	0
Coles, Mr. Henry	0	10	6	Mackie, Mr.	1	1	0
Coles, Mr. Samuel	0	10	6	Overton, Mr.	0	10	0
Fordham, Mr. Thomas	0	10	0	Overton, Mr. William	0	10	0
Humphrys, Rev. Mr.	1	1	0	Pilcher, Mr. W. H.	1	1	0
Humphrys, Mr. Henry	1	1	0	Pilcher, Mr. John	1	1	0
Hanbury, Mr. B.	1	1	0	Smith, Mrs	1	0	0
Izod, Mr. John	0	10	0		20	10	6

WELLS STREET AUXILIARY SOCIETY—REV. DR. WAUGH.

MALE BRANCH.

Collections 24 4 9

FEMALE BRANCH.

By Miss Harvey, *Treasurer*.......................................34 14 0
                                                              ————
                                                              58 18 9
SCHOOLS.

Adelphi Sunday School by Mr. W. Hipkin.....................6 0 0
Barbican Sunday School by Mr. Locke—Boys 1 9 2
                                     Girls 1 19 4
Hill Court, Shoreditch—The Children of Providence Chapel Sunday
  School 2 12 6
Mint Sunday School, by Mr. Thomas Lewis....................14 0 0
Sion Chapel Sunday School 12 19 2
Swallow-street Sabbath School—Teachers 11 8 10
                                Girls 4 3 11
                                Boys 3 6 6

SUBSCRIPTIONS, DONATIONS, &c.

IN THE COUNTIES OF

GREAT BRITAIN AND IRELAND,

EXCLUSIVE OF THOSE IN LONDON,

From April 1st, 1817, to April 1st, 1818.

INCLUDING LIFE SUBSCRIBERS.

BEDFORDSHIRE.

	£	s.	d.
Bedford, Society for promoting the Gospel, by Rev. S. Hillyard	10	0	0
Mr. G. Livius, 1799	10	10	0
Biggleswade, Mr. J. Mann (A)	1	1	0
Harrold, Rev. Mr. West (A)	1	1	0
Roxton, Collection in the little Barn, by Rev. Mr. Metcalf	4	5	6

BERKSHIRE.

	£	s.	d.
Abingdon Auxiliary Society, by Rev. Mr. Wilkins	20	0	0
Maidenhead, Rev. J. Cooke & Congregation	27	14	6
New Chapel, by Rev. G. D. Owen	26	1	3
Newbury, Rev. J. Winter and Congregation, by Rev. Dr. Waugh	16	0	0
Winter, Rev. J. 1798	20	0	0
Ditto 1817	10	0	0
Dryland's, Rev. Mr. by Ditto	6	10	6
Penny Society at Ditto	15	13	4
Coster, Mr. (A)	1	0	0
Donation	0	6	8
Dyer, Mr. J. (A)	2	0	0
Dryland, Rev. Mr. (A)	1	0	0
Gladwyn, Mrs.(A)	1	0	0
	21	0	0

F

	£	s.	d.
Reading, Collection at Castle-street Chapel after two Sermons, by Rev. J. Liefchild	100	3	6
A few Children, by Rev. Mr. Parrott	1	15	0
The Fruits of a Penny Society, collected by Mrs. Tanner	17	10	0
Holmes, Mr...........1798	10	0	0
Ditto 1800	20	0	0
Ryder, Mrs. 1796	10	0	0
Ryder, Mr. 1800	10	0	0
Watkins, Rev. J. ...1813	10	10	0
Welmhurst, Mr. ...1800	10	0	0

	£	s.	d.
Female Society at Rev. A. Douglas's, by Mr. D. Fenton	7	0	0
A Friend, by Mr. J. Bailey	10	0	0
Edwards, Mrs............(A)	1	1	0
Laurie, Rev. W.........(A)	1	1	0
Maberly, Miss...........(A)	1	1	0
Wallingford—Rev. Mr. Harris. Collection by Rev. Dr. Waugh	10	10	0
Young Ladies at Mrs. Lee's School	2	2	11
Mr. Faulkner's School..:...	0	13	0
Windsor, Rev. Mr. Redford and Friends	15	5	0

BUCKINGHAMSHIRE.

	£	s.	d.
Beaconsfield, Rev. J. Harsent and Congregation	7	0	0
Juvenile Society at Mr Gregory's Academy ...	2	2	0
Buckingham Penny Society, by Rev. Mr. Aston :....13	4	8	
Mr. Kirby	2	0	0
Mr. J. Long ......1796......10	10	0	
Chalfont Penny Society, by Mrs. Chandler	1	8	8
Chesham, Rev. S. Surman & Friends	3	3	0
Langley, Mr.W. Nash, 1815 10	0	0	
Marlow, Rev. G. Edwards & Congregation..	6	1	9

Newport Pagnel, By the Rev. T. P. Bull :—

Annual.

	£	s.	d.
Bull, Rev. T. P.	1	1	0
Cripps, Mr. J.	1	1	0
Kilpin, Mr.	1	1	0
Osborn, Mr.	1	1	0
Rogers, Mr.	1	1	0
Ward, Rev. J.	1	1	0
Penny Society	9	0	0
	15	6	0

	£	s.	d.
Olney, Rev. Messrs. Hillyard and Morris :— Collection	5	0	5
Sab. Sch. Children	0	7	8
Miss Mabley, and School	1	3	0
A Friend for Mr. May's School in India	1	0	0
Donations & Sub-scriptions	12	18	5
	20	9	6
Prince Risborough Auxiliary Society in aid of Foreign Missions, by Mr. W. Dorset, Treasurer. One-third of the Ann. Subscrip.	5	8	4
Ditto of a Collection at Bledlow Church, by Rev. Mr. Shepherd, of Westminster, & Rev. Mr. Stephens, Vicar	3	11	8
	9	0	0
Wooburn, Rev. J. Harrison: Collection by Rev. J. Campbell	27	0	0

CAMBRIDGESHIRE.

CAMBRIDGESHIRE AUXILIARY SOCIETY.

Treasurer—Mr. Robert Haylock.

Secretary—Rev. Thomas Towne.

Remittances,	£	s.	d.
1813	174	4	7
1814	192	4	2
1815	198	15	8
1816	223	12	5
1817	214	7	5
1818	193	8	11
	1196	13	2

	£	s.	d.

BARKWAY.

By the Rev. J. Lowe	1	13	4

CAMBRIDGE.

Barrett, Mr. R.	0	10	6
Bradford, Mr. B.	1	0	0
Cook, Mr. T.	1	1	0
Foster, Mr. R.	1	1	0
Haylock, Mr. R.	1	1	0
Kent, Mr. R. W.	1	1	0
Nicklin, Mrs.	0	10	6
Paul, Mr. G.	0	10	6
Searle, Mr. William..i..........	2	2	0
By ditto, Association in the Independent Congregation	19	3	6
Servant,' a Female, Savings of small Sums occasionally obtained......................	1	10	6
Children at Mr. Preston's School...........................	0	3	3¼
	29	14	9¼

DUXFORD.

Pyne, Rev. B. and Friends	11	0	0

EVERSDEN.

Golding, Rev. Mr. & Friends	6	12	1
Rycraft, Mr.	0	10	6
	7	2	7

FOULMIRE.

Miles, Rev. J. and Friends...	12	12	0

HITCHIN.]
Subscriptions.

Field, Mr.	1	1	0
Field, Mr. N.	1	1	0
Field, Mr. H.	0	16	0
James, Mrs.	1	1	0
Japp, Miss........................	0	10	6
Parks, Mr. W.	1	1	0
Sloper, Rev. C.	1	1	0
Ward, Mr............................	1	1	0
Wilshire, Mr. J.	1	1	0
Ward, Mrs.	0	10	6
Sundry small Subscriptions under 10s. per annum	2	17	6

Donations.

A Friend	0	5	0
Manning, Mr.	0	10	0
Quarterly Subscriptions	2	14	6
Weekly ditto.....................	10	17	9
	26	2	3

LINTON.

S. C. by Rev. T. Hopkins......	1	1	0

MELBOURNE.

Rev. W. Carver and Cong. Donation by N. Wedd, Esq.	5	0	0
Collected at the Doors.........	5	19	1

	£	s.	d.

Annual Subscribers.

Campkin, Mr. J.	0	10	6
Carver, Rev. W.	1	1	0
Clear, Mr. H.	1	0	0
Fitch, Mr............................	1	0	0
Mortlock, W. Esq.	1	0	0
Newling, Mr. J.	0	10	6
Scruby, Mr. J.	0	10	6
Stockbridge, Mr. J.	0	10	6
Wallis, Mr. J	0	10	6
Wallis, Mr. G.	0	10	6
Wedd, J. Esq.	1	0	0

Weekly Subscriptions collected by

Charter, Mr. C...................	3	6	1
Campkin, Mr. Joseph	3	1	8
Sell, Mr. H.	1	17	6
Unwin, Mr.	0	18	7½
Wright, Mr. James............	0	7	7
	28	14	6½

ROYSTON *(by Mr. Bunn, Treasurer).*

Association in Rev. J.Towne's Congregation	16	2	6

Subscribers.

Beldam, Mrs. W.................	0	10	6
Beldam, Joseph, Esq.	0	10	6
Butterfield, Mr.	0	10	6
Butterfield, Mrs.	0	10	6
Bunn, Mr..........................	0	10	6
Bonnet, Mr.	1	1	0
Coote, Mr.........	0	10	6
Came, Mr. A.	0	10	6
Dear, Mr.	0	10	6
Ellis, Mr.	0	10	6
Fordham, Miss M	0	10	6
Fordham, Mr. J. W.	0	10	6
Luke, Mr.	0	10	6
Luke, Mrs.	0	10	6
Moule Miss M..:..............	0	10	6
Moule, Mr. W....................	0	10	6
Matthews, Mr...:..............	0	10	0
Phillips, Mr. J...................	0	10	6
Simons, Mr.	0	10	6
Stamford, Mr. J.	0	10	6
Trigg, Mr. J.	0	10	6
Towne, Mrs......................	0	10	6
Towne, Miss.....................	0	10	6
Towne, Rev. T.	0	10	6
Wells, Mr........................	0	10	6
Walbey, Mr. S...................	0	10	6
White, Mr.	0	10	6
	14	14	0

Donations.

Bull, Rev. Samuel	0	10	6
Wells, Mrs.	1	1	0
Small Sums	0	17	8
	2	9	2

	£	s.	d.
Collected by			
Dodkin, Eliza	4	0	2
Haggar, Jemima	3	14	0
Haggar, Mr.	0	8	0
Moule, Miss M.	4	12	4
Proctor, Miss	1	2	9
Proctor, Mr. G.	3	14	9
Stallybrass&Richardson,Mess.	5	0	0
Sabbath School, Female	0	7	0
Wells, Miss	2	12	0

	£	s.	d.
YoungLadies of Mrs.Towne's Seminary	2	1	1½
	27	12	1½
WALKERN.			
Thompson, Rev. William & Friends	2	0	0
	193	8	11

Cambridge, Audley, Rev. J. 1796	20	0	0	Simeon, Rev. J. of King's College, 1803	20	0	0
Bevan, Mr. R. of Trinity College, 1815	10	0	0	Chatteris, Billups, Mr. C. 1817	10	10	0

CORNWALL.

CORNWALL FOREIGN MISSIONARY SOCIETY.

Treasurer—Mr. J. W. M'Dowell.
Secretary—Rev. B. Wildbore.

Falmouth Branch	22	1	7	Truro Branch	11	10	0
Penzance ditto	30	1	0	Bodman ditto	1	5	0
Penryn ditto	21	4	8	Balance from last year	3	8	1
Fowey ditto	4	6	6				
Liskeard ditto	7	0	7	Remittance	90	0	0
Launceston ditto	4	0	0				
Lostwithiel	2	0	0				
Mevagissey ditto	10	2	6	Falmouth, Messrs. Banfield & Co. (A)	1	1	0
St. Ives ditto	1	5	0	Fowey, Mr. G. Williams	2	0	0
St. Maws ditto	2	2	0				

CHESHIRE.

CHESHIRE AUXILIARY SOCIETY.

Treasurer—Mr. J. Williamson.
Secretary—Mr. W. Cross.

Remittances, 1815	150	6	11
1816	367	7	1
1817	312	8	9
1818	254	4	2
	1084	6	11

Bebington, Mr.	1	1	0	Clubbe, Miss S.	1	1	0
Bellis, Mr. Joseph	1	1	0	Colley, Mr. Hugh	1	1	0
Bennett, Mr. N.	1	1	0	Cook, Misses	1	0	0
Booth, Mr.	1	1	0	Cross, Mr. W.	2	2	0
Brassie, Mrs.	1	0	0	Currie, Wm. Esq. M.D.	1	0	0
Bradford, Mr. Thomas	2	2	0	Dodd, Miss	0	10	6
Bridgman Rev. J.	1	1	0	Dodd, Miss S.	0	10	6
Chaloner, Mr.	1	1	0	Dutton, Mr. Peter	2	2	0
Clubbe, Mr.	1	1	0	Dutton, Mr.	1	1	0
Clubbe, Mr.	2	2	0	Eaton, Mr.	1	1	0
Clubbe, Miss	1	1	0	Edelsten, Mr. W.	1	1	0
Clubbe, Miss E.	1	1	0	Hodson, Mr. Thomas	3	3	0

	£	s.	d.
Hitchen, Mr.	1	1	0
Jackson, Mr.	1	1	0
Jones, Mrs.	1	1	0
Jones, Mr. D. F.	2	2	0
Jones, Mr. John	1	1	0
Jones, Mr. James	0	10	6
Lancaster, Mrs.	0	10	6
Lindop, Mr. John	1	1	0
Lloyd, Mr. Hugh	1	1	0
Marratt, Mrs.	0	10	6
Meredith, Mr.	1	1	0
Newell, Mr. Alderman	1	1	0
Parry, Rev. John	1	1	0
Powell, Mr. Edward	1	1	0
Richards, Mr. William	1	1	0
Richards, Mrs. T.	1	1	0
Roberts, Mr. George	1	1	0
Roberts, Mr. William	0	10	0
Smith, Mr. D.	1	1	0
Stuart, Mr.	1	1	0
Walker, Mr. John	1	1	0
Whitebrook, Mr.	1	1	0
Whittell, Mr. Thomas	1	1	0
Williamson, Mr.	2	2	0
Williamson, Miss	1	1	0
Wildig, Mr. George	1	1	0
Sundry Subscrip. under 10s.	0	15	0
	58	6	6

Collections at the Anniversary,
August, 1816.

	£	s.	d.
Chester, Boughton Chapel	12	15	6
Baptist Chapel	1	3	0
Crook's-lane ditto	7	4	2

	£	s.	d.
Welch Calvinistic Methodist Chapel	6	1	7
Queen-street ditto	56	3	9
	38	8	0
Ladies'Penny Society,Queen-street Chapel, 4 quarters	51	11	10½
Young Men's Ditto	5	0	7
Ditto Welch Methodist's Chapel, Ditto	3	8	3
Ladies' Ditto Ditto Octagon Chapel Ditto	9	11	3
Sunday School Children Ditto	1	5	2
Mission. Box at Mrs Lewis's, Draper, Bridge-street	0	18	2¼
Do. at Minshall, by MissPalin	6	0	3
Do. at Harlington, by Rev. W. Silvester	8	0	0
Do. at Delamur and Kelsall, by Mr. Prescott	1	16	0
Penny Society at Tarvin, by Mrs. Jackson	3	0	8
Young Ladies at MissLewis's School, Tarvin	2	12	0
Weekly Subscriptions, by Miss Gamon. Pickton	0	10	11
Penny a Week Society at Northop, by Mr. Williams	9	0	0
Produce of 2 Cherry Trees, by Mr. Williams, Northop	1	6	4
Rev. Rob. Smith and Congregation, Nantwich	8	8	2
	254	4	2

	£	s.	d.
Chester, Misses Clubbe, 1810	10	0	0
Heaton, near Stockport,Cotton Manufactory belonging to Mr. Brown:—Subcriptions by Mr. S. Shawcroft, Treasurer	7	0	0
Knutsford, Rev. J. Turner and Friends	3	0	0
Sheepwash, Cotton Manufactory belonging to Mr. Brown, Subscriptions by Mr. Burgess	8	0	0

STOCKPORT.

Orchard Street Chapel Auxiliary Society—Rev. N. Pugsley.

Treasurer—Miss Mayers.

Annual.

	£	s.	d.		£	s.	d.
A Friend to Missions	1	1	0	Dawson, Mr.	1	1	0
Brown, Mrs.	1	1	0	Downall, Mr.	0	10	6
Brown, Mr.	1	1	0	Dain, Mrs	0	10	6
Brown, P. M. & E.	0	10	6	Fowden, Mr	0	10	6
Beard, Mr.	0	10	6	Fisher, Mr.	0	10	6
Boulton, Miss	0	10	6	Higson, Mr W.	1	1	0
Boulton, W. & J.	0	10	6	Higson, Miss	0	10	6
Broadhurst, Miss E.	0	10	6	Higson, Miss N.	0	10	6
Bramwell, Miss, from her Missionary Basket	0	11	0	Hardy, Mr	1	1	0
Cheetham, Mr.	0	11	0	Howard, Miss	1	1	0
Chesters, Rev. Thomas	0	10	6	Howard, Mr. A.	1	1	0
Chatterton, Mr.	0	10	6	Howard, Mr. John	1	1	0
Drakeford, Miss	1	0	0	Howard, Mr. Jesse	1	1	0
				Howard, Mr.Joseph	0	10	6
				Kirby, Mrs.	0	10	6

	£	s.	d.
Lingard, Mr.	0	10	6
Mayers, Miss	1	1	0
Nabb, Mrs.	0	10	6
Overton, Mr.	0	10	6
Pugsley, Rev. Nathaniel	1	1	0

	£	s.	d.
Walmsley, Mr.	0	10	6
Subscriptions under 10s. and penny a week	27	2	0
	51	15	6

CUMBERLAND.

COLLECTIONS BY REV. MESSRS. COLLISON AND JACKSON.

	£	s.	d.
Alston Moor, Rev. Mr. Harper	5	4	6
Brampton, Scots' Church	5	17	8
Carlisle, Rev. Mr. Whitridge	4	10	0
Do. Sunday School	1	10	0
Rev. Mr. Henderson	3	0	1
Cockermouth, Rev. Mr. Muscatt	5	16	6
Longtown, Rev. Alex. M'Farlane	5	5	7½
Donations	2	2	0
Young Gentlemen at Mr. Thomson's Boarding School	0	5	0
Maryport, Rev. Mr. Dunn	4	8	6
Penrith, Rev. Dr. Thompson	3	15	0
Salkeld, Rev. Mr. Nelson	2	9	0
Whitehaven, Rev. Mr. Rose	1	15	6

	£	s.	d.
Rev. Mr. Cook	6	19	5
M. H. Donation	1	1	0
Wigton, Rev. Mr. Walton	2	10	0
Workington, Rev. Mr. Peel	13	0	0
	69	9	9½
Penrith, Mr. J. Robinson (A)	1	1	0
Whitehaven Auxiliary Society, by Mr. Geo. Vickers, Secretary	14	0	0
Wigton Auxiliary Society (collected by Ladies), by Mr. Wm. Baxter, Treasurer	10	0	0

DERBYSHIRE.

(See Leicestershire Auxiliary.)

	£	s.	d.
Chesterfield Beaver Place Sunday School, by Mr. Cook	4	1	6

DEVONSHIRE.

SOUTH DEVONSHIRE AUXILIARY SOCIETY.

Treasurers—Mr. W. Parr and Mr. Dove.

		£	s.	d.		£	s.	d.
Remittances,	1813	262	8	9				
	1814	120	0	0				
	1815	158	2	6				
	1816	111	8	7				
	1818	154	11	2				
						806	11	0

NORTH DEVON AUXILIARY SOCIETY.

Treasurer—Rev. Mr. Rooker.

		£	s.	d.		£	s.	d.
Remittances,	1814	68	18	10				
	1816	92	3	5				
	1818	60	3	9				
						221	6	0

	£	s.	d.
Bideford	28	17	0
Ilfracombe	16	0	0
South Moulton	10	4	9

	£	s.	d.
Chulmleigh	4	2	0
Puddington	1	0	0
	60	3	9

	£	s.	d.
Ashburton, P. W.	1	0	0
Axminster, Rev. Mr. Small and Congregation	14	11	6
Cawsand, Rev. Mr. Varder &			

	£	s.	d.
Congregation	5	0	0
Hatherleigh, Rev. Mr. Glascott, 1796	10	0	0
Ditto (A)	1	1	0

	£	s.	d.
Honiton Penny Society, by Rev. J. O. Stokes	7	0	0
Kingsbridge, Rev. J. Angear and Friends	7	0	0
Angear, Rev. J.	1	0	0
Holditch, Mrs.	1	1	0
Plymouth Dock, A Friend, by Mr. Garland	3	0	0
Plymouth, A few Friends......	2	0	0
Mr. T. Hodson—1800......100	0	0	
Ditto.............1813......	10	0	0
Ditto.............1814......	10	10	0

	£	s.	d.
Sidmouth, Rev. Mr. Ward and Friends 10	5	0	
Stokenham, Mr Torrens	2	0	0
Tavistock Missionary Society, by Rev. W. Kooker......18	0	0	
Mrs. Brown	1	11	6
Teignmouth Auxiliary Society, by Rev. Mr. Gleed	7	0	0
Totness Penny Society, by the Rev. T. W. Windeatt 10	0	0	

DORSETSHIRE.

DORSET MISSIONARY SOCIETY.

Treasurer—Rev. Dr. Cracknell.

Collection at *Lyme Regis* 15 8 3
Ditto at *Lydling*...... 5 7 0
————20 15 3
Collection at the County Anniversary, March 25, 1818 ....11 11 0
Donations 1 11 0

Annual Subscriptions.

Ayles, Mr 0 10 6
Barling, Mr. 0 10 6
Bartlett, Miss 0 10 6
Blackbeard, Mrs. ... 0 10 6
Couch, Mrs. 0 10 6
Day, Miss 1 1 0

Devenish, Mrs 0 10 6
Hodge, Mr. W...... 0 10 6
Quirk, Captain 1 1 0
Russel, Mr............. 1 1 0
Smith, Mr............. 1 1 0
Sainthill, Mrs. 0 10 6
Tapper, Mrs. 0 10 6
Warne, Mr. 1 1 0
Weston, Mrs. S...... 1 1 0
Williams, Mr. W. Barrister 1 1 0
Wood, Captain 1 1 0
Wood, Geo. Esq. ... 1 1 0
————27 5 6

48 0 9

Beaminster, Mr. D. Gundry, 1812 ....52 10 0
Blandford, by Rev. Messrs. Field and Keynes :—
Penny Subscription by Ladies 53 0 6
Sunday Schools ...1 0 0
Annual Subscrip. 11 11 0
————65 11 6
Birdbush, near Shaftsbury, Rev. J. Jones and Cong. 14 0 6
Bridport. Rev. J. Saltren & Friends 16 0 0
Mr. R. Peters, by him 1 0 0
————17 0 0
Cerne Abbas, Rev. J. Trowbridge and Friends 17 0 0
Charmouth, by Rev. B. Jeans.

Annual.

Barnard, Mr. 1 1 0
Bolton, Mr..........1 1 0
Ferris, Capt. R.N. 1 1 0
Jeanes, Rev. B. ...1 1 0
Lyon, Mr. J. 1 1 0
Love, Mr. & Miss 0 10 0
Collection.............4 17 6
————10 12 6

Dorchester Aux. Soc. by Rev. L. Hall 5 5 0
Mr. Luke, Broadmayne 2 0 0
————7 5 0
Poole, Rev. J. Durant and Congregation.

Annual Subscriptions.

Ashburner, Mrs ...1 1 0
Butler, Mrs. 1 1 0
Bunn, Mr. J. B.......1 1 0
Crew, Mr. T. 1 1 0
Coward, Mr.Thomas 1 1 0
Durant, Rev. T.......2 2 0
Durant, Mr. J. 1 1 0
Friend, Miss 1 1 0
Gollop, Mr. G. jun. 10 0
Gollop, Mr. Wm. ...0 10 0
Gosse, Mr. Thomas 10 0
Hodges, Mr. 0 10 0
Kemp, Mr. G..........1 1 0
Kemp, Miss S. 1 1 0
Kemp, Miss M. 1 1 0
Kemp, Mr. G. jun....1 1 0
Kemp, Mr. James ...1 1 0
Kemp, Mr. Henry...1 1 0
Lance, Mr. W. 0 10 0
Ledgard, Mr. G.W. 5 0 0

	£	s.	d.
Ledgard, Mrs. 1	1	0	
Miller, Mr. R. 1	1	0	
Miller, Mr. T..........1	1	0	
Miller, Mr. J. S.......1	1	0	
Monk, Mr. 1	1	0	
Pretty, Mr. 0	10	0	
Randall, Mr. J. M. 1	1	0	
Sealey, Miss............0	10	0	
Sells, Mr..............0	10	0	
Taverner, Miss 0	10	0	
Wadham, Mr. J......1	1	0	
Wadham, Mr. B. ...1	1	0	
Waterman, Mr. W. 1	1	0	
Welch, Mr. M. K....1	1	0	

	£	s.	d.
Donation 1	0	0	
Penny a Week Sub. 49	0	7	
———85	15	1	
Mr. G. Kemp, 1796...........20	0	0	
Sherborne Auxiliary Society,			
by Rev. J. Weston.			
Subscriptions......24 16 6			
Collection 18 5 10			
———43	2	4	
Swannage Penny Society, by			
Mr. S. March 3	10	0	
Weymouth, Rev. Dr. Crack-			
nell 1812	10	0	0

DURHAM.

Collections by Rev. Messrs. Collison and Jackson.

Barnard Castle, Rev. Mr.
Pratman 6 1 0
Darlington, Rev. Mr. Whit-
tenbury 5 12 0
South Shields, Rev. C. Topack 3 5 6½
South Shields Auxil. Society,
Rev. Dr. Thoburn 4 9 6
Stockton, at the Method. Ch....4 5 5

Sunderland, Rev. J.
Frazer 5 0 3
T. Mason...........7 16 11½
———36 10 8

Sunderland Auxiliary Society,
by Rev. J. Frazer 46 1 2

ESSEX.

Essex Auxiliary Society, by Rev. T. Craig.....................................200 0 0

Barking Penny Soc.
Subscriptions ...10 6 3
Female   Charity
Children 0 14 10
——————11 1 1
Braintree, Ladies' Mis-
sionary Society by
Rev. J. Carter...35 9 10
Col. at Miss. Pray.
Meeting 3 2 4
————38 12 2
Castle Hedingham, Rev. Thos.
Stevenson 10 0 0
Chigwell Row, by Rev. Mr.
West.
Collection at his
Chapel 5 15 6
Sunday Sch. Child.
and Teachers ...0 17 0
——————— 6 12 6
Mr. J. Bellin.........1797 20 0 0
Ditto 1800 10 0 0
Chishill Auxiliary Society, by
Rev. J. Dobson.
Contributions ...20 9 3
Cornwall, Mr. Chis-
hill 0 10 6
Judd, Mrs. Whad-
don 0 10 6
Judd, Mr. J. Do. 0 10 6

Savill, Mrs. Barley
Herts 0 10 6
Savill, Mr. W. ...0 10 6
Wilkinson,   Mr.
Christhall.........0 10 6
——————23 12 3
Colchester, Mr. J. Tabor,
1796 ....100 0 0
Mr. S. Taylor 1817 25 0 0
Debden, Collected at a Barn,
Rev. J. Dorrington 1 0 0
Dedham, Rev. W. B. Cra-
therne...............1813 10 10 0
Dunmow Penny Society, (2
quarters) by Mr. Morton 5 1 0
Epping, Rev. Mr. Alcot,1815 10 10 0
Layton, Mr. R. Smith 10 0 0
Newport Prayer Meeting, by
Rev. J. H. Hopkins...... 4 2 9
Plaistow, Mrs. Vaughan (A) 1 1 0
Rickling Hall, Mr. Spencer,
(A) 2 0 0
Romford, Mr. R. Surridge (A) 1 1 0
Saffron Walden Auxiliary Soc.
by Rev. W. Clayton......14 10 9
Stratford Auxiliary Society,
by Rev. J. Emblem......13 2 11
Walthamstow, Mr. D. Bevan,
1815 ....21 0 0
Woodford, Collection by Mr.
G. Clarke 10 0 0

GLOUCESTERSHIRE.

GLOUCESTERSHIRE AUXILIARY SOCIETY.

Treasurer—Mr.' P. O. Wathen.

Secretary—Rev. John Burder.·

Remittances, 1816	125	0	0			
1817	329	5	10			
1818	253	3	0			
				707	8	10

	£	s.	d.
Cheltenham, Penny a Week			
Society	9	11	6
Mr. Barry, 1810, 10 0 0			
Little Dean Penny Soc.			
by Miss Taylor 5 0 0			
Donation 3 0 0			
	8	0	0
Dursley, Sunday Sch. Teachers			
& Scholars at the Taber-			
nacle, by Miss Taylor ...20 0 0			
Mr. W. Smith (a) 2 2 0			
Ebley Chapel, Rev. S. Davis.			
Ann. Collection...11 3 4			
Subscriptions......17 3 0			
	28	6	4
Frampton and *Framilode* Asso-			
ciation.........................16 16 0			
Forest Green Penny Society,			
by Rev. T. Edkins 9 0 0			
Gloucester, Countess of			
Huntingdon's Ch.			
Rev. T. Thorn 5 8 0			
Rev. W. Bishop's			
Meeting, by Mr.			
J. Wood.........26 6 2			
	31	14	2
Pakon Hill, collected			
by Mrs. Offlay...9 5 0			
Subscrip. & Dona. 9 1 0			
	18	6	0
Painswick, Collection			
at Mission. Pray.			

	£	s.	d.
Meeting, by Mr.			
Wood 6 9 0			
Subscriptions .·,....3 2 0			
	9	11	0
Mr. J. Horlick, by Rev. G.			
Garlick 1 0 0			
Rodborough Tabernacle, Rev.			
J. Rees.			
Anniversary Col. 30 10 6			
Annual Subscrip. 23 1 0			
	53	11	6
Stroud, Old Chapel, Rev. J.			
Burder.			
Anniversary Col. 15 2 3			
Sunday School......2 2 6			
Annual subscrip....9 18 6			
Col. at the Gen.			
Meet. at the As-			
sembly Room ...4 8 10			
	31	12	1
Sunday School at Rev. J.			
Holder's Chapel, by Mr.			
Holder	4	11	10
Stonehouse, by Mr. Elliot......	2	10	0
Tetbury, by Mr. Webber......	2	6	7
Sundry subscrip. and dona....	5	6	0
	253	3	0

Nailsworth, Rev. H. Camp-			
bell, A.M. 10 10 0			
Tewkesbury, Gittens, Mr. (a) 1 0 0			

HAMPSHIRE.

	£	s.	d.
Alton, Rev. C. Howell and			
Friends :			
Ann.Subscriptions 5 2 4			
Collection............2 ·2 4			
Produce of a Mis-			
sionary Box at			
the Chapel Door 1 14 10			
Mr. J. French,			
Holybourne 1 0 0			
Mr. J. Terrall,			
Anstey 1 1 0			
	11	0	6
Andover Penny Society, by			
Rev. Mr. Seaton 24 3 2			
Basingstoke, Rev. J. Jefferson			
and Congregation :			
Penny· Society and Dona-			
tions of Friends 1S 5 0			
Mr. S Toomer, 1800 ......10 0 0			

	£	s.	d.
Cowes, West, (Isle of Wight),			
Penny Society, by Miss			
Donaldson	7	16	0
Rev. R. Adams :			
Sab. School Chil-			
dren & Friends 3 16 9			
Children of Mrs.C. 1 0 0			
Ditto of Mr. E.M. 1 0 0			
Mr. L. and two			
Friends............0 5 6			
Sabbath School at			
East Cowes 3 18 6			
	10	0	9
Fordingbridge, Rev. Mr. Preist-			
ley and Friends............11 0 0			
Gosport, By Rev. D. Bogue,			
D.D.			
Allen, Mr. Jos. ...0 10 0			
Barrow, Mr. 2 2 0			

G

	£	s.	d.
Battershell, Mr. ...1	0	0	
Biddlecomb, Mr....2	2	0	
Blake, Mr. James 0	10	6	
Bogue, Rev. D.			
D.D. ...2	2	0	
Curme, Mr....1	0	0	
Darby, Mr. G. ...0	10	6	
Dodds, Dr. ...1	1	0	
Evening Collection 1	5	9½	
Fryer, Mrs....1	0	0	
Gibson, Mr....1	1	0	
Gilbert, Mr. ...0	0	0	
Goodeve, Mr. J. sen. ...2	2	0	
Goodeve, Mr. J. jun. ...1	1	0	
Goodeve, Mr. B....1	1	0	
Hayson, Mr....0	10	6	
Hayter, Mrs. ...1	1	0	
Hoskins, Mr. J. ...1	1	0	
Hoskins, Mr. ...1	1	0	
Hoskins, Mr. T. jun. ...1	0	0	
Hyslop, Mr. ...0	10	0	
Jack, Mr....0	10	6	
Knight, Mrs. ...0	10	6	
Lamb, Mr. ...1	1	0	
Marshall, Miss E. 0	10	6	
M'Arthur, Mrs....1	0	0	
M'Cloud, Mr. ...0	10	6	
Meredith, Mr. ...1	1	0	
Minchin, Mr. ...5	5	0	
Roberts, Mr. S. ...1	0	0	
Sherrington, Mr....1	0	0	
Sprent, Mrs. ...1	1	0	
Sprent, Mr. G. ...1	1	0	
Voke, Mr. ...1	1	0	
Young, Captain ...1	0	0	
Collection ...18	17	6	
Female Auxiliary Society ...15	5	7	
		74 1 7	
Goodeve, Mr. 1800 ...10	10	0	
Minchin, Mr. T. 1805...10	0	0	

Havant, By Rev. W. Scamp:

	£	s.	d.
Arter, Mr. G. ...1	1	0	
A Friend...1	0	0	
Briant, Mr. John 1	0	0	
Chalkley, Mrs. ...0	10	6	
Clark, Mr. T. J....1	1	0	
Clements, Miss C. 0	10	6	
Dennis, Mr. W....0	10	6	
Ford, Mr. Wm. ...0	10	6	
Hall, Mr....1	1	0	
Hoare, Mr. Wm. 2	0	0	
Hoare, Mrs. Wm. 1	0	0	
Loveder, Mr. J....0	12	0	
Loveder, Mr. P. 0	10	6	
Moodey, Misses ...1	1	0	
Padwick, Mr. T....1	0	0	
Sainsbury, W. & S. 1	1	0	
Sainsbury, Mr. T. 0	15	0	
Scamp, Rev. W....1	1	0	
Thornton, Miss ...1	0	0	

	£	s.	d.
Woods, Mr. S....1	0	0	
White, Mr. W. ...1	0	0	
White, Mrs. ... 1	0	0	
White, Mr. G. ...1	0	0	
White, Miss M....0	10	6	
Waldron, Mrs. ...1	1	0	
B. N....1	0	0	
Collection ...12	6	0	
		36 3 0	

Lymington, Ladies' Penny Missionary Society, by Rev. J. Cobben...6 11 9

Newport (Isle of Wight), Rev. Mr. Tyerman & Friends 8 9 0

	£	s.	d.
Rev. J. Bruce ...			
Weekly Penny Subscriptions ...7	10	6	
Sun. Sch. Teachers and Children ...5	0	0	
		12 10 6	

Petersfield and Harting, by Rev. L. Gore:

	£	s.	d.
Collection at Petersfield ...4	2	3	
Auxiliary Society at ditto ...10	0	0	
Collection at Harting...3	5	9	
		17 8 0	

Portsea, Rev. John Griffin & Friends:

	£	s.	d.
Baker, Mr. ...1	0	0	
Barns, Mr. ...1	0	0	
Buggins, Mrs ...1	0	0	
Cuzens, Mr. W....1	11	6	
Eastman, Mr. ...1	1	0	
Eastman, Mrs. ...1	1	0	
Eastman, Miss ...1	1	0	
Grey, Hon. Sir G. 5	0	0	
Grey, Hon. Lady 5	0	0	
Green, Mr. Penny a Week Subscription ...	7	5	
Griffin, Rev. John 1	1	6	
Guyer, Mr....1	1	0	
Howard, Mr. ...1	1	0	
Hammond, Mr. ...1	1	0	
Jackson, Mr. E....5	5	0	
Jones, Mr. ...1	0	0	
Lang, Mr. ...1	1	0	
Lang, Mrs. ...1	1	0	
Millar, Mr....1	0	0	
Mosberry, R. Esq. Subscription ...2	0	0	
Ditto, Donation ...5	0	0	
Mackie, Mr....1	1	0	
Murry, Miss ...1	0	0	
Napier, Mr. ...1	1	0	
North, Mrs....1	0	0	
Oliver, Mr. ...2	0	0	
Oliver, Mrs. Penny a Week Subscription ...6	5	0	
Santiford, Mrs. ...1	0	0	

	£	s.	d.
Shepherd, Mr.......1	0	0	
Stuart, Captain ...1	1	0	
Shoveller, Mr.......1	1	0	
White, Mr... 1	1	0	
Col. & Subscrip. 26	18	4	
————90	0	4	
Ringwood, Rev. A. Bishop and			
Friends 13	0	0	
Ryde (Isle of Wight), Rev.			
Mr. Gyer and Friends... 3	15	0	
Southampton, Rev. T. Adkins			
and Friends:			

	£	s.	d.
Collection 18	8	3	
Annual Subscrip-			
tions 47	2	0	
Subscriptions of 1d.			
per Week 10	0	0	
————75	10	3	
Titchfield, Rev. Mr. Flower &			
Friends 23	3	6	
Totton, Friends, by Mr. R.			
Davies 2	4	0	
Winchester Female Penny So-			
ciety, one quarter 2	7	0	

HEREFORDSHIRE.

Bromyard, Rev. J. Banfield and Friends	7	0	0
Eignbrook, Rev. T. Williams.................	1	0	0

HERTFORDSHIRE.

St. Albans Auxiliary Society,			
by Rev. J. Raban.........15	5	6	
Rev. J. Raban ....(a) 1	1	0	
Bishop's Stortford, Rev. Mr.			
Chaplin & Congregation 30	0	0	
Buntingford, a Friend 1	0	0	

Bushey, Rev. T. Gilbart and			
Friends 14	10	0	
Ware, Missionary Association,			
by Rev. T. Pavitt.........10	10	0	
Ditto, by Rev. G. North...10	0	0	

HUNTINGDONSHIRE.

HUNTINGDONSHIRE AUXILIARY SOCIETY.

Secretary, Rev. T. Morell.

Remittances, 1815 40	0	0			
1816 15	0	0			
1817 58	1	5			
1818 42	10	0			
			155	11	5
Kimbolton, Rev. Mr. Hogg.................(a)... 1	1	0			

KENT.

Ashford, Mr. Henry Creed... 1	1	0	
Barham Court, Lady Barham,			
1812 12	0	0	
Noel, Hon. C. ....(a) 5	0	0	
Blackheath, Mr. T. Shipman,			
1817 10	10	0	
Canterbury Auxiliary			
Society, by Rev.			
Mr. Gurteen...15	0	0	
Juvenile Ditto ...10	0	0	
————25	0	0	
Friends at a Prayer Meet. 2	0	0	
J. S. and A. K................ 2	2	0	
Chatham Auxiliary Society, by			
Mr. Higgins, Treasurer 22	0	0	
Sunday School, by Messrs.			
Higgins and Hopkins ... 5	15	7	

Hopkins, Mr. Thomas...... 1	1	0	
Brock, Mr. W. ....(a) 1	1	0	
Brock, Mr. E ....(a) 1	1	0	
Moggeridge, Lieut. 10	0	0	
Slatterie, Rev. Mr. ...(a) 1	1	0	
Dartford, a few Friends, by			
Mr. Jennings 4	0	0	
Deal, Religious Conversation			
Society 4	0	0	
Deptford, Mrs. Jewett's Unit-			
ed Friends' Mission. Box 1	7	6	
Deptford, Young, Captain (a) 1	1	0	
Dover Branch Society, by			
Rev. Mr Mather:			
Subscriptions ...17	0	0	
A few Girls of the			
Sunday School...0	4	6	

	£	s.	d.
-Moule, Mr. T. ...1 0 0			
————18	4	6	
W. T............................ 1 0 0			
Eltham, collected by Messrs.			
Smith & Wright 3 9 7			
Smith, Mr. 1 1 0			
———— 4	10	7	

	£	s.	d.
Gravesend, Rev. Mr. Kent &			
Friends :			
A few Monthly			
Subscribers ...18 0 0			
A few Children			
weekly 5 2 6			
Lark, Mr. E. 1 1 0			
————24	3	6

GREENWICH and DEPTFORD AUXILIARY SOCIETY.

Treasurer—Mr. John Dyer.

Secretary—Rev. W. Chapman.

	£	s.	d.
Greenwich-road Chapel, Rev. W. Chapman 25	5	5¼
East-lane Meeting, Rev. G. Scott 17	6	6½
Mr. Venner's School 4	1	5¼
Butt-lane Meeting, Rev. Mr. Barker.............................17	8	8
————64	2	1

	£	s.	d.
Maidstone, Alexander, Mr.			
1804 50	0	0
Margate, Cobb, Mr 1804 ...10	10	0
Monkton, near Margate, by			
Rev. T. Young............ 1	8	0.
Ramsgate, Rev. G. Townsend			
and Congregation.........17	17	6
Rochford, Pattison, Mr. J.			
1796 10	0	0
Sutton Valence, Rev. J. Roaf			
and Friends :			
Penny a Week So-			
ciety 13	19	10
Sun. Sch. Children 2	4	0
Donations of young			
Friends 2	10	0
————18	13	10
Tunbridge, by Rev. T. Lewis :			
Collection............3	7	8
Five Children, One			
Halfpenny per			
week, (Wells) ...0	10	10

	£	s.	d.
Beeching, Mr 1	0	0
Blundell, Mr. 1	0	0
Cressey, Mr. 3	0	0
Luckhurst, Mr. ...1	0	0
———— 9	18	6
Tunbridge Wells, at Rev. Mr.			
Finley's :			
Collection, (1817) 16	13	0
Gough, Rev Mr....4	0	0
Annual Subscriptions.			
Finlay, Rev. Mr. 1	1	0
Dickenson, Mr. S. 1	1	0
Dickenson, Mr. D. 1	1	0
————23	16	0
Woolwich, Rev. J. Bickerdike			
and Congregation......... 6	6	0
Bickerdike, Rev. J.......(a) 1	1	0
Percy, Rev. J. and Con-			
gregation 11	9	6
Parker, Dr. ....(a) 1	1	0
Twiss, Colonel, 1796 10	10	0

LANCASHIRE.

LANCASHIRE AUXILIARY SOCIETY.

Treasurer—Mr. J. H. Heron.

Secretary—Rev. W. Roby.

	£	s.	d.
Remittances, 1815.............................1143	3	6
1816............................. 940	9	10
1817............................. 747	0	0
1818............................. 686	13	2
———— 3517	6	6

	£	s.	d.
Liverpool Branch Society, by			
Mr. John Job			
Bolton, R. Esq. ....(D) 5	0	0
G. Mr. by the Rev. R.			
Philip ....(D) 1	0	0
Lucas, Mr. H..............(D) 1	1	0
Viner, Mr.W...............(D) 1	0	0
Shallcross, Mr. T. ......(D) 1	0	0
Ford, Mrs. Jane.. .....(D) 1	1	0
Job, Mr. John ....(A) 1	0	0

	£	s.	d.
Edwards, Mr. W. ......(A) 1	0	0
Kirk, Mr. George ......(A) 1	1	0
Joynson, Mrs.............(A) 1	1	0
Collection at Bethesda Cha-			
pel, Rev. P. S. Charrier .9	19	9
Weekly Sub.byMissDutton 3	1	8
Young Ladies at MrsFord's 0	7	0
A few Boys at Great			
George Street . Sunday			
School, by Mr. J.Bourne 2	13	0

	£	s.	d.
Collection at the Annual Meeting at Liverpool.			
Pall-mall & Bedford-street Chapel 17		6	6
Gloucester-street Chapel...25		0	0
Newington Ditto 40		1	0
Bethesda Ditto 40		17	0
GreatGeorge-street Ditto	100	1	2
	253	11	1
Saint Helen, from the Rev. J. Sharp and Friends 20		0	0
Rochdale, from the Rev. J.Ely and Friends 10		19	0
From Sunday School Child.	1	8	2
North Meols Branch Society per Mr. Linaker	6	5	6
Rainford Sunday School, and Friends, by Rev. J. Toothall......................	5	0	0
Darwin, from the Rev. J. Townsend and Friends	2	10	0
From the Box in the Brig Albion, of Lywinlyn, per Mr. Davies, of Cardigan	2	12	6
Donation fromMr.J.Davis, a Welch Seaman	1	0	0
A Friend by Mr. Charrier	1	0	0
Wigan, per the Rev. A. Steil. Penny per Week Society...	7	7	1
Collection at Ann. Sermon	13	2	3

	£	s.	d.
Mr. Melling 1811	10	0	0
Darwin, from the Rev. R. Blake and Friends 15		10	0
Haslingden, Rev. P. Ramsay and Friends	2	5	0
Park Chapel, Rev. G. Partington and Friends	2	0	0
Patricroft, Rev. J. Adamson and Friends, a Thank Offering for an abundant Harvest	4	3	0
Clifton, from Friends there...	2	6	0
Mr. Hodgkinson, of Elswick, by the Rev. D. Edwards, of Ditto	1	1	0
Manchester, Rev. W. Roby & Congregation 101		14	3
Manchester Praying Society, Moseley-street	6	0	0
Warrington, Subscriptions per Rev. Mr. Hay 22		4	7
Ditto, by Rev. J. Smedley	4	15	0
Mr. Spear, for a balance of £1 3s. 3d. due from Mill Bank Miss. Association	5	0	0
Bamford Branch, by Rev. J. Grey	6	10	0
Domestic Servant at Mr. J. Fenton's	1	0	0
Remittances............686		13	2

	£	s.	d.
Blackburn, St. Paul's Church, Rev. Mr. Price............30		0	0
Lancaster, Inman, Mr.... (A)	2	0	0
Latchford, near Warrington, for the Lascar Mission, by Miss Allix 20		0	0
Preston Auxiliary Society, by Mr. Hamer, Treasurer. Contributions 71		18	10

	£	s.	d.
Sunday School......1		8	0
Prayer Meeting ...1		19	3
Missionary Box, by Rev. E. Chadwick 0		14	6
Garstang Branch, Mr. Kilshaw ...10		7	0
	86	7	7
Wigan, Melling, Mr. 1811...10		0	0

LEICESTERSHIRE.

LEICESTERSHIRE, DERBYSHIRE, AND NOTTINGHAMSHIRE AUXILIARY MISSIONARY SOCIETY.

Treasurer—Mr. Joseph Nunneley.

Secretary—Rev. J. Alliot.

Remittances, 1815	164	9	2
1816	260	12	2
1817	217	5	2
	642	6	6

	£	s.	d.
Newton Burgoland Sun. School, by Rev. Mr. Ludford ...	4	0	0
Barker Gate, Nottingham, by Rev. Mr. Butcher	6	13	7
Sion Chapel, Nottingham, Rev. Mr. Bryan	5	0	0
Castle Gate, Nottingham, Rev. Mr. Alliot 20		0	0

	£	s.	d.
Congregation, Castle Dennington,Leicestershire...	4	17	6
Belper Male Association 18		4	1½
Ditto Female ditto 10		6	6
Matlock, Rev. J. Wilson	2	0	0
Ditto Penny a Week Subscription, by Miss Wilson	8	14	0

	£	s	d.
Kibworth Congregation, Leicestershire, by Rev. E. Chater	10	0	0
Ashby de la Zouch, by Rev. G. Gouter, penny a week	5	18	6
Bond Street, *Leicester*	10	0	0
Lutterworth Congregation, by Rev. Mr. Hartley	15	0	0
A Friend, for the South African Mission, by Mr. Atherstone	1	1	0
Juvenile Missionary Society, Nottingham, by R. Alliot and C. Thunman, Secretaries	1	3	6
Missionary Box at Miss Cullen's School, Nottingham	1	5	6

	£	s.	d.
Bosworth, Congregation, by Rev. Mr. Mortimer	1	10	0
Cadby, *near Bosworth*, by Mr. Burton	1	0	0
Bosworth Sunday School	0	6	8
Moorgram and Ilkestone, Nottinghamshire, Congregations	6	10	0
Ashbourne Congregation	4	0	0
Mansfield Congregation	11	0	0
Letstone Congregation	2	0	0
Derby Sunday School	0	10	8½
Children at Miss Dawson's School, Derby	0	15	0
Collections at the Annual Meetings, Derby, April 8 & 9	69	8	7¼
	217	5	2¾

LINCOLNSHIRE.

BRIGG AUXILIARY SOCIETY.

Treasurer—Mr W. Goodwin.

Secretary—Rev. Mr. Miles.

	£	s.	d.
Collections at the General Meeting	40	11	0
Penny Subscriptions collected by young Ladies	24	14	0
Sunday School Children	3	12	0
	68	17	0

	£	s.	d.
Gainsborough Auxiliary Society, by Mr. Tidd, Treasurer	24	14	6

	£	s.	d.
Grimsby, Rev. Mr. Smelle and Friends	5	0	0
Juvenile Society, by Ditto	2	0	0

LINCOLN AUXILIARY SOCIETY.

Treasurer—Mr. J. Lupton.

Secretary—Rev. Mr. Gladstone.

	£	s.	d.
At Lincoln Annual Meeting	38	5	6
Annual Subscription	13	11	6
Weekly, by Miss Fluker	0	14	0
Ditto, Miss Lowrie	4	2	0
Children of the Sunday School	0	8	2
Donations	8	14	0
Contributions at Sleaford, by Rev. Mr. Keyworth	8	19	9
Ditto, by Do. at Helpringham	3	8	9
	78	3	8
Pinchbeck, Rev. M. Woodward and Friends	6	12	0

MIDDLESEX.

NORTH MIDDLESEX AND HERTS AUXILIARY SOCIETY.

Treasurer—Mr. W. Radley.

Secretary—Rev. W. Thomas.

Enfield, by Rev. W. Thomas:—			
Adams, Mrs	1	0	0
Addis, Mrs	6	10	0
Bagnall, Mr. T.	1	1	0
Burgoyne, Master	0	10	6
Barber, Mrs.	1	1	0
Baylis, Mr.	2	0	0
B. W.	1	1	0
Child, Mr.	0	10	0
Chubb, Mrs.	0	12	0

Cradock, Mrs	1	1	0
Fauntleroy, Mr.	0	10	0
Fauntleroy, Mrs.	0	10	0
James, Rev. J. Cheshunt Col.	1	0	0
Lachlan, Mr. R.	0	10	0
Mountague, Mrs.	0	10	0
Mummery, Rev. S.	0	10	6
Padman, Mr.	1	1	0
Pupils of Rev. W. Thomas	1	6	6
Phillips, Rev. Mr. Maurice	1	1	0

	£	s.	d.
Ross, Captain	0	10	6
Ross, Mrs.	0	10	6
Radley, Mr.	2	2	0
Radley, Mrs.	1	1	0
Radley, Miss	1	1	0
Radley, Mr. John	1	1	0
Radley, Mrs. J.	1	1	0
Stallwood, Mr.	1	1	0
Shave, Mr.	0	10	6
Sloman, Mr S.	1	0	0
Sloman, Mr. T.	1	1	0
Thomas, Rev. William	1	1	0
Thomas, Mr. W.	0	10	6
Thomas, Miss	0	10	6
Weston, Mr.	1	1	0
Small Subscriptions	1	13	6
	32	1	6

Enfield, by Rev. W. Brown.

	£	s.	d.
Brown, Rev.W.	0	10	6
Baker Street Missionary Association	11	6	0
	11	16	6

PondersEnd, by Rev. J.Knight.

	£	s.	d.
Mrs. Barnjum's young Ladies	1	0	0
Work People of Messrs. Baylis & Co	3	10	2
Knight, Rev. J.	0	10	0
Mears, Mr. W.	0	10	0
Penny a Week Subscriptions	0	14	1
Workmen of Mr. Walls, & Sundries.	0	14	2
	6	18	5

Enfield, by Rev. W. Macdonald :

	£	s.	d.
Macdonald, Rev. W.	0	10	6

	£	s.	d.
Produce of 7 Months' 1d. a Week Subscription at Lady Huntingdon's Chapel, Chase-side	20	1	5
	20	11	11

Cheshunt, by Rev. F. Weybridge.

	£	s.	d.
Crisp, Mrs.	0	10	6
Gentry, Mr.	0	10	6
Gething, Mr.	1	0	0
Moore, Miss	4	0	0
Miss. Prayer Meeting	1	0	7
Sunday School	0	8	6
Weybridge, Rev. F.	1	1	0
Small Subscriptions	4	4	4
	12	15	5

Barnet, by Rev. J. Morison.

	£	s.	d.
Courtnall, Mr.	0	12	0
Hampstead, Mrs.	0	12	0
Hopewell, Mr.	1	1	0
Millson, Mr. for 2 years	1	16	9
Morison, Rev. John	1	1	0
Page, Mr.	1	1	0
Popstring, Mr.	1	0	0
White, Mr.	1	1	0
White, Mrs.	0	10	0
Small Subscriptions	4	12	4
	13	7	1

	£	s.	d.
Southgate, by Rev.W. Lloyd.	13	13	0
Collection at Annual Meeting, at Enfield, after a Sermon by Dr. Collyer	27	13	10
Ditto at the Meeting for Business	5	0	6
	32	14	4
Total	143	18	2

HAMPSTEAD AUXILIARY MISSIONARY SOCIETY.

Treasurer—Mrs. Phillips.

Secretary—Miss Phillips.

	£	s.	d.
Collected at One Penny per Week, by Mr. R. Dixon	3	3	11
Ditto Ditto, by Miss Evans	2	10	0
Ditto Dito, by Miss Reed	1	11	0
Ditto Do. by Miss Stratton	1	8	3
	8	13	2

Collected by the Children of the Sunday School.

Tillyard, Eliza	2	16	2

	£	s.	d.
Nobbs, Eliza	1	18	0
Mason, Mary	1	10	0
Stanmore, Christiana	1	18	0
Partridge. Mary	1	0	0
Peacock, Mary	0	12	0
Haxt, Jane	0	14	0
	10	8	2
Donations	1	17	0
Collected after two Sermons	12	19	10
	33	18	2

	£	s.	d.
Edmonton Penny Society, by			
Miss Warton, Treasurer	11	7	6
Mr. Knowles, 1796	10	10	0
Enfield, Pink, Mr. ......(a)	1	1	0
Feltham, Collection at the			
Chapel School	2	0	4
Hammersmith, Hall, Mrs.			
1815	10	10	0
Scott, Mr. G. 1806	10	0	1
Page, Mr. ......(a)	1	1	0
Hayes Penny Society, by Mr.			
J. Hunt	4	6	8
Mill Hill, Rev. Mr. Phillips			
and Congregation			
Lewis, Mr. A. ......(a)	1	1	0

	£	s.	d.
Thornton, Mr. ......(a)	1	1	0
Thornton, Miss......(a)	1	1	0
Wilson, Mr. ......(a)	1	1	0
Small Sums	1	16	0
Mr. Thorowgood's School	3	0	0
Ponder's End, Walker, Misses (a)	1	1	0
Staines Auxiliary Society, by			
Rev. Mr. Yockney	13	2	0
Croucher, Mr. 1800	20	0	0
Winchmore Hill, Monthly Sub-			
scriptions, by Rev. Mr.			
Humpage	7	0	0
Uxbridge, Rev. G. Redford &			
Friends :			
Annual Collection	37	0	0

MONMOUTHSHIRE.

	£	s.	d.
Pontypool, J. W.	5	0	0
Usk, Hughes, Mr. Thomas ......(a)	5	5	0

NORFOLK.

	£	s.	d.
Foulsham Penny Society, by			
Mr. Fidgett	4	16	0
Guestwick Penny Subscriptions,			
by Miss Sykes	22	19	0
Ditto & Bristow, Rev. J. Sykes			
and Friends	11	17	7
Harleston Auxiliary Society,			
by Rev. T. Fisher :			
Crisp, Mrs. M. ...2 0 0			
Crisp, Mrs. S.......1 1 0			
Devereux, Mr. J. 0 10 6			
Fisher, Rev. T. ...1 1 0			
Lenny, Mrs. D. ...0 10 6			
Pratt, Mr. J. 1 1 0			
Pratt, Mr. W.......1 1 0			

	£	s.	d.
Weekly Subscriptions by			
Crisp, Miss M. ...6 1 8			
Crisp, Miss E.......5 13 4			
	19	0	0
Hindringham Penny Collec-			
tions, by Miss Cook	2	2	0
Lynn Missionary Prayer			
Meeting, Rev. J. Arrow	5	2	0
Norwich Auxiliary Society,			
by Rev. J. Butcher	14	9	0
Old Meeting Missionary			
Fund, Rev. Mr. Hull	30	0	0
Doman, Mr. J. ...1817	10	0	0
Yarmouth Penny Society, Lady			
Huntingdon's Chapel, by			
Rev. G. Steward	6	6	2

NORTHAMPTONSHIRE.

	£	s.	d.
Northamptonshire Association of Independent Ministers, by Mr.			
Inkersole, Treasurer	144	4	1

	£	s.	d.
Cottesbrook, a few Friends, by			
Mr. Jesse Hobson	2	6	0
Hargrave, Rev. J. Longmire,			
A.M. ......(a)	1	0	0

	£	s.	d.
Weedon-Beck Penny Society,			
by Mr. W. Warren,			
Treasurer	5	0	0

NORTHUMBERLAND.

	£	s.	d.
Berwick, Tweedmouth, and			
Spital Union Fellowship			
Meeting, by Rev. Mr.			
Balme	10	0	0
Burns, Mr. Andrew......(a)	1	1	0

	£	s.	d.
Sanderson, Mr. John ...(a)	2	2	0
Hexham, Rev. Mr.			
Scott, by Rev. G.			
Collison	5	0	0
Auxiliary Society	1	11	6
	6	11	6

NEWCASTLE AUXILIARY SOCIETY.

*Treasurer—*Mr. Thomas Bonner.

*Secretary—*Mr. W. Fenwick.

	£	s.	d.		£	s.	d.
Remittances, 1814	94	8	9				
1815	70	0	0				
1816	100	0	0				
1817	95	11	5				
1818	114	2	7¼	474	2	9¼	

	£	s.	d.
Collection at Postern New Chapel, by Rev. Mr. Collison	11	15	0
Ditto at Silver-street Chapel, by Rev. Mr. Jackson	6	2	10½
Ditto at High Bridge Chapel, by ditto	4	2	3½
Ditto at Wall Knoll Chapel, by ditto	1	15	6
Ditto at Gateshead Chapel, by Rev. Mr. Collison	11	3	6
Ditto at Tuthil Stairs Chapel, by ditto	6	0	0
Ditto at General Meeting, Fletcher's long Room	7	3	4½
Collections after the Quarterly Missionary Lectures during the Year	9	1	2¾
Ditto at Monthly Prayer Meetings ditto	11	12	8

Subscriptions.

	£	s.	d.
Atkinson, Mr.	0	10	6
Angus, Mr. J. L.	1	1	0
Andrew, Mr.	0	10	6
Aydon, Messrs.	1	4	0
Brunton's, Mr. B. Executors	1	1	0
Bankier, Mr.	0	10	6
Bonner, Mr. T	1	11	6
Bonner, Hannah	0	10	6

	£	s.	d.
Colhoun, Mr.	1	1	0
Colhoun, Miss	0	12	0
Davison, Rev. R.	0	10	0
Fenwick, Mr. J.	0	10	6
Fairweather, Mr.	1	1	0
Glaholm, Mr. T.	0	10	0
Harvey, Mr. J.	1	1	0
Haggie, Mr. D.	1	1	0
Humble, Mr. T.	0	10	0
Hebron, Mr. R.	0	10	0
Johnson, Mr. C.	0	10	0
Moffett, Mr. T.	0	10	0
Robinson, Mr. D	1	1	0
Sillick, Mrs.	0	10	0
Smith, Rev. J	0	10	6
Scotland, Mr.	1	0	0
Todd, Mr. T.	1	1	0
Turnbull, Rev. R.	0	10	6
Wake, Mr. R.	1	1	0
Wawn, Mr.	1	1	0
Sundry small Sums below 10s.	5	6	8
Ditto additional	0	9	0
Newcastle-upon-Tyne Missionary Association of Young Men	11	9	6
Ditto Female Missionary Association	6	0	0
	114	2	7¼

	£	s.	d.
Newcastle, by Rev. Dr. M‘Indoe	3	7	6
Parkhead, Rev. Mr. Haddock, by Rev. G. Collison	3	2	4
North Shields, Rev. M. Cochraine, by ditto	4	19	6
Tweedmouth, Mr. A. Burns (a)	1	1	0

	£	s.	d.
Wooler Auxiliary Society, by Mr. W. Jobson : Subscriptions	22	13	10
Collections at a Prayer Meeting at Fowbury	1	14	0
	24	7	10

NOTTINGHAMSHIRE

		£	s.	d.
Long Cottingham, Rev. J. Clarke and Friends		4	0	0

(Vide Leicestershire)

OXFORDSHIRE

	£	s.	d.
Banbury, Young Ladies at Mrs. Drury's Seminary, and a few other Friends, by Rev. C. Hubbard	8	8	0
Benson, Weekly Subscriptions by Mr. R. Butler	1	16	4

	£	s.	d.
Bicester, a Society of Friends, by Rev. R. Fletcher	4	6	0
Peppard, Rev. Mr. Walker & Friends	4	0	0
Oxford, Mayow, Mr. (a)	1	1	0
Collingwood, Mr. S. (a)	1	1	0

RUTLANDSHIRE.

	£	s.	d.		£	s.	d.
Oakham Missionary Association, by Rev. G. Foster	10	0	0	Bell, Mrs. ....(a)	1	1	0
				Friend, by Mr. Jelley......	1	1	0
Uppingham, a few Friends, by Rev. J. Green	7	0	0	Kemp, Mr. E. ....(a)	1	1	0

SHROPSHIRE.

	£	s.	d.		£	s.	d.
Ludlow, Rev. Mr. Francis & Congregation	6	12	0	Jones, Mr. L........	1	1	0
Newport, Sun. School, by Misses Silvester and Mr. Croucher 5 12 0				Jones, Mr. T.......	1	0	0
				Kemp, Mr. H.......5	5	5	0
				Lee, J. Esq..........1	1	1	0
Penny Society, by Mr. Markland...4 0 0				Lewin, Mr..........1	1	1	0
Young Ladies of Misses Bullock's Seminary 2 0 0				Olney, Mr..........1	1	1	0
				Parry, Mr. Josiah 1	0	0	0
				Pidduck, Mr. T. ...1	0	0	0
		11 12	0	Weaver, Rev. T....2	2	2	0
Oswestry Auxiliary Society, by Rev. J. Whitridge ...20 0 0				Wilding, Mr. W. 0	10	6	
				Williams, Mr. P. 1	1	1	0
Shrewsbury Auxiliary Society, by Rev. T, Weaver :				Wilson, Mr. J. ...1	0	0	0
				Woodall, Mr. J....0	10	10	6
Blunt, Mr. 1 1 0				Sums under 10s 6d 11	9	9	0
Blunt, Mr.R. jun. 0 10 6							
Cooke, Mr. T. sen. 1 1				*Donations.*			
Cooke, Misses......0 10 6				A Friend, by Rev. T. Weaver 5 0 0			
Craig, J. Esq. 1 1 0							
Deakin, Mr. H. ...1 1 0				Swan Hill Sun.Sch. Boys in ditto ...2 8 0			
Ford, Mr. J. 1 0 0				Ditto, Girls in do. 1 8 3			
Gittins, J. Esq. ...1 1 0				Juv. Mis. Assoc. by Mr. F. Evans 44 5 2			
Gittins, Mr. W. ...1 1 0							
Gittins, Mr. J. ...1 1 0						93 13	5
Gittins, Miss 0 10 6				*Whitchurch*, Rev J. Harris :			
Hiles, Mr. J. 0 10 6				Juvenile Auxiliary, half a year 9 0 0			
James, Mr. T.......1 1 0				Ladies' Pen. Soc. 3 0 0			
						12 0	0

SOMERSETSHIRE.

	£	s.	d.		£	s.	d.
Bath, British and Foreign Mission. Society, by Mr. Evill, Secretary 100 0 0				Davies, Rev. Dr..........(a)	1	1	0
				Gage, Mrs. ....1811...150	0	0	0
Bath,Collected by Miss Smith:				Ditto....................1816...200	0	0	0
Sunday School at Lady Huntingdon's Chapel ...5 12 9				Haweis, Rev. Dr. 1796...500	0	0	0
				Ditto....................1799... 50	0	0	0
Several Ladies ...12 0 0				Ditto....................1800...100	0	0	0
Haweis, Master & Miss..............1 1 0				Ditto.................1804... 45	0	0	0
				Ditto....................1816...500	0	0	0
Smith,Miss, Kingsmead..............1 0 0				Jacques, Mrs.......1812... 10	0	0	0
				Pearson, Mrs.......1814... 10	0	0	0
		19 13	9	Preston, Mrs.......1813... 10	0	0	0
				Breese, Mrs. ....(a)... 10	0	0	0
				Ford, Mrs. ....(a)... 2	2	2	0
Breese, Mrs. E. ...1814... 50 0 0				Sone, Mrs. ....(a)... 1	1	1	0
				Snook, Mr. ....(a)... 1	0	0	0

BRISTOL AUXILIARY SOCIETY—Commenced 1812.

Treasurer—William Skinner.

Secretaries—Rev. W. Waite, A.M. and Rev. S. Lowell.

	£	s.	d.
Remittances, 1813.................................1174	7	0	
1814.............................. 676	9	4	
1815.............................. 625	18	2	
1816.............................. 799	9	1	
1817...... 780	11	3	
1818.............................. 649	16	1	
	4706	10	11

JUVENILE AUXILIARY SOCIETY.

Treasurer—Mr. J. Talbot.

Remittances, 1814..............................185 6 0
1815..............................233 18 8
1816..............................229 5 4
1817..............................190 16 6
1818..............................165 4 10
———1004 11 4

Branch Missionary Society, by Mr. S. Ditchett, Treasurer 51 18 0
Mr. W. Skinner, sundry Donations to the Parent Society ....:........222 10 0
Mr. J. Walcot, 1800...20 0 0
The late Miss L. Green, by Rev. Dr. Ryland................................10 0 0

SOMERSET AUXILIARY SOCIETY.

Treasurer—Mr. W. Cayme.

Remittances, 1814.............................. 70 0 0
1815...............................,.....146 10 0
1817..............................235 10 5
1818.....................:......187 15 9
———639 16 2

	£	s.	d.		£	s.	d.
Borton, St. David, Rev. W.				White, Mrs. E. ...0	10	0	
Reynolds and Congrega.	3	10	0	Subscriptions and			
Bishop's Hull, Rev. Samuel				Donations under			
Greatheed ....(a)	5	0	0	10s. 7	15	6	
Broadway, Rev. T. Pyke and					——34	5	6
Congregation...............	2	2	0				
Bruton, Congregation 5	0	0	*Fulwood,*Rev.T. Gold-			
Chard, Rev. J. Gunn and Con-				ing ....(a) 1	1	0	
gregation.				T.Welman,Esq.(a) 2	2	0	
Bowden, Miss......0	10	6	Hon. Mr. Wel-			
Coles, Mrs. 1	1	0	man............(a) 2	2	0	
Cuff, Mr. G. W....1	1	0	Mrs.J.Welman (a) 2	2	0	
Cuff, Mr. W. 1	1	0	Welman,Mrs.R (a) 2	2	0	
Cuff, Mr. T. 1	1	0	Hawker, Miss (a) 2	0	0	
Cuff, Mr J.........1	1	0	Penny a Week So-			
Cuff, Mr. R. 1	1	0	ciety, by Hon.			
Cook, Mr............0	10	0	Mrs. Welman ...2	8	0	
Collins, Mrs. ..,...1	0	0	Deposited in the			
Deane, Mr. R. ...1	0	0	MissBuncombe's			
Deane, Miss S. ...1	1	0	Mission. House 0	15	2½	
Deane, Mr. Isaac 0	10	0	Sundry small do-			
Gunn, Rev. J......1	1	0	nations 1	17	5	
James, Mrs.........1	1	0		——16	9	7½
Leach, Mr. T.......0	12	0	*Milbourn Port,* Bev. W. Paige			
Lovridge, Miss ...0	10	0	and Congregation......... 3	0	0	
Lovell, Mr..........0	10	0	*Milverton,* Rev. W. Blair and			
Quier, Miss.........0	10	6	Friends 2	0	0	
Rios, Miss 1	1	0	*Somerton,* Rev. S. Pittard and			
Rio, Mr. R. 1	1	0	Friends 2	10	0	
Rio, Mr. T..........1	1	0	*South Petherton,* Rev.			
Rice, Mrs. 0	10	0	J. Bidlake 1	1	0	
Stratton, Mrs......1	1	0	R. Toller, Esq. ...1	1	0	
Sharien, Mr. 1	1	0	J.B.Edmonds,Esq. 1	1	0	
Treasure, Mr. T...1	1	0	J. Axe, Esq. 1	1	0	
Vye, Mrs. 1	0	0	Congregation and			
Vye, Mr.............1	0	0	Friends 19	17	6	
White, Mrs. 1	1	0	Juvenile subscrip. 1	14	0	
White, Mr. J.......1	1	0		——25	15	6

	£	s.	d.
Taunton, Rev. J. & R. Tozer and Congregation, including one year's subscription of a Penny a Week Society	23	10	6
Wellington, Rev. J.H.			
Cuff 1 0 0			
Miss Collart.........1 0 0			
Congregation 6 0 0			
	8	0	0
Wells, Rev. W. Lane and Congregation, Penny a Week subscriptions 18 1 6			
Wincanton, Rev. J. Mountford and Congregation 3 0 0			

	£	s.	d.
Wivelscombe, Rev. J. Buck and Congregation, one year's subscription of Penny a Week Society ...6 7 8¼			
Sunday School, one year's subscription 1 15 9½			
Collection.............8 12 7½			
	16	16	1½
Yeovil, Rev. R. Taylor and Congregation.............18 15 0			
	187	15	9

Taunton, Mr. W. Heudebourk, 1812, Stock, 5 ℣ Cents. 100 0 0

Fairwater House, Mrs. Clarke 2 0 0

STAFFORDSHIRE.

(Vide Warwickshire Auxiliary.)

SUFFOLK.

	£	s.	d.
Beccles Branch Society, Collection at Yarmouth 8	19	4
Bury St. Edmund's, Mr. Kitchener.................................(a) 1	1	0
Hadleigh, Rev. Mr. Cox and Congregation 14	6	9
Ipswich, Mrs. Taylor ....(a) 1	1	0
H. T. by Mr. Hodson 1	0	0

Sudbury,				Ray, Rev. J. M.			
Anonymous 20	0	0		...1	1	0
Barnard, Mrs 2	0	0	Steptoe, Mr. P. Debenham			
Finch, Mr 2	0	0	...50	0	0
Gainsborough, Miss 1	0	0	Steptoe, Mr. N.			
Holman, Mr. 1	1	0	Thorpe.............1	0	0
Holman, Mr. J. 0	10	6	Tozer, Mr W. ...1	0	0
Langley, Mr. Z. Lavenham 1	1	0	Missionary Prayer Meeting.........12	13	3
Mayhew, Mr. T. 2	2	0		95	8	9

Trimley, near Ipswich, Rev. J. Julian, M. A. ....(a) 1 1 0

Wickhambrook, Rev. S. Johnson 9 0 0

SURREY.

Balham, Mr. J. Powell......(a) 1	1	0
Clapham, Anderson, Mr.R. (a) 1	1	0
Phillips, Rev. Mr. ...... (a) 1	1	0
Rogers, Mr. Thos. 1818 ...10	10	0
Stephens, Mr. J....1807 ...10	10	0
Ditto...............1816 ...21	0	0
Batten, Mr. ....(a) 1	1	0
Burrup, Mr. ....(a) 1	1	0
Wilson, Mr. J. B. ....(a) 5	5	0
Ditto...................1818 ...50	0	0
Dorking Mis. Association, by Rev. Mr. Whitehouse ...11	0	0
Collection by Rev. T. Lewis.........8	2	0
A Friend, by Rev. MrWhitehouse 10	0	0
Mr. T. Curtis (a) 1	1	0
	30	3	0

Epsom, Rev. Mr. Atkinson's Collection, by Rev. T. Lewis 6	0	0
Epsom and Ewell Penny Society, 2 quarters 2	15	3
Rev. Mr. Atkinson's Pupils 0	14	4
	9	9	7
Farnham Auxiliary Society, by Rev. J. Johnson 14	0	0
Collection by Rev. T. Lewis 7	0	0
Collection by Rev. J. Johnson and Friends 7	0	0
	28	0	0

	£	s.	d.
Godalming, a few Friends at Hart's Lane, by Mr. J.			
Limbert	3	9	0
Miss E. Cooke ....(a)	1	1	0
Guildford, Rev S. Percy & Cong......17 2 8			
Weekly Subscriptions by do......15 0 0			
Collection by Rev. T. Lewis 8 15 0			
Mr. T. Haydon (a) 1 1 0			
	41	18	8
Hascomb, near Godalming, a Friend	1	0	0
Kingston Auxiliary Society, by Mr. C. Schofield	33	15	6

	£	s.	d.
Leatherhead, Young Gentlemen at Mr. Burrell's School	2	0	0
Mitcham, Mitcham Cottage, Rev. C. E. De Coetlogan	5	0	0
Mortlake Auxiliary Society, by Mr. J Frampton......	6	0	0
Reigate Penny Society, by a few young Ladies, at the Boarding School of Mrs. Burt and Miss Mason ...	4	19	6
Tooting Penny Society, by Rev. J. Tozer	11	0	0
Walton upon Thames, Mr. S. Nightingale ....(a)	1	1	0
Wandsworth, Rev. Mr. Elvey and Friends	15	11	6

SUSSEX.

Brighton, Ladies' Auxiliary Society at Rev. Dr. Styles's Chapel :—			
By Miss Penfold, Treas....30 0 0			
Mr. C. Bond, 1813 ....10 10 0			
Chichester, Rev. Mr. Hunt &			

Congregation	30	0	0
Mr. J. C. Haller ....(a)	1	1	0
East Grinstead, Rev. Mr. Start and Congregation	5	15	1
Heathfield, Rev. Mr. Press & Congregation...............	11	10	6

LEWES.

Old Chapel Juvenile Society, by Rev. J. Kerby	5	0	0

TABERNACLE JUVENILE SOCIETY.

(Established Nov. 6, 1817.—Collected from that Date to March 25, 1818.

MALE BRANCH.

Treasurer, Mr. Henry Hilton.

Secretary—Mr. James Inskip.

Weekly Subscriptions...	5	16	1			
Donations	2	2	6			
				7	18	7

FEMALE BRANCH.

Treasurer—Elizabeth Penfold.

Secretary—Eliza Button.

Weekly Subscriptions	12	5	10			
Donations...	1	3	6			
Missionary Box in a Drawing-room.......................	0	16	2			
				14	5	6
				22	4	1

WARWICKSHIRE.

WARWICKSHIRE, STAFFORDSHIRE, AND WORCESTERSHIRE AUXILIARY MISSIONARY SOCIETY.

Treasurer—Mr. J. Dickenson.

Secretary—Rev. Mr. James.

Remittances,	1816	913	4	9			
	1817	946	3	8			
	1818	735	0	2			
					2594	8	7

	£	s.	d.
Warwick, Rev. J. W. Percy and Congregation.........16		1	0
Coventry, Rev. J. Jerrard and Congregation.................20		0	0
Friends near Coventry, by Mr. Jerrard 3		13	0
Birmingham, late Rev. J. Brewer :			
Livery-street Collection............94	3	6	
Boys' Sun. School 7	18	4	
Girls' ditto 5	0	11	
Ladies at Miss Cope's School ...5	5	0	
————112	7	7	
Rev. J. A. James :			
Carr's-lane Collection 53	9	6	
Subscriptions 41	9	1	
Boys' Sun. School 8	3	1	
Girls' ditto........ 3	15	9	
————106	17	5	
Rev. T. Bennett :			
King-street Collection............21	14	8	
Boys' Sun. School 8	1	9	
Girls' ditto......... 2	3	6	
Branch Society ...8	18	10	
————40	18	9	
Atherstone, Rev. Mr. C. Miller and Congregation ...14		0	0
Foleshill, Rev. N. Rowton and Congregation 13		13	0
Nuneaton, Zion Chapel......... 7		0	0
Chapel End, Rev. J. Dagley and Congregation 5		10	0
Leamington, Rev. Mr. Bermiley and Congregation ... 3		0	0
Donation by the Rev. Mr. Bermiley 1		0	0
Bulkington, Rev. Mr. Sheffield and Congregation 3		0	0
Kenilworth, a few Friends...... 2		3	0
Bedworth, Rev. J. Dix and Congregation 8		8	0
Walsall, Rev. T. Grove and Congregation 52		4	0

	£	s.	d.
Tutbury Branch Society, Rev. B. Brook......................36		5	6
West Bromwich, Rev. J. Hudson and Congregation ...22		7	4
Rev. J. Cooper and Congregation 17		7	4
Wolverhampton Branch Society, Rev. T. Scales ...21		3	4
Uttoxeter Branch Society, per James Bell, Esq.......... 37		2	9
Stafford, Rev. J. Chalmers and Congregation 10		10	0
Lichfield, Rev. W. Salt and Congregation................15		1	0
Stone, Rev. Mr. Williams and Congregation 12		13	0
Alton, Rev. J. Tallis and Friends 2		8	0
Cannock, Rev. J Butteux and Friends 4		6	8
Rugeley, Rev. A. Shanzen and Friends 1		3	0
Hope Chapel, Shelton, Rev. W. Farmer 4		0	0
Cheadle, Sunday School 2		12	0
Gornall, Rev. T. Heathcote and Friends 4		4	0
Breewood and Aston, Rev. Mr. Firnie 6		2	2
Handsworth, Rev. J. Hammond, Collection.........6	6	6	
Rev. J Hammond's School 3	13	6	
————10	0	0	
Worcester, Angel-street Collection..........................50		0	0
Kidderminster, Rev. Y. Helmare and Congregation 30		0	0
Stourbridge, Rev. J. Richards and Congregation.........21		1	4
Dudley, Rev. J. Dawson and Congregation................12		16	0
Lye Waste, Mission. Society 3		0	0
The Young Ladies at Meridan School 1		1	0
	735	0	2

		£	s.	d.
Birmingham, a Friend 21			0	0
Mansfield, Miss 1810......10			0	0
Rugby, Leigh, Sir E. 1796...50			0	0
Ditto, ...1797...20			0	0
Leigh, Lady.........1797...10			0	0

WESTMORELAND.

	£	s.	d.
Kendall, Collection by Rev. Messrs. Collison and Jackson 7	17	6	
Auxiliary Society 10	0	0	
	17	17	6

WILTSHIRE.

	£	s.	d.
Devizes, Rev. Messrs. Sloper and Elliott and Cong.	25	8	9
Frome, Rook-lane Meeting, Subscriptions of a few Friends, by Rev. Mr. Sibree	15	0	0
Hindon, Sun. School Teachers, by Mr. T. B. Sims, Secretary	1	15	0

	£	s.	d.
Salisbury, Society in aid of the Missions, per Rev. A. S. Sleigh	15	0	0
Startley, *Redborn*, and *Corston*, by Rev. S. Pitt	3	0	0
Wilton, Rev. J. Bristow and Congregation	10	0	0

WORCESTERSHIRE.

	£	s.	d.
Blockley, Wilkes, Mr. ......(a)	1	0	0
Peyton, Miss ....(a)	1	1	0
Evesham, Charlett, Mr. R. B. 1817	10	0	0
Pershore, Mr. Brown ......(a)	1	1	0

	£	s.	d.
Worcester, Auxiliary Society, by Rev. Mr. Lake	15	0	0
A Friend, by ditto	5	0	0
Gamage, Mrs............ (a)	1	1	0
Roberts, Mrs.	1	1	0
Smyth, Mr. G. .... (a)	1	1	0

YORKSHIRE.

HULL AND EAST RIDING AUXILIARY SOCIETY.

Treasurer—Mr. James S. Bowden.

Secretaries—Rev. J. Gilbert and Mr. W. Bowden.

		£	s.	d.
Remittances,	1814	316	11	3
	1815	321	8	7
	1816	361	2	9
	1817	292	19	1
	1818	276	18	1
		1568	19	9

Collections at Hull.

	£	s.	d.
At the Rev. Mr. Gilbert's Chapel, by Rev. Messrs. Townsend, Thorpe, and Leifchild	88	1	4
At the Rev. Mr. Morley's Chapel, by Ditto Ditto	70	14	0
At the Wesleyan Methodist Chapel, by Rev. Mr. Thorpe	13	13	6
At the Rev. Mr. Birt's (Baptist) Chapel, by Rev. Mr. Townsend...	7	10	0
At the Public Meeting	9	14	3

Collections at Beverley.

	£	s.	d.
At the Rev. Mr. Mather's Chapel, by Rev. Mr. Leifchild	29	13	3
Beverley Juvenile Society, Rev. Mr. Mather	27	15	4

Weekly Subscriptions.

	£	s.	d.
South Cave, by Rev. Mr. Tapp	3	16	1
Swanland, by the Rev. David Williams	3	3	0
Ellerby, by Mrs. Curlin	1	18	4
Paul, by Mrs. Sanderson	0	3	3

Annual Subscriptions.

	£	s.	d.
Hull, Bowden, Mr. W.	2	2	0
Bowden, Mr. J. S.	2	2	0
Briggs, Mr. W.	2	2	0
Briggs, Mr. R.	1	1	0
Briggs, Mr. J. B.	1	1	0
Burn Mr. W.	1	1	0
Cade, Mr. W.	1	1	0
Carlile, Mr. Thomas	1	1	0
Donaldson, Mr	1	1	0
Gilbert, Rev. Mr.	1	1	0
Gilder, Mr. William	1	1	0
Gilder, Mrs.	1	1	0
Green, Mr. John	1	1	0
Irving, Mr. William	1	1	0
Lambert, Mr. W.	1	1	0
Lambert, Mrs.	1	1	0
Levett, Mr. W.	1	1	0
Levett, Mr. Robert	1	1	0
Lundie, Mr. R.	1	1	0
Nelson, Mrs	1	1	0
Newbald, Mr. Charles	1	1	0
Pexton, Mr. W.	1	1	0
Porters, Mr. James	1	1	0
Rhodes, Mr. F.	1	1	0
Riddell, Mrs. Sen.	1	1	0
Robinson, Mrs. J.	1	1	0
Rust, Mr. W.	2	2	0

	£	s.	d.
Rutherford, Mr. A..........	1	1	0
Shackles, Mr. William ..	1	1	0
Shackles, Mrs. ,........... ...	1	1	0
Tapp, Rev. W.	1	1	0
Terry, Avison; Esq..........	1	1	0
Thompson, T. Esq. M.P.	2	2	0
Thornton, Mrs...............	1	1	0
Thornton, Mr. John........	1	1	0
Todd, Mr. William	1	1	0
Todd, Mr. John	1	1	0
Towers, Mr. W. E..........	1	1	0
Trower, Mrs..................	1	1	0
Wright, Mr. G. S.	2	2	0

	£	s	d.
Wilkinson, Mr. J.	1	1	0
Watson, Mr. Samuel	1	1	0
Watson, T. & J.	1	1	0
Jas. Clark, Easter Offering	0	16	0
Small Subscriptions at Swanland, by Rev. D. Williams...................	1	4	3
A few Friends, by W. F. Towers	0	15	0
Sundry Subscriptions under 10s.	0	19	0
Remittances.........276	18	1	

HULL JUVENILE SOCIETY.

Treasurer—Mr. James Bowden, jun.

Secretaries—Mr. W. Briggs and Mr. W. Bowden, jun.

Remittances,	1813......	90	0	0
	1814......	108	13	3
	1815....................	110	9	9
	1816....................	151	16	4
	1817....................	125	0	0
	1818....................	105	0	0
		690	19	4

WEST RIDING AUXILIARY SOCIETY.

Treasurer—Mr. George Rawson.

Secretary—Rev. William Eccles.

Remittances,	1814...........................	924	9	3
	1815....................	1300	0	0
	1816....................	1600	0	0
	1817........	1432	6	10
	1818.............................	1115	18	9
		6372	14	10

Aggregate Statement of Collections and Contributions to the Auxiliary Missionar
Society for the West Riding of Yorkshire, from the Annual Meeting held at
Huddersfield, 1816, to the Annual Meeting held at Leeds, 1817.

Bingley Branch Society 10	0	0	
Bradford ditto..................20	17	4	
Brighouse ditto 8	0	0	
Cleckheaton ditto 17	16	10½	
Eastwood ditto 4	0	0	
Grafton ditto 3	7	8	
Great Ousebourn ditto............ 4	0	0	
Green Hammerton ditto......... 5	0	0	
Halifax ditto 60	0	0	
Heckmondwike (old Chapel do.) 16	14	7	
Ditto (new Chapel) 10	0	0	
Holmfirth ditto 28	0	0	
Hopton ditto 40	0	0	
Horton (in Craven do.)......... 5	4	0	
Honley ditto 12	0	0	
Huddersfield, Collections at the Annual Meeting ...206	1	10	
Idle Branch Society 8	8	9	
Kipping ditto 12	0	0	
Knaresbro' ditto 25	0	0	
Knottingley ditto................... 3	4	8½	

Leeds Branch Society.........308	6	1	
Linton ditto 1	0		
Marsden ditto 3	7	2	
Morley ditto 33	11		
Ossett ditto 12	0		
Pontifract ditto 48	19		
Pudsey ditto 7	0	0	
Rotherham ditto 68	5		
Sheffield Branch Society.			
Male Juvenile Society of Sheffield & Attercliff ...61	16	0	
Queen Street Female Society ...27	17	1	
Howard Street do. 21	6	10	
Do. Sunday Sch... 2	3	0	
Nether Chapel Female Society ...17	4	6	
Garden Street do. 15	7	0	
Attercliffe do...... 9	3	4	

	£	s.	d.
Scotland Street Female Soc. (Methodist new Connection	6	17	0
	161	14	9

The following Annual Subscribers are included in the above.

	£	s.	d.
Bennet, Mr G.	2	2	0
Browne, Mr. J.	1	1	0
Boden, Mrs. & Misses	0	13	0
Bradley, Mr John	0	12	0
Broadhurst, Mrs.	0	12	0
Butler, Miss	0	12	0
Bower, Mrs.	0	10	6
Bower, Mr. Geo.	0	10	6
Bramall, Misses	0	10	6
Butcher, Mr.	0	10	6
Cam, Miss.	0	12	0
Duff, Mr.	1	1	0
Deakin, Miss J.	1	1	0
Deakin, Miss	0	10	6
Deakin, Miss E.	0	10	6
Deakin, Miss M.	0	10	6
Deakin, Mrs. G.	0	10	6
Eels, Mrs. & Misses	0	13	0
Frith, Miss	0	10	6
Frith, Miss	0	10	6
Three Female Serv. at Miss Greaves's	0	13	0
Greaves, Miss	2	2	0
Greaves, Mr. John	0	15	0
Grayson, Miss	0	10	6
Groves, Miss	0	10	6
Hawksley, Mr.	1	1	0
Hawksley, Mrs. and Daughters	1	11	6
Hague, Mr. Thos	0	16	0

	£	s.	d.
Hind, Mrs.	0	12	0
Hortons, Misses	0	12	0
Hall, Mrs.	0	10	6
Hancock, Misses	0	10	6
Hardstaff, Mr.	0	10	6
Haywood, Miss	0	10	6
Jardine, Mr.	1	1	0
Jobson, Mrs.	0	10	6
Kay, Mrs.	0	10	6
Laycock, Miss	1	1	0
Laws, Misses	0	17	4
Mather, Rev. Jas.	0	10	6
Middleton, Mr.	0	10	6
Nell, Mrs.	0	12	0
Pickford, Mr. John	0	12	0
Parker, Miss	0	10	6
Read, Jos. Esq.	1	1	0
Read, Mrs. & Misses	1	14	8
Rook, Mrs. & Misses	1	1	0
Rowbotham, Mr.	0	12	0
Shepherd, Mrs.	0	12	0
Steer, Mrs.	0	12	0
Stones, Mr.	0	12	0
Smith, Miss	0	10	0
Thompson, Misses	0	10	6
Wilson, Mr John	2	2	0
Waso, Mr.	0	10	6
Wiley, Mrs.	0	10	6

	£	s.	d.
Shipton Branch Society	2	15	2
Stainland ditto	4	6	0¼
Small Subscriptions	2	2	0
Warley ditto	11	2	10¼
West Melton ditto	16	0	0
Wetherby ditto	6	6	0
Wilsden ditto	1	5	0
Wakefield ditto (old Chapel)	41	0	0
Ditto (new Chapel)	54	16	0

NORTH RIDING AUXILIARY SOCIETY.

Treasurer—Mr. Thomas Hinderwell.

Secretaries—Rev. J. T. Holloway, D. D.—Rev. John Arundel.

WHITBY BRANCH—Rev. George Young.

	£	s.	d.
Female Auxiliary Society 1d. Subscrip. and Collections	20	1	0
Juvenile Auxiliary Society (Cliff Lane) Penny Subscription and Collection	13	17	0
Cliff Lane Sabbath School	0	11	6

Annual Subscribers.

	£	s.	d.
Holt, Miss S.	1	1	0
Holt, Mr. John, jun.	1	1	0
Jefferson, Mr. John	0	10	6
Moorsom, Richard, Esq.	1	1	0
Pennock, Mr. John	1	1	0
Skinner, Mrs. J.	0	10	6
Young, Rev. G.	1	1	0

	£	s.	d.
A Friend	1	1	0
	41	16	6

Rev. John Arundel.

	£	s.	d.
Ladies' Missionary Society	20	6	10

Annual Subscriptions.

	£	s.	d.
Miss ——	2	2	0
Arundel, Rev. J.	1	1	0
Scoresley, Mr. W jun.	0	10	6
Marfitt, Mrs	0	10	6
Missionary Box in Sunday School	0	9	2
	25	0	0

BOROUGHBRIDGE BRANCH—By Mr. J. M. Drage, Secretary.

Contributions.

	£	s.	d.
B. Mrs	1	0	0
Fisher, Mr. J.	1	1	0

	£	s.	d.
Friends at Rainton	0	14	6
Ditto at Wormhill Green	0	12	6
Hind Miss (a)	0	10	6

I

	£	s.	d.
Norris, Rev. W.......... (a)	0	10	6
S. Miss	0	10	0
S. Mr .... (a)	0	13	0
Z. Mr.............. ... (a)	1	1	0

	£	s.	d.
Z. Mrs. ...... (a)	0	10	6
Various, one penny			
per week........	0	16	6
	8	0	0

THIRSK BRANCH—*By Mr. T. Squire, Treasurer.*

	£	s.	d.
Penny Subscriptions at Sutton, by Rev. J. Sykes	12	0	7
Ditto at Thirsk, by Rev. H. Panting	6	0	2

	£	s.	d.
Rev. Mr. Brooks at Leybourn	2	0	0
	20	0	9

COLLECTIONS BY REV. G. COLLISON AND T. JACKSON.

	£	s.	d.
Great Ousbourn, Rev J.Jackson	10	7	0
Guisboro', Rev. W. Hinmers	1	4	8
Kirkby Moorside, Rev. J. Eastmead	5	10	0
Malton, Rev Mr. Greenwood	10	0	0
Pickering, Rev. G. Croft....	4	8	0
Auxiliary...............	8	4	8
Seamer Church, Rev. J. T. Holloway, D. D.........	3	1	0
Scarboro', Rev. S. Bottomley	23	19	3

	£	s.	d.
Collection at the General Meeting in the Town Hall	11	5	7
Stokesley, Rev. W. Hinmers	2	11	6
Whitby, Rev. Mr. Young ..	3	10	6
General Meeting at Rev. Mr. Arundel's Chapel..	10	18	6
	95	0	8

	£	s.	d.
Bradford, Mr. T. Holgate, 1799	20	0	0
Collingham, Mrs. Leake, 1813	10	0	0
Gilling, near Richmond, Mr. J. Christian .... (a)	1	1	0
Huddersfield, Mr. Houghton, 1796	10	0	0
Hull, Messrs. G. & J. Eggington, 1796	21	0	0
Rust, Mr. 1812....	10	10	0
Thompson, T. Esq. M. P. 1809	10	0	0
Thornton, Mrs. 1812	10	0	0

	£	s.	d.
Leeds, Mr. Clapham........	50	0	0
Mr. W. Clapham, 1811..	100	0	0
Rotherham, by Rev. J. Bennett, for the Jewish Object...................	4	9	6
Scarborough, Mr. T. Hinderwell............ 1796	10	0	0
Ditto 1800	10	10	0
Yarm, Mr. J. Croker ....(a)	1	1	0
York, Mr. W. Gray ..1796	10	0	0
Mr. Thorpe 1808	10	0	0

WALES.

SOUTH WALES AUXILIARY SOCIETY—By Rev. David Peter, Carmarthen.

	£	s.	d.
Milford, by Rev. Mr. Warlow.			
Collection 9 2 8			
Warlow, Rev. Mr. 1 1 0			
Demack, Mr. W. 1 1 0			
Rogers, Mr. J 1 1 0			
Friend, a 1 0 0			
Foster, Mrs. 0 10 6			
Simleet, Mrs. 0 10 6			
	14	6	8
Haverford West, by Rev. Mr. Bulmer.			
Auxil. Contribu...9 5 3			
Collection 5 14 9			
	15	0	0
Phillips, Mr. G.	1	1	0

	£	s.	d.
Raymond, Mr. T.........	1	1	0
Teurselross and *Rose Market,* by Rev. Mr. Thomas......	6	0	0
St. Florence, by Rev. Mr. Evans................	5	0	0
St. David's, by Rev. Mr. J. Griffiths..............	18	18	6
Trefgarn, by Rev. Mr. B. Griffiths 8 12 0			
Skeel, Rev. Mr (a) 1 0 0			
Nicholas, Mr. T. (a) 1 0 0			
Reynolds, Mr. J. 1 1 0			
	11	13	0
Fishguard, by Rev. Mr. Davis 1 7 0			
Theytson 2 13 0			

	£	s.	d.
Rhosyceiran 2	0	0	
Hicks, Mr. 1	0	0	
James, Mr. 1	0	0	
Meyler, Rev. Mr. 0	10	6	
	8	10	6
Brinberian, by Rev. Mr.			
George 5	16	0	
Hebron, &c. by Rev. Mr.			
Evans............... 7	3	6	
Glandwr, by Rev. Mr. Grif-			
fiths 20	0	0	
Henllan, by Rev. Mr. Loyd 27	12	0	
Trelech, by Rev. Mr. Jones.. 9	2	3½	
Bethlehem, by Rev. Mr. Phil-			
lips 4	5	0	
Lanybre, by Rev.Mr.Rowlands 5	0	0	
Carmarthen, Rev. Mr. Peter.			
Auxiliary Contri. 12	11	0	
Collection 11	13	4½	
Morris, Mr. Jun..5	5	0	
Peter, Rev D. ..1	1		
Evans, Mr. J.....1	1		
Rogers, Mr. J. ..1	1		
Griffiths, Mr. T..1	1		
Thomas, Mr. E...1	1		
Lewis, Mr. J. 1	1		
Rees, Mrs. 2	2		
Profits of a Straw-			
berry Bed, by a			
Lady.........1	12	0	
Edwards, Miss ..1	1	0	
Jenkins, Mrs. 0	10	6	
	41	0	10½
Panteg, by Rev. Mr.			
Davies 4	1	0	
Bwlch Newydd, by Rev.			
Mr. Bowen 3	0	0	
Hermon, by Ditto ..1	5	0	
	4	5	0
Peneader, by Mr. J. Evans .. 6	6	6	
Collected by Rev. Mr. Jones.			
At Crigbar 1	2	0	
At Tabor........1	9	8	
At Hermon......1	9	6	
Benefit Club at La-			
morda 1	15	0	
	5	16	2

	£	s.	d.
Landovery, by Rev. Mr. Je-			
remy 1	12	6	
Capel Rerw, by Rev. Mr. Syl-			
vanus 1	0	0	
Talybont, by Rev. Mr.			
Shadrach 1	7	2	
Lunbadarn, by Ditto 0	14	9	
	2	1	11
Neuaddlwyd Sunday			
School, by Rev.			
Mr. Phillips....8	0	0	
Penrhywgaled, by Do 4	5	7	
	12	5	7
Horeb, by Rev. Mr.			
Jones 5	0	0	
Sunday School, by			
Ditto 2	2	0	
	7	2	0
Saron, by Rev. Mr.			
Jones 4	2	3	
Sunday School, by			
Ditto.........2	3	6	
	6	5	9
Bethel, by Rev. Mr.			
Phillips 2	2	0	
Cardigan, by Rev. Mr. Davies 6	11	1½	
Trewen, Glyn, Hawen,			
and *Wig,* collec-			
tions by Rev.			
Messrs. Evans &			
Griffiths 9	19	3	
Loyd, Mrs.......1	1	0	
Sunday Schools ..8	8	9	
	19	9	0
Newcastle Emlyn, collections			
at the Annual Meeting 23	7	8½	
Lewes, Mr. W. (Llysnew-			
ydd) by Rev. Mr. Jones,			
Trelech 5	5	0	
Loyd, Mrs. Bronwydd .. 5	0	0	
Colby, Miss 1	1	0	
Brigstock, Mrs......... 1	0	0	
Brigstock, Miss Mary.... 0	7	6	
	316	10	1

CARMARTHENSHIRE.

Carmarthen, Mr. Menzies ....(a) 1 1 0
Gower, Bethesda Chapel, Collection by Mr. W. Hammerton..........12 0 0

CARDIGANSHIRE.

Aberystwith, Mr. D. Davies ....(a) 2 2 0

GLAMORGANSHIRE.

Calvinistic Methodists, by Mr. E. Bassett.

	£	s.	d.			£	s.	d.
berthaw 1	18	6		*Dyffryn*.................2	9	0		
urthin...............1	19	6		*Dinaspowis* 0	15	0		

	£	s.	d.
Goppa fach	1	3	0
Gyfylchi	0	13	7
Langyfelach	1	12	0
Lysworney and Lantwit Major	2	16	11
Lantrissent	1	0	0
Merthyr Tidfil	1	11	0
Neath	1	0	0
Newbridge	0	10	0
Oldcastle	1	15	0
Pyle	1	5	0
Pentyrch	1	8	0

	£	s.	d.
Swansea	1	0	0
Salem	1	1	0
St. Fagans	0	14	6
Trehil	2	0	0
Ton yr Efail	1	0	0
Whitchurch	1	5	0
Ystradmynach	1	3	0
	30	0	0

Bridgend Penny Soc. 1 0 0
Mrs. A. Dare 0 10 0
Mrs. Short 0 10 0
————— 2 0 0
Swansea, Rev. Mr. Kemp &
Congregation, at the late

Countess of Hunting-
don's Chapel.
Subscriptions 5 14 6
Collect. by Cards 36 3 6
Do. for Chronicles 2 2 0
—————44 0 0

PEMBROKESHIRE.

Fishguard, Calvinistic
Methodists ...11 8 0
Subscriptions of 1d.
a week, by the
12 Children of
Mr. J. Mortimer,
of Trehowel ..2 12 0
—————14 0 0
Haverford West Tabernacle.
Penny Society ..21 14 1
Sloop Active Mis-

sionary Box....0 11 6
—————22 5 7
Trevine,Calvinistic Methodists 7 6 6
Trevach, Mr. T. Davies .. (a) 1 1 0
Twrgwn, by Rev. E. Morris.
Mrs. Lloyd, of
Bronwydd 5 0 0
Mr J. Lloyd 1 1 0
Trinity Chapel ..1 11 0
Mynyddbach 1 1 0
————— 8 13 0

SOUTH EAST WELCH AUXILIARY SOCIETY.
By Rev. Thomas Luke.

Llanwrtyd, Rev. D. Williams 2 0 0
Second Collection by Ditto 3 0 0
Bethesda Langattoch, Rev. D.
Davies 2 6 6
Second Collection by Ditto 4 0 0
Neath, Rev Mr Bowen 6 0 0
Friends by Ditto 0 9 0
Penhetygwin, Rev. J. Morgan, 3 3 0
Brychgoed, Rev. P. Jenkins.. 4 11 0
Gwynfe, Ditto, Ditto 1 15 0
Altwen, Rev. Mr Davies.... 2 19 0
Groeswen, Rev. Mr. Hughes 3 10 0
Maesmarchog & Hermon, Rev.
Morgan Lewis 1 14 0
Rhyader, Rev. D. Evans 3 6 7
Aber, Rev. D. Lewis........ 2 0 0
Builth, Rev. Mr. Williams .. 2 0 0
Penmain, Rev Mr. Thomas.. 1 16 0
Maesyronnen, Rev. D Jones 1 3 0
BethesdaMerthyr,Rev.M Jones 1 10 6
Talgarth, Rev Mr. Jones.... 3 4 0
Tynycoed, Rev. J. Williams.. 1 0 0
Swansea, Ebenezer Meeting,
by Mr. D. Hughes 8 8 6
Tredustan, Rev. Mr. Lewis .. 1 4 2
Neath, Rev. Mr. Edwards .. 1 1 0

Llangyrnwd, Rev. Mr. Bey-
non................ 0 16 0
Caebach, Rev. David Powell.. 1 0 0
Brecon, Collection at........ 8 2 8½
Ditto at Pontfaen, by Rev.
Mr. Powell 0 18 0
Penny Society, by ditto ..1 11 7
Bridgend, Rev. Mr. Jones .. 2 0 0
Newport, Rev. Mr. Davies .. 5 0 0
Pontypool, Rev. Mr. Jones ... 2 3 7½
Hanover, Rev. E. Davies 6 0 0
Baran, Rev. R. Howell...... 1 3 0
Swansea, Castle Street Meeting.
Annual.
Rev. Thomas Luke........1 1 0
Mr. E Jenkins, White Rock 1 1 0
Mr. Lewin Michael 0 10 6
Mr. Rees Jones 1 1 0
Mr. William Watts 1 1 0
Mr. John Davies 0 10 6
Mrs. Humphreys 0 10 0
L. Weston Dilwyn, Esq. 1 1 0
Mrs. Bruell 1 1 0
Mr. S. Jenkins 0 10 6
————— 99 3 8

NORTH WALES AUXILIARY SOCIETY.
By the Rev. G. Lewis, D. D. of Llanfyllin.

ANGLESEA.	£	s.	d.
Amlwch, Rev. J Evans	2	0	0
Beaumaris and Pentraeth, Ditto	6	0-	0
Cierchiog, R. Roberts	2	0	0
Llanddensant & Llannerchymedd, D. Beynon.............	1	9	6.
Llanfechell and Cemines, O. Thomas	2	0	0
Rhosymeirch, &c. J. Powell..	3	2	0
	17	11	6

CAERNARVONSHIRE.			
Bangor, &c. D. Roberts ..:...16	9	1½
Bethel, D. Griffith 1	1	0
Capelhelig, &c E. Davies...... 1	16	11
Caernarvon, J Griffith....... 4	3	4
Nebo, J. Jones 1	0	0
New Chapel, B. Jones 1	6	3
Pwllheli, Ditto 1	0	2
Salem, W Jones............ 2	3	7½
Saron, W. Hughes 0	7	8
Talsarn, D. Griffiths........ 1	4	8½
	30	12	3½

DENBIGHSHIRE.			
Denbigh, R. Everitt 12	13	9
Llandegle, J Griffith 1	9	0
Llanwrst, P Griffith 2	5	6
Moelfre and Colwyn, T. Jones 4	0	0
Ruthin, E. Lewis........... 0	10	0
Waungoleugoed, W. Jones .. 1	1	4
Wern, &c. W Williams 4	0	0
Wrexham, — Malt 8	3	6
	34	3	1

FLINTSHIRE.			
Bagillt, B. Evans 1	0	0
Halkin Calvinistic Methodist Society 5	11	0

	£	s.	d.
Heol Mostyn, D. Jones......	12	0
Holywell, Ditto............12	5	1
——— Collected at the Annual Meeting, 12th and 13th of August....24	0	2
——— By Sale of Hymn Books 1	1	4
——— Calvinistic Methodist's Sun. Sch. Children 1	16	8
Mold and Buckley 1	2	6
Newmarket, T. Jones 1	0	0
Rhesycae, R Williams...... 2	2	0
	53	10	9

MERIONETHSHIRE.			
Bala, J. Lewis 1	10	6
Bethel, M. Jones 0	12	0
Bronhaulog, J. Davies 2	2	0
Dinas, W. Hughes 1	19	3½
Dolgelley, &c. C. Jones 2	1	0
Llanuwchllyn, M. Jones 1	8	6
Towyn, &c. H. Lloyd 2	4	6
	11	17	9½

MONTGOMERYSHIRE.			
Aberhafesh, J. Davies ...:... 3	7	3½
Drwsynant, W. Hughes 0	16	4
Foel, Ditto...:........... 1	4	4½
Hirnant, M Hughes 0	18	0
Keel, J. Davies 0	16	3
Machynlleth, &c. D. Morgan 16	11	6
Llanbrynmair, J. Roberts.... 4	5	0
Llanfyllin, G. Lewis, D. D. 23	2	10
Pontddolanog, J. Ridge...... 0	14	8¼
Sarney and Domgay, D. Davis 3	3	0
	54	19	3½
Total..202	14	8

ANGLESEA.

	£	s.	d.			£	s.	d.
Aberffraw 10	2	6		Gorslwyd................ 4	7	0
Amlwch 20	4	8½		Gwalchmai 5	0	6
Beaumaris 4	3	9½		Holyhead.............15	5	9½
Bethlehem 10	0	0		Llanerchymedd 13	6	9½
Bethel 3	17	6		Llanrhyddlad 9	13	0½
Bethesda 8	4	6½		Llangristiolus 5	13	3
Bodedern............. 5	3	4½		Llanfair 4	13	0
Bryn Sencin 5	8	3		Llanfwrog 3	15	0
Bryndu 4	0	0		Llangoed................ 3	7	6
Caergeiliog 3	2	3½		Llanfugail 7	12	1½
Dwyran 3	3	0		Llangefni............10	10	0
Gaerwen 8	17	6		Llanallgo................ 5	3	9½
Glasinfryn 7	6	1		Llangwyllog 4	13	3

	£.	s.	d.
Llandegfan	1	7	6
Lledroed	7	13	3
Newbro'	5	0	6
Peniel	3	11	0
Pentre	4	4	6½
Penygarnedd	5	0	0
Penygraigwen	2	1	4
Rhoscolyn	2	6	6¼
Talwrn	4	0	2
Ty Mawr Chapel	6	4	0
Total	229	4	4¾

CAERNARVONSHIRE.

Caernarvon, Miss Ann Owen 1 10 0

Collections by the Calvinistic Methodists in the County of Caernarvon, by the Rev. Evan Richardson.

	£.	s.	d.
Abereirch	1	7	9
Bangor (Graig 17s. 6½d.)	3	19	2½
Bryn'rodyn	3	15	8
Bryn Engan	4	17	6
Bryn Melyn	0	16	5½
Bwlch Derwyn	0	10	0
Caernarvon	10	16	0
Clynog	3	8	7½
Cwm Coryn	0	6	11
Dinas	1	6	5½
Edeyrn	2	6	6
Erw Suran	0	6	5
Four Crosses	1	9	0
Gate House	1	9	0
Garn	0	16	1
Llanllechid	3	14	0
Llandeiniolen	3	15	0
Llanberis	1	12	4
Llanrug	0	14	2½
Llanllyfni	2	12	9½
Llan Engan	2	5	1½
Llanystyndwy	1	4	2½
Llithfaen	0	12	1
Nant	2	6	8
Nevin	2	7	6
Pen-y-caeran	2	9	3
Pen-y-Graig	1	2	0½
Pentre Uchaf	1	7	0
Pwllheli	7	3	3
Rhyd-lios	0	17	8½
Rhyd-bach	1	3	0
Rhyd-clafdy	1	9	0
Terfyn	0	6	5½
Tydmeiliog	3	0	0
Tymawr	2	6	2
Tre-madoe	1	7	11
Uwch-Mynydd	1	8	7
Waen-fawr	2	0	8
Ysgoldy	1	10	3½
	86	6	10

DENBIGHSHIRE.

Congregational Collections by the Calvinistic Methodists, from Mr. Peter Roberts, by Favour of Mr. Gabriel Davies.

	£.	s.	d.
Denbigh Auxiliary	10	10	5
Ditto Collection at the Chap.	4	10	3
Llanrhaidr	5	7	8½
Henllan	3	6	0
Nant glyn and Groes	1	2	0
Tan y fron	0	15	0
Llansanan	1	5	7
Cefn coch Sunday School	1	16	0
Llangerniw	1	0	0
Llanufydd	3	8	9
Cefn Meiriadoc	0	18	7½
Abergele	3	4	0
Mochdre	5	2	11
Llandudno	0	16	6
Llansaintffraed	0	18	11
Rhyddlan	2	9	6
Twl terfyn	0	12	1
Roe	2	16	3
Talybont	0	8	11
Llanrwst Sunday School	6	0	0
Ditto Collection at the Chap.	3	9	10
Llanlidan	0	10	0
Clawddnewydd	0	9	0
Overplus, some places omitted, or a mistake in some of the above items	2	17	11½
	63	16	2½

MERIONETHSHIRE.

Congregational Collections and Subscriptions by the Calvinistic Methodists, transmitted by Mr. Gabriel Davies, of Bala.

	£.	s.	d.
Bala Chapel Collection	10	13	7½
Ditto Ditto Sunday School	5	18	5
Trerhiwaedog	3	0	0
Mrs. Davies's (of Vronhou-			

	£	s.	d.		£	s.	d.
log) Card of Monthly Subscribers	1	10	1	Festiniog	0	5	2½
Llandderfel Chapel Collection on a day appointed for Thanksgiving after Harvest	3	2	0	Maentwrog	0	17	0½
				Penrhyn, two Collections	2	5	1
				Harddlech	0	14	6
				Gwynfryn	1	14	3
Sarnen	0	12	6	Talsarneu	0	14	4¼
Llangown	0	11	8	Dyffryn	1	15	9¼
Talybont	0	11	6	Towyn and Aberdyfi	0	17	11
Park	1	4	3	Dolgelly	7	18	0
Trebenmaen Sunday School	0	11	9½	Barmouth	2	12	9
Tommen Gastell, Ditto	0	10	0	Sion	0	7	3
Penbryn and Llidiardeu	1	1	9	Bryncryg	0	7	6
Ysbytty	1	10	5	Bwlch	1	0	9
Cwmpenan	0	15	5	Llanfihangel	0	6	0
Cerig y dridion	2	3	2½	Carus and Lluyngwiel	0	9	2¼
Llangwm	2	12	0	Llanerchgoediog	0	5	6
Penmachno	0	9	4	Llanarmon	0	14	9¼
Bettws y Coed	0	8	5	Subscriptions	3	3	0
Dolydd elen	0	18	0				
Trawsfynydd	3	0	0		67	13	3¼

	£	s.	d.
Barmouth Sunday School, by Captain Griffiths	3	3	5
Mrs. Meredith ....(a) 1 1 0			
Small Subscriptions 1 1 0			
	2	2	0
Cwmlymonach Sunday School, by Mr. John Jones	1	12	0

MONTGOMERYSHIRE.

Collections by the Calvinistic Methodists in Montgomeryshire, by Mr. Owen Jones.

	£	s.	d.		£	s.	d.
Llanidloes	12	4	9	Cemas	1	14	3
Drefnewydd	1	13	6	Llanwnog	0	14	2
Ceunant	2	15	0	Bont	1	18	9
Llanwyddelen	1	15		Trefeglwys	1	5	0
Llawryglyn	0	9	5	Tregynon	1	13	8¼
Cowarch	0	14	1	Llanwrin	2	7	0¾
Graig	0	7	6	Llanbrynmair	3	3	0½
Brithdir	2	2	0	Bryntail	0	11	6
Bonyfedu and Ochr y foel	0	12	9½	Llanfyllyn	0	18	0
Llanwddyn	0	12	3	Carno	1	5	9
Mallwyd	1	5	6	Glo, &c.	2	7	0
Sarne	0	12	10	Pentyrch	1	18	0
Clochfaen	0	10	9	Penal	0	5	6
Machynlleth	4	5	0	Llanfair	2	13	6
Gwernbant	2	0	0				
Dreowen	1	8	10½		56	4	

SCOTLAND.

	£	s.	d.		£	s.	d.
Aberdeen Auxiliary Society, Rev. J. Philip	50	0	0	Society, by Mr. Jrazer, Treasurer	25	0	0
Juvenile ditto per ditto	7	0	0	*Calton & Bridgton* Asiation for religiousrposes, by Mr. Wollins, Secretary	30	0	0
Alva Missionary Society by Rev. Mr. M'Lachlan	6	12	7				
Avaçh Auxiliary Society, by Mr. M. Urie, Treasurer & Secretary	25	0	0	*Dumbarton* Auxiliaryble & Missionary Soty, by Mr. Glen, Pre	15	0	0
Anderston Missionary Help							

	£	s.	d.
East Lothian Society for propagating Christian Knowledge.			
Black, Mr.........1	1	0	
Cunningham,Mr.0	10	6	
Houden, Mr. R. 1	1	0	
Ritchie,MrHaddington 0	10	6	
Slark, Rev. Mr. Dirleton........1	1	0	
———	4	4	0
Edinburgh Auxiliary Society, by Rev. Mr.Liddle, Secretary 50	0	0	
Mrs. Bailey, Drylaw...... 2	2	0	
Drummond, Mr. J.........1	0	0	
Mr. R. Penton, West Newington 10	0	0	
Elgin Auxiliary Missionary Society, by Rev. N. M'Niel & Mr.J.Collie 10	10	0	
Falkirk United Missionary and Bible Society, by Rev. H. Belfrage...... 9	10	0	
Galston, Ayrshire, Society of Christians of all denominations, by Rev. Dr. Smith.............10	0	0	
Glasgow Auxiliary Society, by Mr.Urie, Treasurer 60	0	0	
Youth's Auxiliary Society, by Mr. M'Gavin 67	0	0	
Greenock & Port Glasgow Bible Society, by Rev. W. Wlson, Secretary 20	0	0	
Greenock Auxiliary Society, by Mr A. Laird........15	0	0	
Female o. by Mr. Laird 15	0	0	

	£	s.	d.
Hamilton Bible and Missionary Society.:........ 5	0	0	
Inch Parish; Aberdeenshire, Monthly Prayer Meet. 4	7	0	
Invergordon Association, by Mr. Hector Holme.....20	0	0	
Kincardine Auxiliary Soc. 10	0	0	
Musselburgh Auxiliary Society, by Rev. A. Black, Secretary 10	0	0	
Oxenham Collection, by Rev. P. Young.........10	0	0	
Paisley Auxiliary Missionary Society, by Mr. J. Carlile, Rev. J. Thomson, Secretary.			
Subscriptions...80	4	0	
Legacy, by Mr. J. Tarbot......5	5	0	
Cambraes Missionary Association, by Rev J. Thomson...8	5	0	
Largs Auxiliary Society, by Mr J.Lyle, Treas. 6	6	0	
———100	0	0	
Perth Juvenile Society, by Mr. T. Bower.........10	0	0	
Perthshire Missionary Society, Rev. J. Willison 30	0	0	
Rothsay, Collection by Rev. S. M'Nab.............12	0	0	
Stewarton Auxiliary Soc. Mr. D.M'Farlane,Sec. 13	0	0	
Tain Northern Missionary Society, by Rev. Mr. M'Intosh............:50	0	0	

Collection made in Scotland by the Rev. Dr. Stewart, Mr. Roby, and Mr. H. F. Burder, in aid of the Funds of the Missionary Society.

Edinburgh. Rev. Dr. Hall's,			
Burgher Denomination.17	10	0½	
Rev. Mr. eddie's, ditto 27	12	9½	
Rev. Mr. othain's, ditto 9	5	0	
Rev. Mr. homson's, Relief Ch'ch............ ..12	0	9	
Rev. Mr. hnson's, ditto 11	1	8½	
Rev. Mr. th's, ditto...10	13	6	
Rev. Mr. ikman's, Independ 14	0	0	
Rev. Mr. yne's, ditto..17	1	6	
Rev. Mr. les's, Baptist 14	0	9	
Rev. Mr. Anderson's, ditto 15	0	0	
Rev.Mr.Laster's, Methodist 10	1	0	
Rev. Mr. theson's, at Leith, Igher......... 6	6	0	
J. S. B. Daion.......... 2	2	0	

Glasgow. Rev. Dr. Dick's,			
Burgher Denomination 33	0	0	
Rev. Messrs. Kidstone & Brashe's, ditto.........40	0	1½	
Rev. Mr. Ewing's Independent.................62	7	6	
Rev. Mr. Wardlaw's, do. 36	2	0	
Rev. Mr. Campbell's, do. 10	6	0½	
East Wood Parish Church, Mr. Logan's.........13	7	2	
Paisley. Rev. Mr. Burns, Low Church.............18	3	2½	
Rev.Mr.Smart's Burgher 10	16	3½	
Greenock. Rev. Dr. Scott's, Established Church...19	7	2	
Rev. Mr. Auld's, Relief Church 9	11	8	
Rev Mr Wilson's,Burgher 5	5	0	

	£	s.	d.
Port Glasgow. A Lady, by Rev. Mr. Hercus........	1	1	0
Dumbarton. Rev. Mr. Grimond's, Relief Church	2	1	7½
Helensburgh. Independent Chapel	4	2	6
Largs. Rev. Mr. Leach's, Burgher	5	9	0
Auxiliary Society.........	5	5	0
Island of Cambraes..........	2	0	0
Beith. Rev. Mr.Anderson's, Relief	6	10	0
Ayr. Rev. Mr. Nicol's, Relief Church.............	9	9	7
Rev. Mr. M'Lean's, Independent...............	2	0	0
Saltcoats. Rev. Mr. Ellis's, Burgher	10	13	0
Hamilton. Rev. Mr. Fletcher's, Burgher.........	2	15	8½
Kilmarnock. Rev. Mr. Hamilton's, High Church	7	7	0
Rev. Mr. Kirkwood's, Relief	2	10	6¼
Rev. Mr. Campbell's, Burgher	7	2	7½
Dunfermline. Rev. Messrs. Husband and M'Farlane	5	5	0
Inverkeithing. Rev. Eben. Brown, Burgher.......	3	0	0
Falkirk. By Rev. Mr. Edwards, Independent...	1	0	1
Ditto, Monthly Prayer Meeting	1	1	0
Do. Collection at Grange Mouth	1	11	8
Linlithgow. By Rev. Mr. Knowles, Independent Prayer Meeting	1	0	0
Do. Auxiliary Juvenile Bible and Missionary Society	2	17	0
Do. Female ditto.........	2	3	0
Borrowstowness. Rev. Mr. Harper's, Burgher.....	4	9	1½
Queensferry. Rev. Mr. Carruther's, Burgher......	5	1	6
Bath Gate. Rev.Mr. Fyfe's, Relief Church	1	2	2½
Whitburn. Donation from Mrs. Brown.............	0	10	6
Buckhaven. Rev. Mr. Telford's, Burgher.........	6	7	0
Pittenween. Rev. Mr. Purdie's, Relief Church...	4	11	0
*Anstruther.*Rev.Mr.Japp's, Independent............	2	17	0
Stirling. Rev. Messrs.			

	£	s.	d.
Smart and Stewart's, Burgher	31	3	6
Rev. Mr. Logan's, Relief, St. Ninian's......	10	0	0
A Young Lady's Charity Box, Stirling.............	1	3	6
Cupar, Fifeshire. At the Burgher Meeting......	2	3	3½
Perth. Rev. Mr. Orme's, Independent	15	7	4
Dundee. Rev.Mr. Lawson's, Relief Church.........	3	8	4½
Ditto, Juvenile Society..	4	0	0
Mr. Russel's, Independ.	11	0	0
Arbroath. Rev. Mr. Anderson's, Independent....	2	0	0
Ditto, Female Juvenile Society	1	10	0
Montrose. Rev.Mr.Cowie's, Independent...........	7	11	0
Aberdeen. Rev.Mr.Philip's, Independent............	30	3	6
Rev. Mr. Penman's......	4	3	0
Rev. J. Murray, Trinity Chapel Association...	20	0	0
Miss. Box in the Family of D. Fordyce, Esq...	1	10	0
Donation of Mr. S. S...	1	1	0
Juvenile-Missionary Society, Old Town......	4	0	0
Female Servant Soc. Donation to aid the Translation of the Scriptures into the Taheitan language	10	0	0
Huntly. Rev. Mr. Hill's, Independent.............	6	13	4
Donation of Mrs. W...	1	1	0
Keith. At Burgher Chapel	3	1	6
A few Friends, by Mr. Duncan..................	2	5	6
Elgin. Rev. Mr. M'Neil's, Independent............	2	3	10
Nairn. Rev. Mr. Dewar's, Independent............	3	17	1½
Donation by Mr. K......	0	10	6
Inverness. Chapel of Ease, Rev. Mr. Martin......	17	5	8
Dunkeld. Rev. Mr. Black's, Independent..........	4	9	1
Little Dunkeld. Bible Soc. by Rev. Dr. Irvine....	5	0	0
Juvenile Missionary Soc.	7	0	0
Rev. Mr. Raeburn's, Bannockburn	4	0	0
Collected at Selkirk, by Rev. Mr. Wilson......	6	0	0
	759	16	10¾

K

IRELAND.

	£	s.	d.
Cork. Missionary Society, by Mr. W. C. Logan, Secretary	20	0	0
Dublin. Female Association by Mrs. Ardill	41	15	0
Union Missionary Prayer Meeting	18	3	0
Juvenile Missionary Society, by Messrs. J. Neven and H. Cooper, Secretaries	15	0	0

	£	s.	d.
Mr. Stephen Seymour	5	0	0
Limerick. Friends of Henry Street Meeting, by Rev. J. Petherick	2	8	0
Tyrone. Auxiliary Soc. by Mr. W. Weir, Treas.	24	0	0
Youghall. Collection at a Prayer Meeting, by the late Rev. T. Gordon	4	0	0

NEWFOUNDLAND.

	£	s.	d.
Carboncar. Mr. Tullock	7	0	0
St. John's Signal Hill Auxiliary Society by Lieut.			

	£	s.	d.
Vicars, of the Royal Engineers	15	7	10

SUNDRIES.

	£	s.	d.
Pimlico, Chelsea, & Brompton united Prayer Meeting, including Buckingham, Ranelagh, Cook's Ground, & Trevor Chapels, by Rev. Mr. Dunn	20	16	6
Collection at Chandler Street Chapel, after a Sermon by Rev. J. Leifchild	10	2	6
Missionary Box on board the Sloop Eleanor, of Holyhead	1	0	0
A Friend in the Country	1	0	0
A Friend to Missions	1	0	0
W. B. a Donation	0	5	6
Widow Lady, by Mr. Pawling	0	10	0
R. Z.	5	0	0
F. S.	1	1	0
A Friend	0	5	0
Aliquis	5	0	0
R. S. G.	1	1	0
A Friend, by Rev. Dr. Nicol	1	0	0
R. S. 3s. Mrs. Watson 1s. 6d. G. G. £1	1	4	6
Produce of a missionary			

	£	s.	d.
box at Stoney Stratford Independ. Meeting House	2	0	0
Produce of a Necklace by a young female Friend	0	15	0
A few young Men at a Biscuit Baker's	1	14	6
Anonymous	2	0	0
J. C.	5	0	0
N. C.	0	12	0
R. of M.	1	0	0
I. S. A.	1	0	0
A Lady, by Rev. J. Honeywell	2	0	0
Mrs. Hartley, a free-will offering	5	0	0
Mrs. Denniss	1	1	0
Picture of the Cession of Matavai, sold 3 copies	3	3	0
T. S.	0	10	6
M. Wilson, Bethnal Green, collected in a Pagan Temple	0	10	2
J. J.	0	10	6
By Mrs. Smith, of Chelsea, Mr. H. Burgess 0 10 6 Mr. Smith 1 0 0 A few Friends 1 19 0	3	9	6

	£	s.	d.
Omicron	1	1	0
A Friend, by Rev. Mr.			
James £1—poorBoy 2s	1	2	0
Sacred Edict..................	0	7	6
T. G. W.	1	1	0
W. A. S.	1	0	0
A poor Woman's mite......	2	10	0
A few Bookbinders and			
Friends, by Mr. Allen	1	11	2
J. B. City Road...............	1	0	0
S. M.	15	0	0
C. H.	2	0	0
A Lady, by Mr. Smith, jun	1	1	0
B., by Rev. R. Fairbrother	1	0	0
I. F. B.	0	10	0
Secreta Approva	1	0	0
D. W...........................	1	0	0
Knill's Missionary Tem-			
ple, at Mr. Nisbett's,			
including family fines	8	8	0
Friends at Collier's Rents	5	8	4
S. L., Weathersfield	1	0	0
C. D.	1	0	0
Two Ladies, on reading			
Rev. Dr. Chalmers's			
Sermon preached be-			
fore the Dundee Mis-			
sionary Society, by			
Mr. Hatchard	30	0	0
The Epsom Club	1	0	0
A Friend to Missions, by			
Mr. J. Lang...............	10	0	0
Do. for Bethelsdorp, by do.	10	0	0
R. I.	10	0	0
H. of A.	1	0	0
Orphan Sch.Boys,City-road	0	17	0
W. C.	1	0	0
Mr. W. D. Surgeon, R.N.	1	0	0
Mrs. M. at the Ordination			
of Missionaries at Is-			
lington	1	0	0
B. W., by the late Mr.			
Flint, Camberwell	1	0	0
S. S., by Mr. Hodson......	1	1	0
Books sold at the Mission-			
ary Rooms	2	13	3
For Books, by Mr. Tarn...	1	12	6
Mrs. Bolton, a Donation...	2	0	0
Missionary Box, Old Jewry	7	8	9
A few young Ladies at Miss			
Holton's School, by			
Rev. W. Clayton......	1	1	0
Mrs.B. byRev. J.Townsend	1	0	0
The Deacons of Trinity			

	£	s.	d.
Chapel, Rev. T. Smith	5	5	0
Journeymen Hair-dressers			
at Mr. Ross's, 4th an-			
nual Subscription	4	0	0
Penny Society,by Mr.Budd			
Rosoman Row.........	2	2	0
Weekly Subscriptions of a			
small Family, by T.			
Sard, Collector	1	3	0
Mrs. Lavrock, Deptford...	0	10	0
Rev. Dr. Steinkopff, Collec-			
tion at a Prayer Meet-			
ing held at his Church			
in the Savoy	5	0	0
An old Director's mite......	10	10	0
A Friend of Rev. T. Lewis,			
of Islington, towards			
100 Malay Testaments	25	0	0
Mr. B. Tucker, Donation	1	0	0
Subscriptions and Dona-			
tions, by E. & G. Fox	1	2	5
M. O.	3		0
M. R.	5		0
G. A. S.	5	0	0
J. B.	1		0
E. D. Walworth. produce			
of a Missionary Box	1	1	0
R. G.	3	0	0
Few Friends at Sion Chapel	2	18	0
A female Missionary Fund			
by Miss Kinnerley ...	4	12	0
Prayer Meeting at Mr.			
Kesterton's in the Boro'	7	0	0
Missionary Prayer Meeting,			
Upper Mary-le-bone,			
by Mrs. Moss	6	15	0
A few Friends meeting at			
409, Oxford Street, by			
Miss M. A. Mott......	2	0	0
Rev. C. Berry, Hatfield	1	0	0
Mrs. Hamilton..............	1	0	0
E. Jones, by Mr. Richards	1	0	0
Mrs. Gale, Old Bailey......	1	0	0
Mr. W. D. Moxley, by			
Rev. Dr. Bogue	1	1	0
Mr. Shepherd, Reading (a)	1	1	0
Mr. S. Maberly, ditto...(a)	2	2	0
Rev. F. H. Maberly, Ches-			
terto n ....(a)	1	1	0
Baron B.Von Lerber, Berne	2	0	0
A Friend at West Cowes...	0	6	0
Mr. Fenton, Reading...(a)	1	1	0
Mr. Kirkpatrick, Newport,			
Isle of Wight ......(a)	1	1	0

The Secretaries of the Auxiliary Societies which are regularly organized, are requested to send to No. 8, Old Jewry, London (with the Accounts correctly arranged of the ensuing Year), the NAMES *of the Officers of their respective Societies.*

DISBURSEMENTS

In the Year ended April 1, 1818.

𝕸issions.

	£	s.	d.	£	s.	d.
SOUTH SEA ISLANDS.						
For Equipments, &c.	496	7	0			
Bills drawn on the Treasurer, for supplies at New South Wales	1559	12	5			
				2055	19	5
SOUTH AFRICA.						
For sundry Articles sent to the several Missions	350	10	11			
Bills drawn at Cape Town	2553	4	6			
				2903	15	5
INDIA.						
Madras and Bengal	2340	10	0			
Surat—Equipments 187 19 7						
Bills for Salaries 950 0 0	1137	19	7			
				3478	9	7
CHINA. Bills drawn by Dr. Morrison	500	0	0			
MALACCA.						
For the Equipment and Conveyance of Missionaries	1836	7	0			
Bills drawn on the Treasurer	480	0	0			
				2316	7	0
AMBOYNA	126	14	0			
MADAGASCAR.						
For the Equipment and Conveyance of Missionaries	660	11	6			
ISLE OF FRANCE.—Bills drawn by Mr. Le Brun	262	10	0			
WEST INDIES.						
Demerary—For the Support of Missions at George Town and Le Resouvenir	550	16	0			
Trinidad—Equipment and Conveyance of Mr. & Mrs. Mercer 197 14 5						
Bills drawn by Mr. T. Adam 405 0 0	602	14	5			
Antigua—For Schools	21	0	0			
Carried forward	£13,478	17	4			

Brought forward £13478 17 4

NORTH AMERICA.

Quebec	60	0	0				
Canada	40	0	0				
Newfoundland..........	70	0	0				
				170	0	0	

EUROPE.

Malta	296	10	0				
France	100	0	0				
Belgium	91	13	4				
				488	3	4	

SIBERIA.

For the Equipment and Passage of two Missionaries to St. Petersburg, and from thence to Irkoutsk......	776	8	5	
For the Instruction of Lascars in England	64	8	9	

THE SOCIETY'S SEMINARY AT GOSPORT.

For the Support, Clothing, and Instruction of the Students	1784	8	4				
For the Instruction of Missionaries at other Places ...	407	2	5				
For Travelling Expenses of Missionaries and Candidates, Board while in Town, and other necessary Charges...	326	2	2				
				2517	12	11	

THE SOCIETY'S PUBLICATIONS, viz. Reports, Transactions, Addresses, &c.*

For Paper...	276	10	0				
Printing	319	10	9				
Stitching, &c.	106	0	4				
				702	1	1	

CHARGES OF MANAGEMENT.

Expenses of Auxiliary Societies, Travelling Expenses of Ministers in their Service, &c.	484	2	6¼				
Salaries, Poundage, Rent, Coals, and other expenses at the Old Jewry...............	555	12	7				
At the Annual Meeting in London, Travelling Expenses of Ministers, &c........	104	16	5				
Postages, Carriage of Parcels, and sundry small Charges	631	0	2				
				1775	11	8¼	

Total of Disbursements, carried to General Statement......£19,973 3 6¼

* Bills due for Books and Printing when this Account was made up, not then received, amounting to £749 10s. 1d.

GENERAL STATEMENT.

TREASURER TO THE MISSIONARY SOCIETY.

Dr.	£	s.	d.
1817.			
To Balance from last Year's Account..............	1,119	14	9¾
To Amount of Subscriptions, Collections, Donations, &c.............	18,685	17	10¼
To Legacies....................	1,473	13	11
To Dividends on Stock............	1,978	15	9
	22,138	7	6¼
Repaid by the American Board for Foreign Missions	200	0	0
	£23,458	2	4

Cr.	£	s.	d.
By Disbursements, as per preceding List.............	19,973	3	6¼
By the purchase of Stock (in application of Legacies)	898	8	9
By Exchequer Bills purchased.....	2,498	11	8
	23,370	3	11¼
By Balance in favour of the Society..............	87	18	4¾
	£23,458	2	4

We, the Auditors, have examined this Account, and do find that on the 1st of April, 1818, there was a Balance due to the Society of £87 18 4¾—That the Society possessed Stock, in the 3 per Cent. Consolidated Annuities, £16,690—in Reduced Annuities, 3 per Cents. £2,650—4 per Cent. Annuities, £17,000—5 per Cent. Annuities, £7,100—together with Exchequer Bills, amounting to £10,500.

JAMES MUSTON.
GEORGE GAVILLER.
THOMAS B. OLDFIELD.
JOHN FENN.

May 5, 1818.

APPENDIX.

SOUTH AFRICA.

	Rd.	S.	St.
Bethelsdorp Auxiliary Missionary Society, by Mr. Messer	261	2	0
Caledon.—Subscriptions, by Mr. Seidenfaden	198	5	2
Cape Town.—Subscriptions, &c. paid into the Hands of Mr. R. Beck, for 1817	2473	2	0
Stellenbosch.—Ditto, by Mr. F. Rossoun	400	0	0
Cape Town.—Ab. Faure, Esq....1814	1000	0	0
Graaff Reinet Auxiliary Society, by Mr. A. Van Lingen, Treas.	685	0	0

MADRAS.

Missionaries' Friend Society, by Mr. Vansomerin, Treasurer,
paid into the Hands of Messrs. Hunter, Hay, and Co.
Madras..Star Pagodas

1814	30	0	0
1815	90	0	0
1816	150	0	0
1817	250	0	0
	520	0	0

BELLARY.

Auxiliary Society, by the Rev. J. Hands.

Pious Soldiers in the 84th Regiment of Foot....Star Pag.	80	13	60
Ditto in the 69th Ditto	21	25	60
Mr. Paterson, Assistant Surgeon	3	0	0
Mr. Oliver, Master of the Charity School	2	28	0

CALCUTTA.

BENGAL AUXILIARY MISSIONARY SOCIETY.

Collection..S. R.	231	4	0
The Missionaries labouring in Bengal under the Patronage of the London Missionary Society	1000	0	0
Judge Harrington	100	0	0
Mrs. Harrington	100	0	0
Lieut. Stewart	250	0	0
Six other Donations	45	0	0
Lieut. Peevor	24	0	0
Chinsurah, by Rev. R. May	56	1	1
J. Gilbert, Esq.	50	0	0
	2016	5	1

J. H. Harrington, Esq....1813....R. D.	500	0	0
W. Morrison, Esq. late of Calcutta....1815	100	0	0
Dr. Stewart, Bombay....1817	100	0	0

COLLECTIONS AT THE ANNUAL MEETING, LONDON, 1818.

Surrey Chapel	£422	12	10
Tabernacle	178	9	0
Albion Chapel	28	0	0
Spa Fields Chapel	116	17	3
Tottenham Court Chapel	146	14	0
St. Bride's Church	131	0	9
Sion Chapel	116	1	0
Silver Street Chapel	37	10	3
Orange Street Chapel	85	0	0
Total	£1262	5	1

LEGACIES.

	£	s.	d.
1800. Mrs. Sarah Walmsley, late of Bampton, Yorkshire, a legacy paid by Mr. J. Bateman	21	0	0
Mr. Archibald Laird, late of Greenock	10	0	0
1802. Mrs. Mackay, late of Whitby	10	0	0
1804. Mr. Robert Douglas, late of Kingsland	50	0	0
Mr. Henry Poole, late of Woodford	50	0	0
Mrs. Sarah Tewsbury, late of East Halworth	100	0	0
Mrs. Catherine Fleureau, High-street, St. Giles's, Reduced 3 per Cents	400	0	0
1805. Mr. Raybolt, late of London	100	0	0
Mr. John Binns, late of Threadneedle-street	200	0	0
Mr. George Ramsay, late of Kingsland-road	10	0	0
Mr. George Whittenbury, late of Manchester	100	0	0
Mr. Alexander Ross, jun. late of Aberdeen	50	0	0
1807. Mr. Benjamin Cole, late of Homerton	100	0	0
Mrs. Catherine Farr, late of Hoxton	100	0	0
Mr. Aitkin, late of Greenock	100	0	0
Mrs. Workman, late of Bristol	18	0	0
1808. Mr. Thomas Carter, late of Peckham	250	0	0
Mrs. C. Daubuz, late of Falmouth	10	0	0
Mr. S. Dodkin, late of Basingbourn	100	0	0
Mrs. Mary Tilt, late of Stourbridge	50	0	0
1810. Mrs. Appleton, late of Cecil-street, Strand, produce of £100 stock	69	7	9
Mrs. Martha Basset, late of Newbury	20	0	0
Mr. Richard Clark, late of Westminster	100	0	0

	£	s.	d.
Mr. Charles Ward, late of Chipping Norton......	50	0	0
Mr. Thomas Hawkes, late of Piccadilly, 4 per Cent. Annuities...............	2000	0	0
Mr. Atkins, late of Blackheath, Reduced 3 p Cents............er	100	0	0
1811. Mr. Andrew Knies, late of Wellclose-square......	50	0	0
Rev. John Clark, late of Trowbridge...............	100	0	0
Miss Stringer, late of Watlington, Oxfordshire...	100	0	0
Mrs. Margaret Elder, late of Redman's Row......	98	15	0
Mrs. E. Pentycross, late of Wallingford, 4 per Cent Annuities...............	100	0	0
1812. Mr. Gillespie, late near Down, Perthshire.........	17	3	11
Mrs. Sarah Roberts, late of Upper Ealing	50	0	0
Mrs. Pratt, late of Teignmouth......................	3	3	0
Mr. Peter Lemaire, late of Castle-street, Borough	5	0	0
1813. Mrs. Compigné, late of Camberwell, by Mr. Compigné...............	200	0	0
Samuel Pinder, Esq. late of Falcon-square.........	50	0	0
1814. Mrs. Ann Henry, late of Moorhouse, N. B.......	54	18	6
Mrs.Mary Powell, late of Presgwyn, near Oswestry	22	10	0
Mr. William Jones, late of Carter-street...........	14	8	9
Mrs. Roberts, late of Charterhouse-square.........	50	0	0
1815. Legacy by the will of Henry Stone, late of Thorne, in the County of Hereford, Esq. deceased........	500	0	0
Paid by Messrs. Charles Forster, George Breillat, and John Dawson, residuary Legatees under the same will.			
Mr. Thomas Jones, late of the City of Chester...	200	0	0
Mr. Edward Goff, late of Scotland-yard, London, a legacy by him...............	100	0	0
Duty paid by Messrs. Boyce, West, and Lockett, Executors.			
Mrs. Alison Hamilton, widow, late of Edinburgh	16	10	0
Henry Toogood, Esq. late of Warminster.........	100	0	0
1816. Mr. William West, late of Northampton.........	50	0	0
Rev. B. Bloomfield, late Missionary at Malta.....	15	0	0
Mr. Augustus Savory Jenkins, late of Ashton, Wilts, Reduced 3 per Cents......................	200	0	0
1817. Mrs. Alice Lowe, by her will—The Rev. Thomas Jackson and Mr. John Morrison, Executors, Reduced 3 per Cents......................	200	0	0
Four years and a half dividends on the above Stock	24	6	0
Mrs. S. Chamberlain, late of Moorfields............	20	0	0
Mr. Charles Turner, late of Gilcomston, near Aberdeen, by Rev. J. Philip, Executor...........	20	0	0
Mr. Isaac Diss, late of Colchester....................	20	0	0
Mr. Francis Chaloner, late of Kirby Moorside, by Rev Mr. Eastmead...............	100	0	0
Mr. Samuel Bracy, late of Bishopsgate, by Mr. James Rowell...............	20	0	0
Mrs. Sheldon, late of London, by Mr. Maberly...	100	0	0
Mrs. Mary Unwin, of Castle Hedingham, Essex, by her will—Dr. Abraham Wilkinson, of Russell-square, Executor (after deduction of Legacy Duty) Reduced 3 per Cents......................	450	0	0

L

	£	s.	d.
1818. Mr. Joseph Parry, late of Shrewsbury	1000	0	0
And from the Residue of his Estate	1000	0	0
Executors, Rev. Thomas Weaver, Mr. Parry, and Mr. Lee.			
Mr. Richardson, late of Havant—Executor, Mr. Butler	100	0	0
Dr. James Nasmyth, late of Edinburgh	100	0	0
Mr. Joseph Adam, late of Napton on the Hill, Warwickshire—one eighth part of clear Residue of his Estate	45	16	3
Mrs. Hannah Vertue, late of Sutton Place, Hackney, Executors—Mr. Peter Guillebaud and Mr. Josiah Walley—3 per Cents	100	0	0
Mrs. Mary Mather, late of North-street, City Road—Executors, Mr. John Mather, Mr. Thomas Gadd, and Mr. Thomas Bolman Browne	100	0	0
Mr. Richard Packer, late of St. Ann's-hill—Executors, Mr. Packer and Mr. Pierpoint	19	19	0
Mr. Joseph Strathie, late of Auchterden, near Perth—Executors, Mr. James Morris and Mr. David Thomson	100	0	0
Mr. Abraham Spurlock, late of Bristol	5	0	0
Mr. William Dodds, late of Holloway Down. —Executors, Mr. Thomas Old, Mr. Richard Frances, Mr. Samuel Pealey, and Mr. Thomas W. Dodds	50	0	0
Rev. Cornelius Winter, late of Painswick	50	0	0
Mr. George Thring, late of John-street, Tottenham-court-road—Executrix, Mrs. Alice Thring	30	0	0
Mrs. Jane Gibbs, late of Little Bartholomew-close—Executors, Mr. John Coward and Mr. John Barlow	10	0	0
Mrs. Margaret Cooper, late of Kingston—Executors, Rev. John Clayton and Mr. Robert Steven, 3 per Cents	500	0	0
Mr. William Hodson, late of Islington—Executors, Mr. Samuel Elliott, Mr. George Farr, and Mr. Edward Hodson, 4 per Cents	300	0	0

Many benevolent persons, desirous of promoting the welfare the MISSIONARY SOCIETY, have bequeathed various sums of money thereto, by their last Wills; but by omitting to point out the particular Society for which they intended them, or by a loose or unguarded form of Bequest, considerable difficulties have arisen, and the Institution has been in danger of losing some of the proposed Legacies. To prevent this in future, the Directors of the Missionary Society beg leave to recommend the following

𝔉orm of a 𝔅equest.

———

" *Item.*—I do hereby give and bequeath unto the Treasurer for the time being, of a certain voluntary Society, formed in London in the year 1795, entitled THE MISSIONARY SOCIETY, USUALLY CALLED THE LONDON MISSIONARY SOCIETY, the sum of pounds, of lawful money of the United Kingdom of Great Britain and Ireland, current in Great Britain, to be paid within   months next after my decease, out of such part only of my personal estate as shall not consist of chattels real, upon trust to be applied towards the carrying on the purposes of the said Society: and I do hereby direct and declare, that the Receipt of the Treasurer for the time being of the said Society, for the said Legacy, shall be a sufficient discharge to my Executors for the same."

ND - #0143 - 071024 - C0 - 229/152/9 - PB - 9780243103324 - Gloss Lamination